Natural
Emirates

Natural Emirates

Wildlife and Environment of the United Arab Emirates

TRIDENT PRESS

Published by Trident Press Ltd
Text copyright © 1996: Trident Press Ltd
Pictures copyright © 1996: Mediatec LLC. & Listed Photographers
Layout & Design © 1996: Trident Press Ltd

Editors: Dr Peter J. Vine and Ibrahim Al Abed (Arabic edition)
Original Art: Judy Roberts
Commissioned photographers: Hanne and Jens Eriksen
English edition typesetting: Johan Hofsteenge
Arabic edition typing: Omar Abeedo
Arabic translators: Makawi Khalifa, Abbas Al Zubair

Published with the cooperation of the Higher Committee of the United Arab
    Emirates Silver Jubilee and the Ministry of Information and Culture, PO Box
    17, Abu Dhabi, U.A.E.

Trident Press Ltd., 2-5 Old Bond Street, London W1X3TB

British Library Cataloguing in Publication Data
A CIP catalogue record for this book is available from the British Library.
ISBN: 1-900724-02-2

ILLUSTRATION ACKNOWLEDGEMENTS

The following list is arranged in order of first appearance of each pictorial
source.
All paintings and sketches are by Judy Roberts.

Photographs
Hanne and Jens Eriksen: pp. 13, 14,15, 17,18, 19, 52, 53, 54, 55, 56, 59, 60, 61, 62,
    63, 64, 65, 69, 70, 71, 74, 77, 78, 85, 91, 93, 96, 97, 98, 100, 101, 102, 122, 137,
    141 (baby turtles only), 143, 150, 151, 152, 153, 154, 155, 156, 157, 158, 159,
    160, 161, 162, 163, 164, 165, 166, 214, 215, 217, 230, 231 and houbara on front
    cover, plus flower, tree, and gazelle at Sir Bani Yas on back cover.
Alex Smailes: pp 16, 67, 68, 147, 168, 170, 171, 176, 177, 178, 180, 181, 187, 190,
    191, 193, 197, 198.
Gary Feulner: pp 21, 22, 23, 24, 25, 27, 28, 30, 31, 32, 33, 34, 35, 36, 40.
Duncan Willets: 26.
Chris. and Tilde Stuart: 40, 126, 129, 130, 132, 134216, 217, 218, 223, 225, 226,
    232. and agama lizard on back cover.
Peter Whybrow and The Natural History Museum: 42, 44, 45, 46, 47, 48, 49, 50.
Charles Crowell: 56, 57, 58, 66, 79, 229.
Christian Gross: 59 (baby gazelle), 122 (viper and gecko), 123, 125, 129
    (monitor lizard), 131, 219 (hyaena), 220 (fox), 221 (caracal), 224 (mouse-
    tailed bat).
Kevin Hyland and Christian Gross: 124, 127, 128, 218 (hare), 222 (young
    wildcats), 225 (lesser jerboa)
Robert Baldwin: 76, 80, 81, 82, 139, 140, 141, 142, 144, 148, 201, 203, 204, 205,
    206, 208, 209, 211, 212.
Marijcke Jongbloed: 86, 87, 88, 89, 90, 92, 93 (purple cactus flower), 94, 108, 113,
    115, 116, 118, 119, 129, 133, 222, 233, 236, 237, 238.
Mike Gillett: 101, 104, 105, 106.
Barbara Tigar and Patrick Osborne: 110, 111, 114.
Adam Woolfitt: 169, 228, 235.
Peter Vine: 172, 183.
Jeremy Stafford-Deitsch: 174, 194.
Hans Sjoeholm: 185.
Jurgen Kuchinke: 188.
Hagen Schmid: 189.
F. J. Jackson: 192
Paul Bates and The Harrison Museum: 219, 221, 222 (sand cat), 224 (sheath-
    tailed bat), 226 (sundevall's jird).

Contents

The Natural History Movement — Peter Hellyer — 11

Geology of the United Arab Emirates — Gary Feulner — 21

The Fossil Record — Peter Whybrow, Andrew Smith & Andrew Hill — 41

Habitats and their Protection — Richard Hornby — 51

    Sir Bani Yas — Peter Vine — 58

    Khor Kalba — Marijcke Jongbloed — 70

The Sea Shore — Robert Baldwin — 75

Plant Life — Marijcke Jongbloed — 83

Insects — Mike Gillett — 95

Terrestrial Arthropods (excluding insects) — Barbara Tigar — 107

Terrestrial Reptiles and Amphibians — Christian Gross — 121

Marine Reptiles — Robert Baldwin — 135

Birds & Birdwatching — Colin Richardson — 149

Marine Fish — Mike Shepley — 167

Marine Mammals — Robert Baldwin — 199

Terrestrial Mammals — Christian Gross — 213

Traditions and Wildlife — Christian Gross & Marijcke Jongbloed — 227

Appendix   Birds' Checklist — Colin Richardson — 239

    Index — 244

THE AUTHORS

Peter Hellyer is a long-term resident of Abu Dhabi and past chairman of the Emirates Natural History Group (ENHG). As Managing Editor of Emirates News he has played a leading role in focussing national and international attention on the UAE's rich wildlife. He is also editor of *Tribulus* , the journal of the ENHG, which has gained a reputation for its scientific reporting of natural history research in the UAE. In addition to his strong interest in natural history he is an avid amateur archaeologist and co-ordinator of the Abu Dhabi Islands Archaeological Survey.

Gary Feulner holds degrees in geology from Princeton University and Yale University in the United States. He is a longtime resident of the UAE and currently serves as Chairman of the Dubai Natural History Group. He is a keen outdoorsman who has walked extensively in the UAE, exploring many of the country's remote off-road locations.

Peter J. Whybrow is a Senior Research Scientist in the Department of Palaeontology at the Natural History Museum in London. A graduate from the University of Reading he has undertaken palaeontological work throughout Arabia and in Pakistan, Turkey and Africa. Amongst his scientific publications are 12 papers on the palaeontology of Arabia.

Andrew Smith is a Senior Research Scientist in the Department of Palaeontology at the Natural History Museum in London. Andrew graduated from the University of Edinburgh and is a Fellow of the Royal Society of Edinburgh. His main interests are the morpho-logical and molecular phylogeny of sea urchins and he has recently published on the Cretaceous echinoids from the United Arab Emirates-Oman border region.

Andrew Hill is Professor of Anthropology at Yale University, USA, and a graduate of Bedford College, University of London. Andrew has directed palaeontological field work in Kenya for nearly 20 years and has many publications on fossils from East Africa. His main interest lies in discovering and identifiying African primates from 16 million years ago.

Richard Hornby is a biologist with expertise in various aspects of wildlife and land management. After gaining his Ph.D. in ornithology he enjoyed a long career with the nature conservancy and its successor bodies in Southern England. In 1993 he moved to Abu Dhabi as the first general manager of the National Avian Research Centre, after which he has worked as an environmental consutant on a range of wildlife related projects in the UAE. He has been the chairman of Emirates Natural History Group (Abu Dhabi) since 1994.

Robert Baldwin is a marine ecologist and author with a special interest in southern Arabia. He has undertaken coastal survey work in both the UAE and Oman and recently spent a year based in Abu Dhabi whilst researching and writing a book on the whales and dolphins of the UAE. A keen diver and underwater photog-rapher, Robert is pursuing his studies on Arabian marinelife and is firmly committed to furthering conservation within the region.

Mike Gillett is married with three children. Originally from Birmingham, he has worked as a biochemist in several London medical schools and in the Federal University of Pernambuco in Brazil. Since 1991, he has been an Associate Professor of Biochemistry in the Faculty of Medicine at the UAE University in Al Ain.

Christian Gross has lived in the UAE since 1979 and is author of Mammals of the Southern Gulf, and co-author of Falconry and Birds of Prey in the Gulf. His Animal Management Consultancy company is involved in a number of interpretative projects in the Emirates, including the new Desert Park and Breeding Centre in association with Sharjah Natural History Museum.

Marijcke Jongbloed is an amateur naturalist, having only discovered this hobby during her thirteen years residency in the UAE. Author of several books on UAE's natural history and founder of the Arabian Leopard Trust, she recently concluded her career in medicine to become manager of the Sharjah Natural History Museum and Desert Park.

Colin Richardson came to Dubai in 1976 to pursue his career as an architect. He has been compiling Emirates Bird Report since 1987, has written a number of scientific papers on Arabian ornithology, and is author of *The Birds of the United Arab Emirates*. He established the Gulf's first and only and birdwatching tour agency and looks after visiting businessmen and tour groups who have an interest in discovering the natural emirates, through observation of its varied bird life. Colin is secretary of the Emirates Bird Records Committee and is a founder member and Bird Coordinator of the Dubai Natural History Group.

Peter Vine holds a Ph.D. in marine biology and currently works as an author and publisher. His books include *Red Sea Invertebrates, The Red Sea, Red Sea Explorers* and *Red Sea Safety*. He is also co-author of the award winning title: *Tides of War* and has more than twenty volumes published under his name, including *The United Arab Emirates*, in which he wrote extensively on the UAE's culture, history, wildlife and development. As Managing Editor of Trident Press, he continues to combine his love of nature with his enthusiasm for publishing.

Mike Shepley is a commercial film maker who divides his time between living in Dubai and Scotland. Since completing a commissioned study of reef and pelagic fishes of the UAE for H.H. Sheikh Mohamed bin Rashid Al Maktoum in 1985/86, he has continued his observations of the Arabian Gulf and east coast, both above and below water. A former Scottish Open, British National and European fishing champion he has contributed to over a hundred books on fish and angling. He is mainly engaged with wildlife and recreational tourism film production.

Barbara Tigar is a professional biologist with degree qualifications in environmental biology and applied entomology. She has worked in the UK, Lesotho, Mexico and recently spent three years at the National Avian Research Centre in Abu Dhabi, where she studied the feeding ecology of houbara bustard. She is now living in Scotland where she is writing-up her houbara research work for publication and submission towards a PhD thesis at London University and in her spare time creating a garden from a section of neglected and exposed Scottish hillside. Barbara has had her work published in numerous scientific journals, on subjects ranging from biological control to conservation.

FOREWORD

I HAD THE GREAT PLEASURE of visiting this country for the first time officially in May 1996, a quarter of a century after its political emergence as the "United Arab Emirates" under the leadership of H.H. Sheikh Zayed Bin Sultan Al Nahyan, the "Green Prince".

This political birth was accompanied by remarkable growth and development in all sectors thanks to the UAE's enormous oil resources, which were put to use in vital areas of production and in building economic, educational and social infrastructures.

Over a period of only two decades, the settlements and villages spread out between the sands of the Arabian desert, and the shores of the Gulf were transformed into developed capitals and urban centres as part of a modern and unifying political plan.

A comparison of the model of the city of Abu Dhabi in the fifties and the capital as it stands today underscores the extensive scope and the unique nature of achievements in civil engineering and urban planning.

A few statistics in sensitive and significant areas such as education and agriculture illustrate the extent and depth of the qualitative and quantitative advances made. In the seventies, school enrolment was 20,000, while today it has reached half a million. In agriculture, the number of palm trees was increased from a few hundred thousand to some 22 million trees. The mud-built villages strewn along the arid coast have become modern urban cities that play a sensitive and important economic and political role on the international scene.

I also learned of the great interest of the Government in caring for the country's important archaeological sites and in protecting a number of areas rich in natural and cultural heritage, such as Sir Bani Yas where one of the oldest churches and urban settlements in the Arabian Peninsula were discovered.

Over and above these economic and national achievements, I was particularly impressed by the attention to folklore and handicrafts promotion, as well – I wish to emphasize this – as the progressive role that women play in the United Arab Emirates.

I also had the opportunity to share my impressions with H. H. Sheikh Zayed during a long and cordial meeting in which we discussed the various areas of co-operation between UNESCO and the UAE.

The United Arab Emirates is currently a member of UNESCO's Executive Board and has become the Organization's partner in a number of significant projects in the Arab region - such as "Kitab fi Jarida", which will promote the spread of culture and creativity in all Arab States, and the "Sheikh Zayed Bin Sultan International Award for Cultural Heritage and Social Traditions" established with the aim of safeguarding human and cultural values. These and other actions are a model of fruitful co-operation with UNESCO towards the achievement of its noble objectives of spreading education and promoting culture so that the defences of peace may be constructed in the minds of people worldwide.

Federico Mayor
Director General UNESCO

THE NATURAL HISTORY MOVEMENT

Peter Hellyer

Our knowledge of the UAE's natural history owes much to the collection of data, records and specimens by enthusiastic part-time naturalists who were based in the region, and to the efforts of scientists who came to visit them. The Bombay Natural History Museum and the British Natural History Museum in London, for example, still have specimens of birds and animals collected by Surgeon Major A.S.G. Jayakar of the Indian Army, who lived in Muscat from 1885 to 1891, and was the first person to introduce to science the Arabian tahr, *Hemitragus jayakari*, an endangered goat-like animal which can still be found in the higher mountains of Fujairah.

Written data about the country's natural history can be found in notes penned by various officials who visited the region. Captain Atkins Hamerton, for example, the first European known to have visited the area of the Al Ain oasis, in 1840, noted that

The Brymee dates are considered superior to any produced in the province of Oman. Wheat grown in the valley is of a fine description, but does not appear to be much cultivated. Fruit, such as oranges and lemons, grapes, figs, mangoes, olives and pomegranates, grow in great perfection. Coffee, too, was formerly cultivated on the hill Hafeet, but ... its growth has been abandoned.[1]

Lieutenant Colonel S.B. Miles, British Political Agent and Consul in Muscat, who travelled extensively in parts of southern Arabia between 1872 and 1886, visiting the Al Ain oasis in 1875, referred, in a posthumously published book, to the presence of Arabian oryx, *Oryx leucoryx*, the cape hare, *Capus lepensis*, and gazelle, *Gazella* sp., in the desert areas of Abu Dhabi.[2] The type specimen of one of Arabia's lizards, *Mesalina brevirostris* Blanford 1874, was also collected from one of the UAE's Tunb islands around this time, representing the first formal scientific description on record of an animal from the Emirates.

J.G. Lorimer, author of the Gazetteer of the Persian Gulf, Oman and Central Arabia, compiled between 1905 and 1908, recorded a list of fish to be found in the waters of the Arabian Gulf, but offered relatively little additional biological information. As recently as 1954, following an expedition to the Dubai and Sharjah area by the Peabody Museum at Harvard University, the total list of mollusc species for the Trucial Coast only amounted to 64 species.[3] One reason for the paucity of records was that data from field work was frequently not published. Between 1922 and 1935, for example, an English naturalist collected extensively in the Arabian Gulf, including the waters of the Trucial Coast, but published nothing at all until 1958. Another collector, Ronald Codrai, representative in the Trucial Coast for the Iraq Petroleum Company, forerunner of the Abu Dhabi Company for Onshore Oil Operations, ADCO, sent his shells to a scientist, F. Haas, who published them in the specialist journal *Nautilus* in 1954.[4]

Information in the scientific literature on the UAE's birdlife was even scarcer. A possible nesting, in the 1920s, by barn swallows, *Hirundo rustica*, on the UAE island of Greater Tunb, was mentioned by Lieutenant Colonel Sir Arnold Wilson, a British Political Resident in the Gulf.[5] Almost 70 years later, its status has still to be confirmed, although it is suspected to have bred in Ras al-Khaimah.[6] One unusual confirmed bird record from the 1930s was that of a white stork, *Ciconia ciconia*, ringed in Kaliningrad (then Konisgberg, in East Prussia), in June 1936, and found dead in the Al Ain area in September of the same year.[7] A few years later, in 1944, D.F. Vesey-Fitzgerald collected a specimen of the toad *Bufo dhufarensis* in the Al Ain area, apparently the first scientific record of amphibians from the UAE.[8]

After the Second World War, the Emirates, still known as the Trucial States, were gradually opened up to the outside world as a result of the commencement of oil exploration, and more Europeans visited the inland regions, either on oil company business, or for other reasons. Among these was Wilfred Thesiger, who explored much of southern Arabia in connection with his work for the Anti-Desert Locust Unit. Spending a few days on and around Jebel Hafit, Thesiger was the first westerner to record the presence of the Arabian tahr in the area, and also the first European to see a live specimen, it having originally been described from two skins and skulls purchased by Dr. Jayakar in Muscat in 18921. He also referred to the presence of wolves and hyaenas on the mountain, and noted that a leopard had been there several

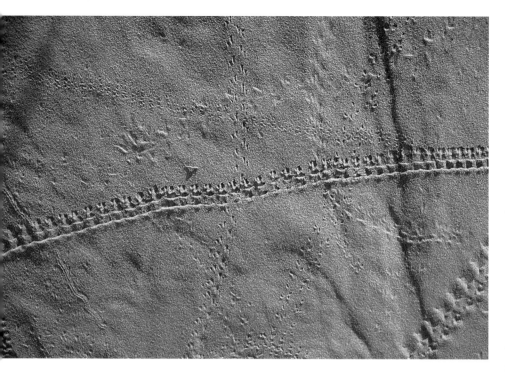

they will move about in cars and will keep in touch with the outside world by wireless. They will bring back results far more interesting than mine, but they will never know the spirit of the land, nor the greatness of the Arabs. [10]

By the early 1950s, as the oil industry began to grow, the oil companies displayed a greater interest in the geology of the country, calling upon scientists for assistance. They also provided facilities for scientists and naturalists who visited in a private capacity. D.F. Vesey-Fitzgerald, for example, undertook a survey of wildlife in the Bainuna area of Abu Dhabi between 1950 and 1952, during which he found evidence of the previous presence of the Arabian race of the ostrich, *Struthio camelus syriacus*, now extinct.[11] A team of geologists and geomorphologists from Imperial College, London, visited Abu Dhabi on several occasions between 1961 and 1965 to study the coastal sabkha salt flats, inter-tidal flats and shallow inshore waters and coral banks. They also used the opportunity to collect more mollusc specimens, obtaining, and subsequently publishing a total of 198 species, of which five were new to science[12] The team's leader and colleagues also wrote a number of papers on the geology of Abu Dhabi's sabkhas, though they attracted little attention outside geological circles.[13]

Again with assistance from the local oil industry, a leading British ornithologist, visited Abu Dhabi and Dubai in 1965, putting together a preliminary bird list for the country, and, inter alia, also noting that the house sparrow, *Passer domesticus*, had not yet appeared in Abu Dhabi, where today it is an abundant resident, although he saw them in Sharjah.

During the 1960s and early 1970s, further scientific missions visited, usually in collaboration with the oil industry. A number of first confirmed sightings of mammal and other species date from this time. A caracal, *Caracal caracal*, collected in 1968 near Swaihan by a visiting UK mammal specialist, remains the only known record of this endangered member of the cat family from the heart of the UAE desert, and provides useful evidence of the recent contraction of its range to the fastnesses of the mountains. In 1970, a former British Political Agent, Donald Hawley, published a book on the Trucial States with a short appendix on the country's flora.[14]

years earlier, but "I noticed few birds other than the vultures (probably mainly Egyptian vulture, *Neophron percnopterus*) wheeling over the precipices and an infrequent falcon; I saw no raven." In a subsequent paper following a third journey in 1948-49,[9] Thesiger recorded the presence of what he described as tawny eagles, probably of the race now described as a separate species, the steppe eagle, *Aquila nipalensis*, in the Al Khatam area.

Thesiger also collected plants for London's Natural History Museum, and published a list of flora from Jebel Hafit in his 1949 *Geographical Journal* paper. The papers themselves had a restricted circulation however whilst his collection of fauna and flora in London, though available to researchers there, was little studied and less known. Indeed, no catalogue of his collections is yet available anywhere in the UAE.

In his introduction to Arabian Sands, Thesiger writes:

I went to Southern Arabia only just in time. Others will go there to study geology, archaeology, the birds, the plants, the animals, even to study the Arabs themselves; but

Further valuable data, on birds at least, was collected by Major Michael Gallagher and colleagues in 1970 and 1971. Other reptile collecting in the mid-1960s produced three additional type specimens of reptiles, *Stendactylus leptosymbotes*, from Ras Ghanadha *and Acanthodactylus gongorhyncatus* from Bida Azan in Abu Dhabi, both published in 1967,[15] *and Lacerta cyanura*, from Ras al-Khaimah's Wadi Shawkah, published in 1972.

While a corpus of scientific data was thus gradually being amassed, it was of little value to the Emirates itself. Collected by transient foreign visitors, it remained uncoordinated and largely unavailable to UAE residents, being published in scientific journals overseas, stored in museum collections, like that of the Natural History Museum in London, or simply remaining in the personal papers of those who had carried out the work. A large number of records of birds seen on the islands of Das, Zirku and Qarnein in the early 1960s by an oil company employee, for example, only came to light by accident in the early 1990s. Yet to be properly studied, it contains valuable information about breeding seabirds on Das and Zirku before commencement of the construction of oil facilities.

Whilst extensive knowledge existed among the country's citizens most of this remained unpublished, communicated orally between those for whom the information was of direct practical value. Fishermen and hunters, for example, had detailed knowledge of a wide area of natural history, such as what species of birds or mammals could be expected to be seen, where they bred, when particular species of fish, turtles or dolphins could be found and so on. Not surprisingly, at a time of great social, economic and industrial change, study of the country's wildlife and environment was a low priority.

Expatriates took an active role in making scientific recordings of the UAE's wildlife, leading at quite an early stage to production of a UAE Bird List. By 1973 the number of bird species recorded on Abu Dhabi island had reached 134. During this period a small network of keen naturalists began to communicate their interest in the Emirates' natural history, both among themselves and to members of the general public, culminating in establishment of the Abu Dhabi-based Emirates Natural History Group. The aims of the Group were "*to encourage and assist its members in the study and appreciation of the natural history of Abu Dhabi, the United Arab Emirates, the Middle East and the world at large.*" These objectives were pursued in three distinct but related ways, through public meetings twice a month, through the production of a thrice-yearly duplicated Bulletin, first issued in March 1977, which continued to appear until 1989, when it was replaced by a bi-annual printed journal *Tribulus*; and through encouraging members and others to get out and about in the country to make recordings of anything they saw.

Group Recorders were appointed for different areas of natural history, such as birds, flora, mammals, fishes and archaeology, the latter always part of the Group's interests. The uniqueness and quality of the data they collected resulted in strong links being forged between the ENHG and overseas academic institutions such as Britain's Royal Botanic Gardens at Kew and Edinburgh. After a year, the ENHG had a total of 200 members, confirming of founders belief that there was a substantial interest in the country's natural history.

Many ENHG members worked for Abu Dhabi's oil companies, in particular ADMA-OPCO, which also provided a variety of support, including use of the company post office box, access to duplicating facilities for the bulletin and subsequently, in 1980, a room for use as an office and storeroom for the rapidly growing collection of shells, insects, birds, bees, plants and whatever else Group members picked up on their trips. In recent years the oil sector, led by the Abu Dhabi National Oil Company, ADNOC, and its group of companies, including ADMA-OPCO and its onshore counterpart, the Abu Dhabi Company for Onshore Oil Operations, ADCO, has continued to provide support both to the ENHG and others for studies of the country's environment and natural history.

There were soon signs of a growing interest among UAE nationals in the country's wildlife, led by the country's President and Ruler of Abu Dhabi, Sheikh Zayed bin Sultan Al Nahyan. Brought up in the ways of his Bedouin forefathers,

Sheikh Zayed learned to shoot by the time he was 12, and to hunt with falcons by the time he was 16. By the age of 25, however, he stopped shooting, and in the half a century that has followed has confined himself to falconry.

In his book *Falconry as a Sport: Our Arab Heritage*, he explained the reasons for his change of heart.

One day I set out on a hunting expedition in open country, he recalled. *My game was a large herd of gazelle spread over a wide area. I followed them and began shooting. Three hours later, I stopped to count my bag, and found I had shot fourteen gazelle. I pondered over this a long time. I realised that hunting with a gun was no more than an outright attack on animals and a cause of their rapid extinction. I changed my mind, and decided to restrict myself to falconry only.*[16]

By the early 1960s, when he was Ruler's Representative in the Eastern Region of Abu Dhabi, based in Al Ain, Sheikh Zayed realised that unrestricted hunting was threatening to wipe out the last few remaining Arabian Oryx in the desert, and arranged for four animals to be captured and brought to him in Al Ain. To house them, he ordered the setting aside of an area for the country's first zoo, now, over thirty years later, the largest in the Middle East, while several hundred oryx can presently be found both in the zoo and in private collections within the Emirates, all descended from those original animals from the wild.

Like many of those who hunt, by whatever means, Sheikh Zayed was also keenly interested in the preservation of wildlife. In 1976, combining his interests, he arranged for the first-ever International Conference on Falconry and Conservation to be held in Abu Dhabi, attended by falconers, natural historians and conservationists from throughout the region, as well as from Europe, the United States and other countries. One by-product of the conference was the issuing of a law banning hunting in the territory of Abu Dhabi, the forerunner of more extensive legislation on a federal level in subsequent years, while the conference itself provided clear leadership on the necessity of conserving the country's environment and wildlife.

The establishment, in 1977, of the Emirates University, based in Al Ain, also provided an important boost for a national focus upon wildlife and the environment with expansion into fields of pure science accompanied by creation of specialist units such as the Desert and Marine Environment Research Centre. The late 1970s and early 1980s saw an explosive growth of interest in the country's natural history. A first full UAE Bird List was compiled, initially being maintained by the Ornithological Society of the Middle East in London, with additions being made annually. Work by founder members of ENHG extended the knowledge of reptiles and plants, whilst other work included extensive studies of the bees and wasps to be found in the country, leading to the discovery, in the course of the 1980s, of several species that were new to science.

The ENHG Bulletin displayed the breadth of interest of its members, with articles on topics ranging from plants to insects, fish to marine mammals, birds to archaeology. In 1979, a branch of the ENHG, later to become a fully-fledged organisation, was established in Al Ain, while in 1984 a Dubai Natural History Group was also formed. The groups' reputation among the international scientific community also strengthened despite the fact that most members were not formally trained. Increasingly the groups were called upon to assist visiting scientists, and articles in the ENHG Bulletin, and later The Gazelle, newsletter of the Dubai group, gained in stature. Particular beneficiaries from the late 1980s onwards were palaeontologists from London's Natural History Museum and Yale University and a variety of foreign archaeological missions, particularly in the northern emirates.

At a government level, too, interest in the study, and protection of the country's environment continued to develop. In 1983, for example, a federal law on hunting, Law No. 9/1983, was issued banning the hunting of, or the collection of, the eggs of all wild birds, with the exception of cormorants, which were perceived by the fishing community as posing a threat to their livelihood. The law also banned the hunting of gazelles, hares and spiny-tailed agamids (the large *dhub* lizard). Though implementation of the law proved difficult, particularly in more remote areas, and although it was by no means all-encompassing, no mention being made, for example, of endangered species of the cat family, it represented a major step forward in the creation of a legal framework of protection. Further ministerial decrees from the Ministry of

Agriculture and Fisheries also provided protection for marine turtles and for dugongs, although once again implementation was difficult.

In 1987 the Chancellor of the University, Sheikh Nahyan bin Mubarak al Nahyan, became Patron of the ENHG and of its sister body in Al Ain. The following year he drew the attention of President Sheikh Zayed to the importance of the mangrove forest to the immediate east of Abu Dhabi island as a refuge for breeding and migrant birds as well as for a variety of breeding fish. The President responded by immediately declaring the area a nature reserve, and by ordering the preservation of the mangroves and their surrounding habitat. Similar approaches by the Dubai Natural History Group, aided by a 1987 study of wintering wader birds, also led to the designation of Dubai Creek, (Khor Dubai) as a wildlife sanctuary, at the initiative of Sheikh Mohammed bin Rashid Al Maktoum, now Crown Prince of Dubai.

17

In the early 1980s Sheikh Zayed created a private wildlife park on the offshore island of Sir Bani Yas. A major focus of this project was on the breeding, in a predator-free environment, of endangered local species, such as the Arabian oryx, *Oryx leucoryx*, the sand gazelle, *Gazella subgutterosa*, and the Arabian gazelle, *Gazella gazella*. As stocks increased to healthy levels, a programme of release into large protected areas in the deserts of western Abu Dhabi was initiated. In addition to Al Ain Zoo, which logged up some successes in captive breeding of endangered Arabian species, other private zoos were also established, with Sheikh Khalifa bin Zayed Al Nahyan and Sheikh Mohammed bin Rashid Al Maktoum building up particularly impressive collections.

The mid-1980s saw the first results of research undertaken by resident Arab and expatriate scientists. At the Emirates University, for example, botanical studies carried out by Professor A.A. Ghonaimy on the flora of the Al Ain region, led in 1985 to the production of the first book on the country's flora. [17] This was followed by the first detailed illustrated checklist of the flora of the whole country. Written by Rob Western with the assistance of the Royal Botanic Gardens in Edinburgh, this 1989 publication, was funded by the University on the instructions of its Chancellor, Sheikh Nahyan .[18] In his Foreword to Western's book, Sheikh Nahyan formally recognised the importance of the role played by keen amateur naturalists.

The Emirates University has made a point of encouraging original research on the country. If we of the Emirates do not study ourselves and our land, we cannot expect others to do it for us. The long story of historical and scientific research, however, has always shown that it is not merely the full-time academic who contributed to the expanding of the frontiers of knowledge. There has always been, and there will always be, a place for the talented and dedicated amateur.

Other research which attracted less public attention, was also being carried out into some of the country's endangered animals. In 1985, for example, a captive breeding programme for the Gordon's wildcat, *Felis sylvestris gordoni*, the first such programme anywhere in the world, was established by Christian Gross and Marijcke Jongbloed, with the collaboration of Dubai Zoo. Over the

course of the next five years, over 30 cats were bred in an international programme that also involved zoos in Oman, the United States and Europe. The project's administrators also carried out research into the status of two other endangered cats, the caracal lynx, *Caracal caracal schmitzi*, and the Arabian leopard, *Panthera pardus nimr*, which was to lead eventually to the formation of the Arabian Leopard Trust. Today, operating from the Sharjah Natural History Museum under the patronage of Sharjah Ruler Dr. Sheikh

Sultan bin Mohammed Al Qassimi, the Trust is the focal point of a peninsula-wide programme to protect and breed the leopard, perhaps Arabia's most endangered animal, with only around 100 believed to exist in the wild.

Increasing confidence and skills among the UAE's resident expatriate birdwatchers resulted in them taking over upkeep of the official UAE Bird List from F.E. Warr, who had maintained it in London from the late 1970s. An Emirates Bird Records Committee was set up, adopting the same strict rules for assessing descriptions of rare birds as those used elsewhere. As a result, ornithology in the Emirates has now attained recognised international standards, one result of which has been the gradual development of a professionally-run bird watching tour business that brings well over a million dirhams a year to the UAE's growing travel industry.

In 1990 the Emirates Natural History Group launched *Tribulus*, a biannual magazine, to replace its former duplicated bulletin. This has consistently attracted contributions not only from serious amateur enthusiasts, but also from professional scientists, ranging from veterinary surgeons, reporting the first cases of rabies in the UAE, to archaeologists, palaeontologists, botanists and ornithologists. It remains the only regular scientific journal to be published in any language on the archaeology and natural history of the Emirates, and is increasingly quoted by other journals overseas. Publication of the magazine was made possible through financial support provided by a number of major companies operating in Abu Dhabi.

ADCO and ADNOC began, from 1988, to fund palaeontological research, undertaken by scientists from the Natural History Museum of London and Yale University, into the Miocene outcrops in Abu Dhabi's Western Region. This work led, as is described elsewhere in this book, to the discovery of the most significant deposits anywhere in the world of late Miocene terrestrial fossils. Both ADCO and ADNOC, as well as other firms like Union National Bank and British Petroleum, extended support to the Abu Dhabi Islands Archaeological Survey Project, created in 1991 on the instructions of President Sheikh Zayed. In 1995 the Union National Bank sponsored a year-long scientific survey of the cetaceans (whales and dolphins) of the UAE's offshore waters, the first such

study ever undertaken. Local scientists also benefited from commercial support. In 1994, for example, Shell made a major grant to the Desert and Marine Environment Centre of the Emirates University for a study of the mangroves along the UAE's coastline, yielding valuable information on the significance of the mangroves as a spawning ground for commercially-important fish species, as well as on other aspects of their ecological significance.

In 1989, the National Avian Research Centre (NARC) was created by Emiri decree in Abu Dhabi, charged with investigating the breeding biology and habitat preferences of the houbara bustard, *Chlamydotis undulata macqueenii*, and of the preferred species of falcons for hunting: the saker, *Falco cherrug* and the peregrine, *Falco peregrinus*. NARC, chaired by UAE Chief of Staff Sheikh Mohammed bin Zayed Al Nahyan, and with a complement of professional ornithologists, botanists and other scientists, rapidly moved into studies of the broader UAE habitat. A book on the breeding birds of the Emirates, compiled by NARC's staff ornithologist, was published in early 1996, with the support of ADNOC.[19]

The Federal Environmental Agency (FEA) was established in 1993 with a remit *to protect and develop the environment within the state; establish the necessary plans and policies to protect the environment against the harmful effects arising from activities inflicting damage to human health, agricultural crops, land and marine life, (and) other natural resources.*[20]

Federal legislation on the protection of the environment and wildlife was issued during 1996, and the FEA has now established a Biodiversity Conservation Committee, to report on and monitor the status of the UAE's endangered flora and fauna.

Other initiatives have been taken at the level of individual emirates. In 1994, for example, the Ruler of Sharjah, Dr. Sheikh Sultan bin Mohammed Al Qassimi, issued an Emiri decree giving the Arabian Leopard Trust legal status as an official body. This was followed, in 1995, with the opening of the first public museum in the country dedicated to the study of natural history. Also in 1995, the Ruler of Fujairah, Sheikh Hamad bin Mohammed Al Sharqi, issued an Emiri decree establishing the country's first offshore marine reserves, to protect the environmentally valuable coral reefs off the UAE's east coast.

Whilst amateur naturalists still have, and always will have, a valuable role to play, fully trained scientists, both from within the UAE and internationally, are now taking the lead in important biological and environmental studies. The original natural history groups, now joined by more recently established organisations such as the Environment Friends Society, the Emirates Environmental Group (Dubai) and the Abu Dhabi Environmental Group, have adapted to changing circumstances and set out to complement the work of the scientists, and to educate both their own members and the public at large.

Development of the study of natural history in the Emirates has paralleled other aspects of the country's growth. Whereas a quarter of a century ago, virtually all study of the UAE's natural history had been undertaken, or was being undertaken, by visitors from overseas, with the results being obtainable only overseas, now most research is undertaken by locally based individuals, both nationals and expatriates, sometimes in collaboration with foreign scientific institutions. Whilst all those concerned with the study and protection of the country's environment would agree that there is much more yet to be done, it is nevertheless clear that in this, as in so much else, it is local initiative - government, commercial and private, that is together determining the future of the United Arab Emirates. For the surviving pioneers of the UAE's natural history movement, that is a matter of some considerable satisfaction.

[1] In *Selections from the Records of the Bombay Government*. New Series. No. XXIV, 1856, republished by The Oleander Press, 1985. p. 117 [PV0]

[2] Miles, S.B. (1919). *The Countries and Tribes of the Persian Gulf*. Garnet Press, London, edition, 1994, p. 439.

[3] Biggs, H.E.J., (1973). 'The Marine Mollusca of the Trucial Coast', *Bulletin of the British Museum (Natural History), Zoology*: Vol 24 No. 8, December 1973.

[4] Haas, F. 1954. 'Some marine shells from the Persian Gulf collected by Ronald Codrai', *Nautilus* 68: 46-49.

[5] *The Geographical Journal*, Vol LXIV No. 3 1927.

[6] Aspinall, S.J. (1996). *Status and Conservation of The Breeding Birds of the United Arab Emirates*, Hobby Publications, Liverpool & Dubai.

[7] Warr, F.E. (1981). 'UAE Bird Recoveries', in *Bulletin of the Emirates Natural History Group* No. 13, March 1981, p. 6

[8] Balletto, E., Cherchi, M.A. & Gasperetti, J. (1985) 'Amphibians of the Arabian Peninsula', in *Fauna and Flora of Saudi Arabia*, Vol 7. p. 336.

[9] Thesiger, W., (1950). 'Desert Borderlands of Oman' in *The Geographical Journal*, Vol. CXVI nos. 4-6, 1950, pp. 137-168.

[10] Thesiger, W (1994). *Arabian Sands*, op. cit, p. 13.

[11] Vesey-Fitzgerald, D.F., Oryx 1: 232-235

[12] in Biggs (1973), op. cit.

[13] e.g. Evans, G., Kendall, C.G. St. C. & Skipwith, Sir Patrick A. D'E (1964). 'Origin of the coastal flats, the Sabkha of the Trucial Coast, Persian Gulf'. *Nature*, Lond. 202:759-761

[14] Hawley, D.F. (1970), *The Trucial States*, Allen & Unwin, London. Appendix A, pp. 296-299.

[15] Leviton, A.E. & Anderson, S.C. (1967). 'Survey of the reptiles of the Sheikhdom of Abu Dhabi, Part 2: Systematic account of the collection of reptiles made in the Sheikhdom of Abu Dhabi by John Gasperetti'. *Proceedings of the California Academy of Sciences* (4): 35: 157-192.

[16] Al Nahyan, Zayed bin Sultan, (1977). *Falconry as a Sport: Our Arab Heritage*, cited in Emirates News, August 6, 1994.

[17] Ghonaimy, A.A. (1985): *Ecology and Flora of the Al Ain Region*. United Arab Emirates University

[18] Western, A.R. (1989*): The Flora of the United Arab Emirates: An Introduction*. United Arab Emirates University.

[19] Aspinall, S.J. (1996). op. cit.

[20] Federal Law No. 7 of 1993 establishing the Federal Environmental Agency, (Article 4), in *Tribulus*, Bulletin of the Emirates Natural History Group, Vol 3.2. (October 1993), p. 27.

GEOLOGY OF THE UNITED ARAB EMIRATES

Gary Feulner

Opposite Page:
The author on a trail
in the northernmost
Hajar Mountains,
called the Ru'us Al-
Jibal, where the thick
carbonate sediments
of the Tethys Ocean
are well exposed.

G EOLOGICALLY, THE UAE OCCUPIES a corner of the Arabian Platform, a body of continental rock that has remained relatively stable since the Cambrian Period more than 500 million years ago (Fig. 1). From a geological standpoint, the Arabian Platform encompasses not only present day Arabia but also the shallow Arabian Gulf (which is not a true ocean basin) and the rocks of the coastal Zagros Mountains of Iran. For most of its history, the Arabian Platform has been part of the larger Afro-Arabian continent, and the two have behaved as a unit in response to plate tectonic movements (Fig. 2). Only about 25 million years ago, with the initial opening of the Red Sea, did Arabia begin to separate from the African plate.

The Precambrian history of the UAE, like that of eastern Arabia generally, is somewhat speculative. Precambrian rocks do not outcrop, nor are they known from drilling information. Limited exposures of Precambrian rocks in neighbouring Saudi Arabia and the Sultanate of Oman indicate that this region participated in the late Precambrian glaciations that are known from geologic evidence in many disparate parts of the present day globe.

Since the middle Cambrian Period, not long after the first appearance of abundant fossilizable life forms, the area that now constitutes the UAE has been primarily an area of coastline or shallow coastal seas at or near the edge of the Afro-Arabian continent. Cambrian sediments on both sides of the Arabian Gulf suggest that the region was at that time the site of incipient rifting of a larger continent to form a new ocean basin. This may account for the UAE's position at the margin of the Afro-Arabian continent.

Movement of the Afro-Arabian plate during the Palaeozoic twice caused Arabia to pass near the

Burrow casts and the
enigmatic fossil
Cruziana (at lower
left), believed to be
trilobite tracks, from
the scarce Palaeozoic
rocks of the UAE.

Fig. 2.
The Afro-Arabian Plate,
highlighting the UAE.

Fig. 1.
The Geological Time Scale.

South Pole (in the Ordovician and Carboniferous), and the UAE may have become glaciated. Since the end of the Palaeozoic, however, the UAE has remained in tropical or subtropical latitudes. Moreover, despite its travels, this area appears to have remained tectonically relatively stable, and the geologic history of the UAE has therefore been primarily a history of the advance and retreat of the sea.

THE OIL RESERVOIRS

Over time, sediments accumulated on the coast and continental shelf that was to become the UAE. Limited pre-Permian exposures in the UAE reveal fine-grained, shallow water terrigenous sediments (silts and shales). These were probably relatively thin overall and may have been largely removed by intermittent emergence and erosion. Later, in the tropical Mesozoic seas, thick

Fig. 3.
The Tethys Ocean in the Triassic.

sequences of carbonate rocks – limestones ($CaCO_3$) and dolomites ($CaMg(CO_3)_2$) – were deposited. The late Permian and Mesozoic seas of the UAE were part of an ocean that opened north of Arabia during that time, separating the Afro-Arabian continent from the Eurasian continent. This palaeo-ocean is known to geologists as Tethys and at one time it extended westward to the present-day Mediterranean countries and eastward to the Himalayas (Fig. 3).

Fossiliferous limestones and dolomites of Jurassic to late Cretaceous age (*c*.210 to *c*.85 million years ago) are the rocks in which the UAE's abundant oil reserves are typically found. Some of these rocks represent depositional environments very much like today's Arabian Gulf shores, but they are now buried at depths of approximately 2,500m to 7,000m. In particular, the lower part of the Mesozoic sequence includes sabkha deposits indicative of a restricted shallow water environment.

It is ironic that the enormously important petroleum reservoir rocks of the UAE are nowhere exposed at the surface. But apart from the rocks of the Hajar Mountains, there is little surface outcrop of any kind throughout eastern Arabia, and most of what is known in detail of the geologic history of the Arabian Platform in this area comes from drilling and seismic information. Two persistent regional structural features noted by petroleum geologists are a major ridge running NE-SW through the Qatar peninsula and a parallel and adjacent major trough running through western Abu Dhabi and into the Empty Quarter. Subsurface structures may be very gentle, but gradients of as little as 2% can be sufficient to permit migration and entrapment of crude oil.

From left:
The mountains of the Ru'us Al-Jibal drop steeply to the sea.

The sediments found in the Ru'us Al-Jibal correlate with oil-bearing strata buried thousands of metres beneath the surface in the western UAE.

The purple-brown patina known as "rock varnish" covers ancient gravel plains. It is now known to be caused by manganese-fixing bacteria.

Shallow water sedimentation continued through the early Tertiary over most of the UAE, but regional uplift began in the late Oligocene (*c.*25 million years ago). Subsequent Miocene sediments consist of salt and gypsum, and the area has been mostly emergent since the end of the Miocene (*c.*5 million years ago). In the west of Abu Dhabi are exposures of terrestrial deposits and fossils of late Miocene age (*c.*6 million years ago) which indicate an environment of riverine savannah at that time.

The land emerged above sea level at various times throughout the earlier Mesozoic and Tertiary depositional history, but in the form of low lying land-masses, as occur today. These periods, when the sea did not cover the land, are evidenced by occasional identifiable breaks in the otherwise continuous sequence of sedimentary layers and by sedimentary features indicating surface erosion, such as the development of palaeo-soils. One such example is a regional gap in marine sedimentation which occurs at the Cretaceous-Tertiary boundary. Since the mid-Cretaceous (*c.*100 million years ago), local topographic highs (and major structural traps for petroleum) have been created by salt domes rising from thick Cambrian salt deposits that underlie many areas of the southern Arabian Gulf at depths of more than 6,000m. Today these salt domes are responsible for certain coastal hills, such as Jebel Dhana and Jebel Ali, and for many of the UAE's offshore islands, such as Sir Bani Yas, Das, Zirku, and Sir Abu Nu'air.

MOUNTAIN BUILDING

The exception to this placid but productive history lies in the Hajar Mountains in the east of the country and along the border with the Sultanate of Oman. There, earth movements driven by plate tectonics caused the ocean floor of the deep ocean then lying to the north-east to be forced over the edge of the Arabian Platform and its cover of shallow water sediments. This process created a structure of massive superposed sheets (called *nappes*) of diverse rock types that now appear to have been shuffled, like cards, on a grand scale. The result was fortuitous for geologists, as the Hajar Mountains constitute the world's finest and most extensive surface exposure of rocks of the oceanic crust.

These nappes were emplaced during the late Cretaceous, from about 90-70 million years ago. Mountains were created at that time and this affected sedimentation in adjacent areas, including the Northern Emirates. However, those original mountains were rapidly eroded, and to the south in Oman the area again became a site of shallow marine deposition by the end of the Cretaceous.

The wadis at the tip of the Musandam Peninsula have been flooded by a combination of tectonic subsidence and the post-glacial rise in global sea level.

25

In the UAE, some parts of the Hajar Mountains may have remained above sea-level ever since their origin in the Cretaceous. Nevertheless, their present height and rugged topography is a product of renewed uplift and erosion due to regional forces commencing at the end of the Oligocene (*c*.25 million years ago) and continuing to the present. This regional uplift is believed to be related to the ongoing convergence of the Afro-Arabian and Eurasian plates, which is responsible for the Zagros Mountains of Iran and other Alpine-Himalayan chains, and to the opening of the Red Sea.

Geologically recent events such as Pleistocene glaciation and its associated effects on climate and sea level have put the finishing touches on the present day geology of the UAE as a whole.

THE DESERT

Most of the surface of the present day UAE is a sand desert, stretching from the Arabian Gulf coast south to the unbroken and uninhabited sands of the Empty Quarter, and east to the gravel plains bordering the Hajar Mountains. The desert is a geologically recent feature, the result of prolonged subaerial erosion and deposition in an arid environment. The sands overlie the thick, oil-rich sedimentary strata of the Arabian Platform which constitutes the bedrock of most of the UAE, but the oil producing rocks are nowhere exposed at the surface, and are known only from drilling.

Typical Aklé Dune Pattern

The desert sands vary in both composition and form. Near the coast the sand consists mostly of calcareous material ($CaCO_3$) derived from the carbonate bedrock, seashells and coral reefs of the coast. Further inland, the sand consists predominantly of quartz grains. Quartz (SiO_2) is the most common rock-forming mineral and is a stable end product of the chemical weathering of most rock types other than carbonates. However, even the well-weathered and well-winnowed quartz grains of the desert sands normally contain surface impurities or infra-crystalline impurities which may impart different colours.

In many areas near the coast, the sand is stabilized by vegetation, although the natural flora has been altered in recent times by extensive grazing of domesticated animals. Further inland the sands may be quite barren, as few plants can successfully colonize the mobile dunes.

DUNE PATTERNS

Sand dune formation is controlled by a combination of wind strength and direction, and sediment supply. In detail, however, the formation of dune patterns is complex and remains poorly understood. Within a given area the dune pattern may be quite regular, but also very intricate. Physical features are typically created on several different scales: giant sand ridges on a scale of hundreds of metres to a few kilometres, sand dunes measured in metres to tens of metres, and ripples on a scale of centimetres to a metre or more. This

hierarchy can be readily observed in the deserts of the UAE.

Since dune patterns vary with wind direction, seasonal or occasional variations in wind direction introduce new elements into the overall pattern. These elements may reinforce or cancel each other, in the same manner as ocean waves. In addition, because sand dunes cannot move or change as quickly as ocean waves, past history may play a significant part in what we see today. Despite relatively consistent prevailing wind directions in the present day UAE, dune patterns and alignment vary considerably from area to area.

In an attempt to find order in complexity, geologists have recognized certain basic types of dune forms. Many of these are well illustrated in the UAE, although hybrid or intermediate forms are probably the norm. *Barchan dunes* are perhaps the simplest. These are individual crescent shaped dunes, convex

in the upwind direction, having a relatively gentle upwind slope but a steep slip face downwind. They tend to form in areas where the sediment supply is limited and are most often seen atop gravel plains or salt flats. They may form fields of up to several dozen, advancing across the flats.

Transverse dunes are elongated sand ridges that form perpendicular to the prevailing wind direction. Most of the active dunes seen in the UAE are of this general type. Typically they occur in parallel arrays with elongated troughs between. Beyond this, they may be quite variable. The crestlines may be relatively straight, or sinuous or cuspate, and oblique elements are normally present. Like barchans, transverse dunes are asymmetrical, having relatively gentle upwind slopes and steep slip faces on the downwind side.

In the UAE, very large transverse dune ridges are developed in and around the Liwa oasis and in the Manadir area in the extreme south-east of the country, along the border with Oman. In Manadir, the major sand ridges are locally called *'irqs* ("ergs") and are individually named. In both of these areas the sand ridges may reach heights of 100 metres or more above the adjacent basin floor, and smaller, subsidiary dune patterns are developed on the main ridges.

In the Manadir area the main sand ridges are relatively straight and are separated by elongated, continuous *sabkha* or salt flats. In contrast, the Liwa dunes are a textbook example of the so-called *aklé* pattern, in which the main ridges are sinuous and adjacent ridges are "out of phase" by half a wavelength, so that the trough between them is divided into a chain of broad basins separated by narrow gaps. The gaps are often filled by tongues of low sand, thereby creating a pattern of discontinuous rounded basins.

Longitudinal dunes are formed parallel to the prevailing wind direction, with slip faces on both sides. Their mode of formation is not well understood but is thought to involve helical flow of air along the troughs between them. In the UAE longitudinal dunes are well developed only in the extreme south-west, where access is difficult, but they continue for hundreds of kilometres into the Empty Quarter.

Far Left: *The wind sculpted desert features on many scales.*

Left: *"Fossil" dunes sands were cemented at a time when ground water levels were higher than today.*

27

Top Right: *An inland sabkha lake after rains at Qaraytiysah, in the Eastern Desert.*

Bottom Left: *Giant dune ridges and sabkha flats at Liwa.*

Bottom Right: *Between Abu Dhabi and Liwa, tongues of pale sand resembling a choppy sea of dunes seem to be advancing along broad troughs between higher, flatter ridges of red sand.*

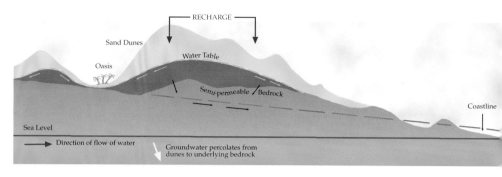

Fig. 4. *Cross-section of an Oasis.*

THE EFFECTS OF CLIMATIC CHANGE

The largest dune features of the present day UAE, including the major transverse dunes of Liwa and Manadir, the smaller eroded dune ridges of the Northern Emirates, and the longitudinal dunes of the south-west, are believed to date from the most recent glacial period, more than 10,000 years ago. Glaciation in northern latitudes contributed to sand dune development in the UAE in two ways. First, glaciation compressed the width of the climatic zones between the glaciers and the equator, leading to a stronger global wind regime. Second, glaciation caused a fall in global sea level which largely emptied the Arabian Gulf and so exposed a tremendous volume of loose sediment to serve as source material for dunes. A glacial origin for these major features is consistent with the fact that they do not seem to be aligned with today's prevailing winds.

The present day wind regime appears to be transporting material from the coast inland and reworking the surface of the major earlier structures without, so far, removing or reorienting them. For example, one may observe between Abu Dhabi and the Liwa oasis that extensive tongues of pale sand resembling a choppy sea of dunes (aligned NE-SW) are filling in broad troughs between higher, flatter ridges of red sand (aligned WNW-ESE). The latter are known as *suruq*, or easy travel zones, and are interpreted as the eroded cores of older, larger ridges. Further inland, however, the major transverse dune ridges of Liwa and Manadir are neither in motion nor are they being eroded at the present time, although the smaller dunes on their surfaces conform to present day winds.

The crests of both barchans and transverse dunes are normally very sharp, but after rain they may be flattened or rounded. The prevailing wind direction in the UAE today is from the north-west, so that most active dunes are aligned NE-SW, with their steep faces to the south-east. A major subsidiary wind direction, however, is from the south-east. Occasional strong south-east winds have the effect of creating temporary "reverse" crests at the tops of dunes otherwise oriented to north-west winds. This phenomenon causes particular difficulty for drivers in the dunes.

In addition to changes in wind regime, the UAE deserts have experienced changes in rainfall at various times in the past. This is indicated by the widespread occurrence of outcrops of lightly cemented, cross-bedded dune sands. These were cemented by the precipitation of calcium carbonate and other salts from ground water at a time when the water table was higher than it is today. Other evidence of higher rainfall in the past includes playa lake sediments, horizons containing abundant fossil roots and burrows, fossil reeds, crocodile bone, freshwater mollusc shells and trails, and fragments of ostrich eggshell. Occasional gravel deposits, often preserved as low, flat-topped hills or *mesas*, testify to the presence of rivers.

Some of these features may be attributable to the alternation of so-called pluvial (wet) and inter-pluvial (dry) periods recognized elsewhere and believed to correlate with the stages of Pleistocene glaciation. Arid conditions in the UAE predated the Pleistocene, however. The widespread Miocene deposits of the Baynunah Formation (*c.*6-7 million years old) in the west of Abu Dhabi are interpreted as a major river system that watered a semi-arid, subtropical savannah. The Baynunah formation contains the fossilized remains of early relatives of elephants, hippopotamus, horses, cows, crocodiles, turtles and other animals. The intervening Pliocene is not known from the UAE, but was a period of drought in both East Africa and the Mediterranean.

Paradoxically, the dune sands of the UAE have actually facilitated human habitation in the desert environment. This is because the porous sands serve as a reservoir for what little water does fall, allowing it to collect above impermeable bedrock or subsurface crust and protecting it from evaporation. Where the resulting water table is close to the surface, wells may be dug for human use, and small scale agriculture may be possible (Fig. 5). The best example in the UAE is the Liwa oasis, which was a seasonal home to many Abu Dhabi families until the discovery of oil.

Algal mats form on coastal sabkha at the upper limit of normal high tides.

SABKHA ENVIRONMENTS

Sabkha is the Arabic term for low-lying saline flats subject to periodic inundation. Three types are recognized, based on their environment of formation. All are found in the UAE. Coastal sabkha, as the name implies, forms at or near the marine shoreline. Fluvio-lacustrine (i.e. river-lake) sabkha is formed in association with riverine drainage patterns in arid areas. Inland or interdune sabkha is found in low-lying basins within the sand desert.

All sabkhas share certain characteristics. Although they are restricted to hot, arid regions, the sabkha surface is always very close to the local water table, usually within about a metre. Groundwater is drawn towards the surface by capillary action and evaporates in the upper subsurface in response to the high temperatures. There it deposits dissolved salts, including calcium carbonate, gypsum ($CaSO_4$-$2H_2O$), anhydrite ($CaSO_4$) and sodium chloride or halite (NaCl), which precipitate in that order. These salts create a hard, impermeable crust in a zone about half a metre below the surface. This crust, along with high salinity, discourages all plant growth. The crust also impedes the drainage of surface water, so that

after rains the sabkhas flood. The surface water then evaporates over time, often leaving behind a dazzling white crust of salt.

When dry, the sabkha is firm and suitable for vehicle transportation, but after rains it is notoriously treacherous. Sabkha is not quicksand, however, and the subsurface crust will ultimately support the weight of humans, animals and ordinary vehicles, although this may be small comfort to one who is mired in it. The explorer Wilfred Thesiger relied on this knowledge to cross the Sabkha Matti in the western UAE by camel in 1948, after a week of rain.

COASTAL SABKHA

The UAE is famous among geologists worldwide for its coastal sabkha, which dominates the coastline west of Abu Dhabi island. Here the sabkha may extend more than 15 kilometres inland. The coastal sabkha is extremely flat but most of the surface is nevertheless above the level of normal high tides, so that it is flooded only by a combination of storm surge and spring tides, or by heavy rains.

Cross-sections through the sabkha show a characteristic sequence (from bottom to top) of algal layers, calcareous mud, gypsum, anhydrite and occasional salt (Fig. 5). This sequence reflects the growth of the coastal sabkha. Gelatinous mats of blue-green algae develop in the high intertidal zone and trap fine calcareous sediment brought in by the tides. Lower in the intertidal zone, a species of crab builds burrows which cement the surface of the calcareous mud over large areas. Gypsum crystals form within the sediments at the water table. Little by little, these processes raise the level of the land surface and cause the shoreline to advance seaward. It is estimated that the Abu Dhabi coastline has prograded (i.e. advanced seaward) approximately 25 kilometres in this way over the past 5000 years.

Study of the coastal sabkha has also yielded an answer to the "dolomite problem." *Dolomite* ($CaMg(CO_3)_2$) is known from the geologic record as a common mineral, sometimes the dominant mineral, in carbonate rocks of shallow water origin. Because sedimentary deposition of dolomite is unknown in any present day environments, it was widely assumed that dolomite is

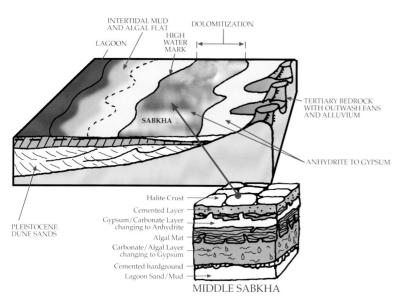

INTERTIDAL MUD AND ALGAL FLAT

DOLOMITIZATION

HIGH WATER MARK

LAGOON

SABKHA

TERTIARY BEDROCK WITH OUTWASH FANS AND ALLUVIUM

ANHYDRITE TO GYPSUM

PLEISTOCENE DUNE SANDS

Halite Crust
Cemented Layer
Gypsum/Carbonate Layer changing to Anhydrite
Algal Mat
Carbonate/Algal Layer changing to Gypsum
Cemented hardground
Lagoon Sand/Mud

MIDDLE SABKHA

Far Left:
Fig 5. Cross section of coastal sabkha.

Left: *Rain or storm surge may flood sabkha for several kilometres above normal high tides.*

Salt polygons form by surface evaporation and capillary action.

the last glaciation the Sabkha Matti was covered by sand dunes, but these have been almost entirely removed by the prevailing north-west winds since the rising post-glacial sea level cut off northerly sediment sources.

formed by chemical alteration of calcium carbonate ($CaCO_3$), which is widely deposited in warm seas, soon after its deposition. The problem was that no present day environments were known in which alteration to dolomite was taking place, either. Now it is recognized that dolomitization occurs extensively in the sabkha environment, beginning above the normal high tide zone. Further inland the upper sabkha sediments may be entirely replaced by finely crystalline dolomite.

THE SABKHA MATTI

The Sabkha Matti is a large and well known sabkha located in the extreme west of the UAE, extending more than 100 kilometres inland (Fig. 5). Until recently it was the bane of overland travellers. The Sabkha Matti is classified as a fluvio-lacustrine sabkha because it has now been identified as the probable confluence and estuary of several rivers which drained the Empty Quarter in earlier, wetter times. Groundwater percolating in buried watersheds may help to account for the location and extent of the present day sabkha here. During

Wrinkled sabkha surface in the Manadir area of the Eastern Desert.

INTERDUNE SABKHA

The UAE's best example of interdune sabkha occurs in the Liwa area, where the sinuous giant dune ridges enclose myriad sabkha flats. After heavy rains these flats may remain flooded for weeks or months. The Liwa area is one of several noted for its *sand roses*. These are attractive natural formations resembling stone flowers. They consist of interlocking flat polyhedrons of gypsum-cemented sand, formed by subsurface precipitation just above the groundwater level. Typically, layers of sand roses are found weathering out of low dunes somewhat above the present day sabkha surface.

Throughout the Liwa area, the sabkha flats testify to the historical proximity of groundwater (Fig. 5). South-east of the Liwa oasis, old wells are preserved in which the water level remains within two metres below the surface. Within the oasis area itself, however, local residents report that water levels have dropped to 10 metres or more as a result of increasing agricultural demand.

The elongated parallel sabkhas of the Manadir area, in the extreme south-east of the country, are larger than those of Liwa and are probably intermediate between interdune sabkha and fluvio-lacustrine sabkha, since it seems likely that their hydrology is at least partly controlled by surface and subsurface runoff from the Hajar Mountains to the east. As in Liwa, some of these sabkhas are now being filled with soil in preparation for agricultural use.

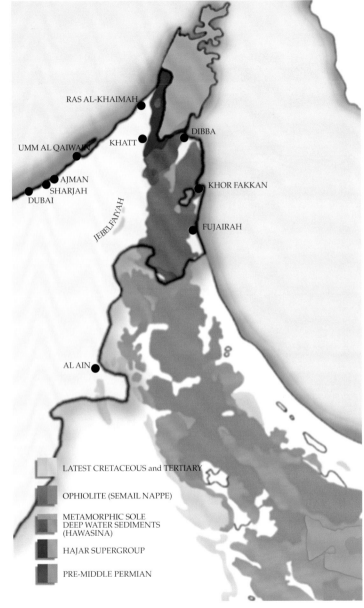

RAS AL-KHAIMAH

DIBBA

UMM AL QAIWAIN   KHATT

KHOR FAKKAN

AJMAN
SHARJAH
DUBAI

JEBEL FAIYAH

FUJAIRAH

AL AIN

LATEST CRETACEOUS and TERTIARY

OPHIOLITE (SEMAIL NAPPE)

METAMORPHIC SOLE
DEEP WATER SEDIMENTS
(HAWASINA)

HAJAR SUPERGROUP

PRE-MIDDLE PERMIAN

Fig. 6.
Geological map of the Hajar Mountains.

Pillow lavas are formed when lava erupts in deep water, typically at mid-ocean ridges where new oceanic crust is being formed.

The Ru'us Al-Jibal at sunset: this area has been uplifted by more than 2000 metres in the past 25 million years.

THE HAJAR MOUNTAINS

The Hajar Mountains parallel the east coast of the UAE. At their highest point in the north, in the Musandam Peninsula, they reach a height of 2000 metres. There the mountain slopes drop directly into the sea. This area is known locally as the *Ru'us Al-Jibal*, literally the "heads of the mountains." The Ru'us Al-Jibal exposes the thick sequence of Mesozoic carbonates of the Arabian Platform which correlates with the principal oil bearing strata that lie deeply buried to the west.

To the south of the Ru'us Al-Jibal the Hajar Mountains consist of a complex of igneous and sedimentary rocks which represent the upper mantle, oceanic crust and deep ocean sediments of the ocean that once lay to the north-east. The igneous rocks of the mantle and oceanic crust are collectively called *ophiolites*. The ophiolites of the UAE now lie above the rocks of the Arabian Platform. The Hajar Mountains constitute the world's most extensive surface exposure of ophiolites. For this reason they are of tremendous interest to geologists.

The distinctive geology of the Hajar Mountains is best understood by reviewing the plate tectonic history of the area. This consists of five principal stages described below. Figure 7 depicts these stages and Figure 8 summarizes the resulting structural sequence and the nature of the rocks that can be seen in the Hajar Mountains today. Figure 6 shows the present distribution of the principal rock units.

33

Ocean Formation and Deep Water Sedimentation
(Permian to Late Cretaceous)

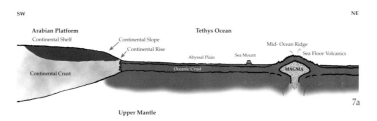

7a

The colourful deep water sediments of the Hawasina basin are thrust against the grey carbonates of the Ru'us al-Jibal in Wadi Khabb.

The opening of the Tethys Ocean occurred along a mid-ocean ridge situated to the north-east of the Arabian Platform. Here new oceanic crust was created as adjacent plates of the lithosphere diverged. This crust consisted of a suite of related igneous rocks formed at various depths under the mid-ocean ridge by partial melting of mantle rock, and characterized by the extrusion of volcanics at the ocean floor.

As the Tethys continued to open, deep ocean sediments accumulated on the continental rise and continental slope of the Arabian Platform, and on the abyssal plain of the new ocean. These sediments included radiolarian cherts, fine muds and, nearer the Arabian Platform, occasional beds of mixed coarser material deposited by underwater landslides and dense, sediment laden flows called 'turbidity currents'. Seamounts (extinct subsea volcanoes) were also created in association with the mid-ocean ridge and coral atolls were established on some of these.

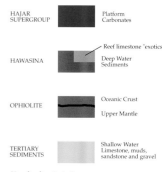

Key for figs 7a to 7e

Subduction of the Afro-Arabian Plate
(Mid-to Late Cretaceous)

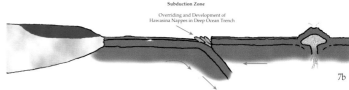

7b

In the mid to late Cretaceous, about 95 million years ago, a subduction zone formed in the Tethys Ocean between the mid-ocean ridge and the margin of the Arabian Platform, roughly parallel to the two and lying more than 400 kilometres to the north-east of the present day coast. This subduction zone dipped to the north-east. Here the plate carrying the Afro-Arabian continent was subducted beneath the oceanic crust of the Tethys at a deep ocean trench, and the upper mantle and oceanic crust of the Afro-Arabian plate, plus a thin veneer of deep ocean sediments, were resorbed into the deeper mantle.

Abortive Subduction of the Arabian Platform and Obduction of Oceanic Crust (Late Cretaceous)

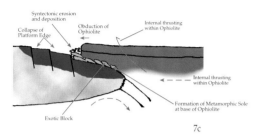

7c

The subduction process proceeded routinely until enough of the Afro-Arabian plate had been subducted to bring the Arabian Platform itself into the subduction zone. Subduction cannot accommodate the relatively light (i.e. less dense) rocks that constitute continental crust, and the arrival of the Arabian Platform therefore caused the subduction zone to 'jam'. The situation was ultimately resolved by the formation of a new, parallel subduction zone further to the north-east, in order to accommodate the continuing global convergence of the adjacent plates. However, in the initial process of trying to subduct the edge of the Arabian Platform, the distinctive geology of the Hajar Mountains was formed.

At a subduction zone, not all of the descending plate is subducted and resorbed. At least part of the veneer of deep ocean sediments is often scraped off and piled up in front of the overriding plate. This process was accentuated as the Arabian Platform approached the subduction zone. The effect of successive underthrusting and scraping off of sediments in the subduction zone was to create a pile of overlapping sheets of deep water sediments, with those formed nearest to the continent (south-west) at the bottom and those formed farthest away (north-east) on top.

In the final phases of the abortive subduction, the leading edge of the Arabian Platform was forced under the edge of the overriding plate. Correspondingly, the overriding plate, consisting of upper mantle and oceanic crust, was forced over the edge of the Arabian Platform and over the overlapping layers of deep water sediments that had accumulated in the trench between them. To some extent those sediments acted as a lubricating layer which facilitated this movement. The phenomenon of thrusting of a sheet of oceanic crust onto the adjacent continent at a subduction zone is called *obduction*. This process seems to have begun approximately 90 million years ago and continued until about 70 million years ago.

The foregoing description is somewhat oversimplified, because the ophiolites of the Hajar Mountains appear to represent a piece of oceanic crust that originally contained within it major lateral offsets like those of the present-day mid-Atlantic ridge, which are known as transform faults. These offsets are preserved today as the transverse structural alignments that mark many of the major wadi systems that cross the Hajar Mountains, such as Wadi Hatta and the so-called Dibba Zone at the southern edge of the Ru'us Al-Jibal. Both of these areas are structurally very complex.

Serpentinized peridotite is the most common rock type found within the ophiolite. The dark peridotite, originally formed in the upper mantle, is typically altered to a pale green platy mineral called serpentine.

Blocks of white reef limestone called "exotics" often cap hills within the deep water Hawasina basin sediments.

The emplacement of the ophiolite nappe, originally more than 10 kilometres thick, involved considerable shearing along its base, which is exposed along most of the western front of the mountains. In addition, the mantle rocks were invaded by hydrothermal fluids both in their initial environment beneath a mid-ocean ridge and during their subsequent transport and emplacement. This has resulted in extensive veining and alteration of the mantle rocks to a mineral called *serpentine* – a fibrous, platy greenish-white mineral of the mica family, related to asbestos. It is from such serpentinization that surface exposures of mantle rocks like those in the Hajar Mountains and elsewhere have received the name "ophiolites", which means "snake (or serpentine) rocks".

The End of Subduction and Isostatic Uplift
(Latest Cretaceous)

After emplacement of the ophiolite nappe, subduction finally ceased in this area and a new subduction zone was created further to the north-east. Freed from the forces of subduction, the thick pile of superimposed rocks that had been accumulated by subduction and obduction at the edge of the Arabian Platform rose isostatically, since all of the rocks involved are lighter than the underlying mantle. This uplift completed the detachment of the obducted ophiolite, and may also have been responsible for some additional movement of the nappes in response to gravity.

Isostatic
Rebound

7d

Isostatic uplift caused the area to rise above sea level and it was subsequently eroded. In the UAE, shallow water sediments from the latest Cretaceous and early Tertiary can be found overlapping the edge of today's mountain front, indicating that some if not all of the present day mountain region was again submerged at that time. Late Cretaceous and early Tertiary sediments found near Al-Ain and Jebel Fayah are known for their abundant shallow-water marine fossils, including rudists (large solitary coral-like bivalve), echinoids (sea urchins and sand dollars), gastropods (snails) and nummulites (large foraminifera).

Regional Uplift and Erosion

(Oligocene to Present)

The Hajar Mountains, as we know them , are the result of uplift, deformation and erosion under arid or semi-arid conditions, beginning in the late Oligocene (c. 25 million years ago) and continuing to the present day. This uplift is thought to be related to movements of the crustal plates and consequent slow-motion collision (i.e. tectonic convergence) of the Eurasian plate, Afro-Arabian plate and other marginal plates, including the Indian plate. The same movements are also responsible for mountain building in the Alps, the Zagros and the Himalayas, and the opening of the Red Sea.

Whereas the original emplacement of the ophiolite involved a substantial component of horizontal movement, amounting to hundreds of kilometres, the post-Oligocene phase of uplift and deformation seems to have involved mainly compressive movements characterized by open folding and vertical faulting. Such features are well displayed in the resistant carbonate strata of the Ru'us Al-Jibal, where the overall uplift since the Oligocene has been more than 2000 metres. Evidence of this deformation may also be seen or inferred elsewhere, as at Jebel Fayah, Jebel Rowdhah or Jebel Hafit, where it involves sediments deposited after emplacement of the ophiolite nappe. Low angle thrust faulting

on a scale of at least several kilometres is also known to have occurred. The best example is in Wadi Haqil near Ras al-Khaimah, where the Ru'us Al-Jibal carbonates are seen to be thrust westward over deep water sediments which are presumed originally to have been thrust over the carbonates.

Erosion of the Hajar Mountains has produced the broad gravel plains that border the mountains on both east and west, and that fill major valleys. Within the mountains themselves, erosion has proceeded by the alternation of cutting and filling. At present we are in a phase of cutting down, and in virtually any mountain wadi south of the Ru'us Al-Jibal, one can observe that the current wadi bed is frequently bordered by the steep walls of higher gravel terraces (up to as much as 30 metres higher). These walls provide excellent cross sections for the study of sedimentary processes in the wadi environment, processes that continue today. The surfaces of the gravel terraces have typically remained undisturbed for a long time, and now display a deep purple-brown patina known as *rock varnish* (a.k.a. desert varnish), which is caused by manganese-fixing bacteria.

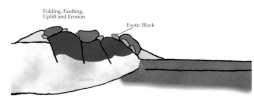

Folding, Faulting,
Uplift and Erosion

Exotic Block

7e

Further study must be awaited in order to determine whether the alternating phases of cutting and filling are the result of variations in regional precipitation or regional uplift, or both, or some other factor. However, it seems clear that erosion of the mountains and deposition of gravels has been greatest when the climate has been wettest, and that precipitation levels known from recent and historic times are not sufficient to account for gravels of the size and scale that exist.

A final but distinctive touch is the effect of Pleistocene glaciation on the mountains of the northernmost Musandam Peninsula. At the peak of glaciation, global sea level was more than 100 metres lower than today, and the wadis of the peninsula established a base level in this environment. Thereafter, rising sea level coupled with regional subsidence of the Arabian Gulf flooded the wadis at the tip of the peninsula, creating the unique and scenic arid fjords of that area.

Figure 8.
Structural Units and Rock Types of the Hajar Mountains.
(from top to bottom of the structural sequence)

POST-OBDUCTION SEDIMENTS

This unit consists of shallow water sediments deposited after emplacement of the ophiolite nappe. Various subunits are recognized by geologists. They range in age from latest Cretaceous to Miocene and include both clastics (sandstones and shales) and carbonates. These sediments were deposited unconformably on top of the underlying units and have themselves been folded or tilted and eroded by post-Oligocene uplift and deformation. This can readily be observed at Jebel Fayah or Jebel Rowdhah in the Northern Emirates, or at Jebel Hafit or Fossil Valley near Al-Ain. These sediments are known for their abundant shallow water marine fossils, including rudists (large solitary coral-like bivalves), echinoids (sea urchins and sand dollars), gastropods (snails) and nummulites (large foraminifera).

-    -   -   *unconformable sedimentary contact*   -   -   -

OPHIOLITE NAPPE

At the top of the main structural sequence lies the ophiolite nappe, often called the *Semail nappe* by geologists. This nappe consists of a sheet of the upper mantle and oceanic crust dated at *c.*90-100 million years old. The total original thickness of the ophiolite nappe was some 15 kilometers, including more than 10 kilometers of upper mantle.

OCEANIC CRUST:

At the top of the ophiolite, the rocks of the oceanic crust normally occur in a regular sequence, from top to bottom, as follows:

(a) **Lavas and pillow lavas**: These are usually basalts and were extruded at the mid-ocean ridge. Pillow lavas are lavas erupted under deep water, which cool quickly at their surface while flowing, forming distinctive pillow-like lobes. Occasionally, deep water sediments (usually cherts or thin-bedded limestones) are associated with the pillow lavas.

(b) **Sheeted Dykes**: These are sets of parallel intrusive "walls" of diabase or diorite (an igneous rock also of basaltic composition) which were emplaced vertically and served as feeders for lavas at the mid-ocean ridge.

(c) **Gabbros and layered gabbros**: These are coarsely crystalline rocks which solidified in magma chambers under the mid-ocean ridge. They are composed principally of pyroxene and calcic feldspar and are therefore relatively low in silica, but not as low as mantle rocks, having a range of chemical composition equivalent to basalt.

Gabbros are common along the east coast and in Wadi Hiluw, but in the UAE the top of the ophiolite nappe has generally been eroded and the rocks of the upper oceanic crust are therefore absent. Sheeted dykes are found only at the mouth of Wadi Hiluw and pillow lavas are known only from isolated outcrops.

Like ophiolites elsewhere, the ophiolites of the UAE contain localized deposits of copper ore. Many of these were mined in antiquity and may now be recognized by the presence of slag from nearby smelting.

UPPER MANTLE:

The compositional transition from oceanic crust to upper mantle has long been recognized seismically. The abrupt change in seismic velocities that occurs at this horizon is known as the Mohorovicic discontinuity or "Moho." In the Hajar Mountains it is possible to walk below the Moho.

The primary constituent of the upper mantle is a dark rock called (generically) *peridotite*, which is made up of the mineral *olivine* and one or more types of *pyroxene*, with minor trace minerals such as chrome spinel. The precise composition (and therefore the technical name) is variable. The most common peridotite in the Hajar Mountains is called *harzburgite,* but *wehrlite* and *lherzolite* are also found.

Mantle rock is distinctively low in silica (SiO_2) and high in magnesium and iron, relative to ordinary rocks. Mantle peridotites may contain occasional pods of relatively pure olivine or of relatively pure *chromite*. The latter may permit mining of chromium on a small scale.

Mantle peridotites are well exposed along the road from Dhaid to Masafi and from Masafi to Dibba, as well as in the area south of Hatta, but alteration to serpentine is common. In many places near the base of the ophiolite nappe, the mantle peridotites have also been extensively fractured and/or silicified. This is especially so along the western front of the mountains.

-   -   -   *tectonic/metamorphic contact*   -   -   -

METAMORPHIC SOLE

At various sites the emplacement of the ophiolite nappe was accompanied by localized contact metamorphism of the rocks at its base, involving both the underlying sediments and the ophiolite itself. Metamorphism was sometimes sufficient to produce garnet schists or amphibolites. This *metamorphic sole* is well exposed as silver-white rocks along the main road north of the town of Masafi. The rocks exposed there are principally schists and marbles, the metamorphic products of clastics and carbonates, respectively, in the underlying sediments.

-   -   -   *tectonic/metamorphic contact*   -   -   -

HAWASINA SEDIMENTS

This unit consists of the deep ocean sediments that were deposited in the Tethys Ocean and imbricated at the subduction zone. They are late Permian through late Cretaceous in age, and are therefore contemporaneous with the shallow water carbonates of the Arabian Platform, which they now overlie. A number of individual subunits have been identified and mapped, but the internal structure is often very complex due to the movement and deformation that these rocks have undergone.

The Hawasina sediments include red and green cherts (sometimes composed of radiolarians), thin-bedded mudstones and carbonates, fissile shales, turbidites, continental slope and rise clastics including conglomerates of slumped and redeposited shelf limestones, and occasional volcanic rocks. These sediments are often very colorful. They are best seen in the UAE at Jebel Wamm, west of the Dibba plains, or in the areas south and east of Tawiyyan or east of Hatta. They can also be observed just over the Oman border in the area of Wadi Sumayni.

At the top of the Hawasina sediments in certain places are large blocks of white reef limestone, called *exotics*, which are resistant and tend to form the summits of large or small peaks. They are typically associated with volcanic rocks and are thought to represent coral atolls that formed atop seamounts. No major exotics occur within the UAE, but good examples can be seen just over the Oman border at Jebel Ghaweel and near the villages of Shiyah and Shuwayhah, on the track from Jebel Rowdhah to Mahdhah.

-   -   -   *tectonic contact*   -   -   -

ARABIAN PLATFORM

The lowest unit observed, structurally, is the Arabian Platform itself, represented in the UAE by the thick late Permian to late Cretaceous shallow water carbonates (limestones and dolomites) exposed in the Ru'us Al-Jibal. These are known collectively to geologists as the *Hajar Supergroup* and include numerous subunits. They can be correlated with the principal oil-bearing strata that lie deeply buried to the west. Various horizons throughout the Hajar Supergroup contain shallow water marine fossils, including abundant bivalves and gastropods, rarer brachiopods, crinoids and cephalopods, and locally abundant pipe corals and trace fossils.

The pre-Permian basement of the Arabian Platform is known in the UAE only from localized and fragmentary outcrops of Paleozoic shallow water elastics near the village of Al-Ghail, which have been collectively called the Rann Formation. Scarce fossils have indicated ages ranging from Ordovician to Devonian. The carbonates of the Ru'us Al-Jibal are presumed to have been deposited unconformably above the pre-Permian basement.

The Fossil Record

Peter Whybrow, Andrew Smith & Andrew Hill

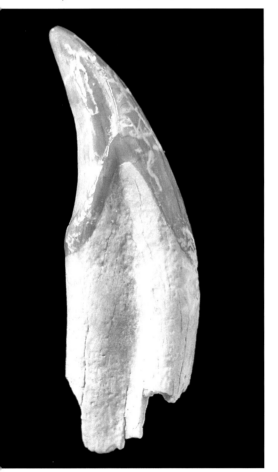

Tooth of an 8 million year old monkey-like fossil from the Miocene of Abu Dhabi.

Since 1979 an international team of palaeontologists and geologists have taken part in a research project in the United Arab Emirates led by the Natural History Museum, London. Their work has added a considerable data base of knowledge to the ancient heritage of the Emirates and the project has received support from the Abu Dhabi Company for Onshore Oil Operations (ADCO) and the United Arab Emirates Ministry for Higher Education and Scientific Research. The research project embraces three themes. The first theme is the geology and palaeontology of the Miocene (a geological time period from 23 million to 5 million years ago) rocks found in the Western Region of Abu Dhabi. The second theme is about the Eocene to Oligocene (30 to 50 million years ago) environment and fossils found at Jebel Hafit, and the final theme concerns the geology and palaeontology of the Cretaceous rocks (about 70 million years old) found in the Eastern Region of the United Arab Emirates bordering the foothills of the Hajar Mountains. In addition, preliminary studies have been carried out on the 150 million year old fossils found in the Musandam region of the United Arab Emirates.

Before examining the results of the three research themes so far, it is useful to outline the tectonic (structure of the earth's crust) history of Arabia so as to give an idea of why this part of the world - especially the United Arab Emirates - is important for international geological and palaeontological studies.

Continents on the Move

As is discussed in the previous chapter the world's land masses have not always been in the place where they are today. During the past 700 million years they have moved, broken apart and joined together. The earth's crustal plates include the land masses - continental plates - and the material beneath the oceans - oceanic plates. This movement of continental plates continues today and some plates, such as the Arabian continental plate drifting away from Africa, travel at a rate of 5 centimetres a year. At the margins of these plates there are two types of phenomena; "active" events caused by colliding plates and "passive" events where the plates are spreading apart. The term "active" is derived from the mechanism that returns material back into the earth's upper mantle. Material of an oceanic plate is more dense than that of a continental plate, so that when the two collide the oceanic plate is forced beneath the continental plate. This process, called subduction, can result in the formation of mountain ranges such as the Zagros mountains of Iran and activities associated with this process are deep-seated earthquakes and intense volcanicity, sometimes with catastrophic results.

When the "active" and "passive" margins have been identified, and by using data from the earth's past magnetic fields that have been fossilised within the iron minerals of basalts found at the margins of spreading oceanic plates, the positions of the land masses can be plotted for various parts of geological time. The results from this plotting is called palaeogeography.

Following its splitting away from South America about 140 million years ago, the massive continental plate of Africa, the northeastern part of which was to become Arabia, steadily moved northeastwards. This movement was due to sea floor spreading along the mid-Atlantic ridge - a "passive" plate margin. During the late Cretaceous (about 70 million years ago) the rocks of ancient Nubia, linking Arabia with Egypt at that time, began to drift apart to form the beginnings of what is now the Red Sea rift. At this time Arabia was still isolated from both Europe and Asia by a seaway named the Tethys that once connected the ancient Mediterranean with the Arabian Gulf and the Indian Ocean. Twenty three million years ago, approximately, the pace of movement of Arabia away from Africa increased by an anticlockwise motion to the northeast that closed the Tethys sea. This event prompted the formation of the Zagros and Taurus Mountains of Iran and Turkey respectively and, in Arabia, most of the volcanicity linked with this movement was confined to the southern Red Sea area, namely the Republic of Yemen and the Kingdom of Saudi Arabia. A land connection to Africa was still in place in southwestern Arabia; the Ethiopian-Yemen isthmus existed until Pliocene times (about 5 million years ago) when the Red Sea was connected to the Mediterranean but cut off from the Gulf of Aden. This land bridge allowed migrations of terrestrial animals to and from Africa and Asia via Arabia.

Two major events for geological science are therefore exhibited in Arabia and particularly in the United Arab Emirates. The first occurred at the time just before the dinosaurs became extinct, 70 million years ago, and was the emergence of oceanic crust in what are now the foothills of the Hajar Mountains. Around the islands formed by this event shallow water, marine carbonates were deposited (see, Ancient Seas). This habitat supported a unique and diverse assemblage of invertebrate animals ranging from echinoids and corals to bizarre molluscs called rudists. Their fossilised remains can now be found at Jebel Huwayyah, Jebel Rawdah and Jebel Buhays.

The second event (about 23 million years ago) focuses on the disconnection of the Tethys seaway by the northeastern movement of the Arabian continental plate in Mesopotamia and the Arabian Gulf to form a land bridge, possibly located between Qatar and the coastal Fars region of Iran. After this disconnection, Tethys ceased to exist. Land animals from both Africa and Asia had the opportunity for intercontinental dispersal via Arabia and it is probable that these changes to Middle East geography also changed the flow of river systems in northwestern Africa and in Mesopotamia allowing animals in freshwater habitats, such as fish, turtles, crocodiles and aquatic mammals, to disperse into new ecosystems. The remains of these animals can be found, but rarely, in the Western Region of the Emirate of Abu Dhabi.

Consequently, the United Arab Emirates is palaeontologically unique for it has the finest locations for discovering Middle East Cretaceous marine inverte-brates and late Miocene Arabian continental vertebrate fossils.

EMIRATES GEOLOGY AND PALAEONTOLOGY

Overall, the surface geology of the Emirates can be divided into three regions. These are, a) the offshore islands, b) the generally flat western interior from the international border at As Sila to, roughly, the Dubai-Al Ain road and c) the region west of that road to include Al Ain, the northern Emirates and the emirate of Fujairah.

OFFSHORE ISLANDS

The first geological survey by Europeans of what is now the United Arab Emirates appears to have taken place in the 1850's when Captain C. G. Constable of Her Majesty's Indian Navy sailed from Bombay to chart the islands lying offshore from Abu Dhabi, Dubai and the northern emirates. In his reports (Bombay Asiatic Journal, 1859 and 1860) he distinguishes the Persian side of the Gulf from the Arabian side where at Aboo Moosa (Abu Musa) and Surree (Sirri) he describes a white calcareous grit that he termed "Milliolite", probably Pleistocene or recently formed beach rock - a hardened mass of sand and shells cemented by carbonate. He was intrigued by seeing what he thought were the products of volcanoes - iron ore, gypsum, salt, sulphur and diorite (a rock similar to basalt) - that he had found on other islands such as Daus (Das), Arzenie (Arzana), Dalmy (Dalma), Jirnain, Seir Abonade (Sir Abu Nu'ai). He states that ". . . specimens of 'peacock-iron-ore' from Dalmy are as beautiful as any that I have ever seen from the island of Elba". He goes on to comment ". . . doubtless there are points . . . on the mainland . . . where the volcanic rock projects above the surface . . . [such as] Sir Beni Yas, and the headland close to it [presumably Jebel Dhanna] is on a level almost with the sea, [and] as far inland as the eye can reach, barren and uninhabited . . .". We now know these so-called volcanic rocks and minerals, called the Hormuz Formation, are about 550 million years old and have been brought to the surface by Cambrian salt to form a salt diapir (or salt plug) and have no link with volcanoes. Unfortunately, Constable did not record finding any fossils on the offshore islands.

Reconstruction of life in Abu Dhabi 8 million years ago. A sabre-toothed cat attacks a primitive three-toed horse, Hipparion. Parts of both animals have been found as fossils.

In October, 1859, he sailed further up the coast to "Koweyt" where the boat passed through large sheets of "... oily substance... Our Arab Pilot... was certain there were springs of it near this part... but he did not know how to collect it or he could make a fortune by it". Coincidentally, the birth of the modern petroleum industry is marked in the same year - 1859 - by the successful shallow exploration well in Pennsylvania, U.S.A.

THE WESTERN INTERIOR

The vast area south from the Arabian Gulf coast that borders the Rub al-Khali especially around the Liwa area, where huge dunes cover any geological feature, has only rare rock outcrops. These mainly occur in the coastal region

to the north of the Abu Dhabi to As Sila road in the area from Tarif to Jebel Dhanna. Here the jebels and sea cliff localities expose rocks of Miocene age called the Baynunah and Shuwaihat Formations. Rare vertebrate fossils have been found in these rocks. Near to As Sila itself, marine carbonates outcrop at the foot of the escarpment and these are about 16 million years old and are similar to limestones of the Dam Formation found in the Kingdom of Saudi Arabia. In the Emirates these rocks are sometimes known as the Lower Fars or Gachsaran Formation and were deposited in a shallow, tropical sea. Poorly preserved fossils such as gastropods and bivalves can, with difficulty, be found.

LIFE IN AN ANCIENT MIOCENE LAND - ABU DHABI 8 MILLION YEARS AGO

Numerous channels, about 10 metres wide, formed the river system, itself about one kilometre in width. The water in the channels was deep, clear, sometimes fast flowing and had probably originated in the western highlands of Arabia. This habitat was ideal for the freshwater bivalve molluscs that lived in the river and their larvae were distributed widely throughout the system in the gills of the numerous catfish that shared the environment. The channel banks, formed of sandy-gravels that had been deposited when the river was in flood, perhaps during monsoonal rains, were home to 4 metre long crocodiles.

A gerbil had burrowed into the channel bank and it was having a very disturbed night. That day a cat the size of a leopard had killed a horse, and part of its carcass - one of its three-toed legs - was now being noisily crunched by a group of hyaenas. Equally noisy were the hippos. They were hungry and hesitant about leaving the river so as to get to their grassy feeding area in a woodland. Here, a group of four-tusked elephants had decided that the woodland was too good a feeding area to pass by. Disturbed and anxious, the gerbil decided to make a run for a quieter place but as it dashed away from the noisy feeding habits of the larger mammals it was snatched, caught and crunched between the strong jaws of a badger-like carnivore. Its skull lay shattered for some days until, after having been cleaned by ants, it became scattered into the river by the north-northeast wind and subsequently buried by sediments.

Later, much later, in fact 8 million years later, the gerbil's teeth were excavated from sandstone by palaeontologists and given a new scientific name. The gerbil became *Abudhabia baynunensis*, a Latin name derived from the Baynunah region of the Emirate of Abu Dhabi where it was found in 1992.

This reconstruction of life in Abu Dhabi 8 million years ago is not entirely fanciful. Although we can never know exactly what happened to faunas and floras in the geological past and how they utilised their environment, the reconstruction is based on the hard evidence from the fossils themselves and how, in part, their modern relatives are believed to live.

Although palaeontological studies had been carried out on Miocene rocks in East Africa (during the 1920's) and in Asia (Pakistan during the 1830's), Arabia, during this early period of discovery and exploration, appeared to be completely barren of vertebrate fossils. The Arabian continental plate embraces an area that includes all the countries of Arabia together with Jordan, Syria and Iraq west of the River Tigris, and consequently occupies a central palaeogeographical position between the better known Miocene vertebrate fossil localities of Africa and Asia. This gap in our knowledge of Arabian fossil vertebrates was vast, both in terms of geological time and the geography of the Middle East during the Miocene, and was especially frustrating as it was known (as mentioned above) that Arabia had been part of Africa for some considerable time and had only recently, 23 million years ago, joined with Asia. Therefore, prior to the 1970's there was no fossil evidence that animals had used Arabia as a "corridor" for intercontinental dispersal.

Our lack of knowledge of Arabia's past animal life changed in 1974 when, like seeing the dark side of the moon for the first time, Natural History Museum [then the British Museum (Natural History)] palaeontologists discovered a whole fauna of fossil vertebrates from the eastern region of the Kingdom of Saudi Arabia. These fossils were dated at about 16 million years old and their discovery prompted further work along the eastern coastline of the peninsula.

In 1979 one of the present authors (PJW), a palaeontologist from the Natural History Museum, London, visited Jebel Dhanna in Abu Dhabi's Western Region and discovered some fossil horse teeth weathering out of soft sandstones. These teeth, belonging to the first known fossil horses from Arabia, were from an extinct animal called *Hipparion*, about the size of a small pony that had three toes to each of its feet. *Hipparion* is unknown in the Old World before 11 million years but geological maps of the Western Region indicated that the rocks were equivalent in time to rocks previously described from Saudi Arabia and dated at about 16 million years old. The horse fossils disproved the evidence detailed on the geological maps and showed that the Emirate of Abu Dhabi had the only known record of fossiliferous late Miocene rocks from the whole of the Arabian Peninsula.

The Miocene exposures in the Western Region had received little attention from oil company geologists - they have little economic potential. However, their potential for the scientific and cultural heritage of the United Arab

Outcrops of the 8 million year old Baynunah Formation in the Western Region, Abu Dhabi. Inset: Reconstruction of life around the Miocene river. Hippos, crocodiles, primitive giraffes and acacia-like trees have all been found as fragmented fossils.

Molar tooth of a primitive Miocene elephant from Abu Dhabi.

45

Emirates was, and still is, considerable. An international team of specialist palaeontologists and geologists was led by the Natural History Museum and Yale University with the support of the ADCO. Besides collecting and identifying fossils and discovering other fossiliferous localities, other aims of the project were to collect rock samples for analysis; to measure the thickness and record the types of rock exposed, sandstones and clays amongst others; to date the rocks and to provide names for the geological sequence. Over several years, 35 scientists have participated in the project and an area of nearly 200 square kilometres has now been thoroughly examined out of a possible 10,000 square kilometres.

So what are the results of this project so far? The Miocene rocks have been divided into two formations - the Baynunah and the Shuwaihat Formations named after the places where they are best exposed. The Shuwaihat Formation outcrops at sea level in some of the coastal exposures and mainly consists of fossilised aeolian sands. These rocks seem to lack any fossils that can be used for dating purposes, but by careful stratigraphic work it is believed that rocks of the Shuwaihat Formation might be of the

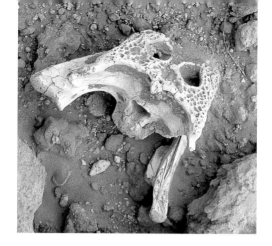

far, four species of invertebrates; two species of plants; three species of fish; eight species of reptiles; two species of birds and 31 species of mammals have been identified. Of these one species of fish and two mammal species are new to science. There may be other new fossil species but critical parts of the skeleton have not yet been discovered to confirm the diagnosis. No complete fossil skeletons have yet been found. The collected material (more than 800 identified specimens) consists mainly of isolated bones and teeth - themselves sometimes fragmented and incomplete. By comparing this fauna with other faunas discovered in east and north Africa, it is likely that the fossils from Abu Dhabi represent animals that lived during a time period of between 6 and 8 million years ago. It is hoped that better material will be found during the duration of the project that will continue until the year 2000.

same age as similar rocks found in Saudi Arabia. Thus, their age might be about 14 million years old. Confirming evidence for this date, plus or minus a few million years, comes from detailed analysis of the imprint of the earth's magnetic field on the iron minerals in the sandstone: magnetochronology.

After the aeolian sands of the Shuwaihat Formation had become rock, a regional river system evolved. This river may have been part of an extension into the lower part of the Arabian Gulf of the Tigris-Euphrates delta, or, more likely, the river originated from the western interior of Arabia flowing into an estuary located in the region presently known as Sabkha Matti. The sands, gravels and clays deposited by this river form the Baynunah Formation that overlies the Shuwaihat Formation in the Western Region. The Baynunah Formation contains fossils and, so

Opposite Page, left: Fragmented 8 million year old vertebrate fossils weathering out of the Baynunah Formation, emirate of Abu Dhabi

Top right: Lower jaw of a hippopotamus that thrived in the Miocene river.

Bottom right: A beautifully preserved partial skull of cattle-like mammal that once roamed the area of Abu Dhabi.

This Page, top: Fragmented skull of an 8 million year old crocodile, similar to today's Nile crocodile.

Bottom: Fossilised sand dunes of the Shuwaihat Formation.

47

ANCIENT SEAS

The magnificent mountain of Jebel Hafit overlooks the lush garden city of Al Ain. The rocks of the jebel have been subject to intense folding resulting in a structure like an elongated dome of which the central part has been eroded away; this structure is called an anticline. Jebel Hafit rocks are of lower Eocene to middle Oligocene age - 50 to 30 million years old.

THE JEBEL HAFIT SEA - 30 MILLION YEARS AGO.

The Tethys seaway stretched across this part of the Emirates linking the Indian Ocean with the Mediterranean and the sea covered most of northern Africa, Jordan, Syria and Iraq. Parts of Turkey, the Balkans and part of Greece together formed an island and the Asian mainland (southwestern Iran) was about 1000 kilometres from the Arabian coastline. At this time most of the northern Emirates, Dubai and the Hajar Mountains were an island and marine life flourished in the shallow tropical Tethyan sea around shoals and in lagoons.

Microscopic animals make up the bulk of the marine fossils to be found at Jebel Hafit. These fossils are important to oil exploration as their presence in various time horizons in a bore hole core can tell the oil geologist the age of the rocks in which they are found. Distribution across the Middle East of one such microfossil found at Jebel Hafit, *Nummulites*, is important to the oil industry as the Asmari Limestone in which *Nummulites* species are found, is a key geological horizon.

JEBEL HAFIT FOSSILS

At the foot of Jebel Hafit, near where the road from the cement works passes through a man-made gorge, numerous fossils of *Nummulites*, almost the size of a bottle-top, can be found. With them, lying loose on the scree slopes, are fragments of branching corals, oysters and gastropods, rare sea urchins and, even rarer, remains of barnacles and crab claws. At the northern part of the jebel north

In the nearshore sands lived a specialised community of burrowing sea-urchins (Faujasia eccentripora Lees). These lived just beneath the surface and obtained their food by eating sediment grains.

In amongst the patch-reefs and shallow rocky bottoms there lived a great variety of sea urchins. All are well-preserved although they have lost their defensive armament of spines. This is Glyphopneustes hattaensis Ali.

48

towards Al Ain, south of the Khalid bin Sultan road, eroded flanks of the anticline are exposed in the wadi. Here very hard, massive limestones are preserved with their beds in a near vertical position. Numerous coral "heads" are found here, some quite large about 60 centimetres in diameter.

THE EASTERN MOUNTAINS
The Cretaceous sea - 70 million years ago

The geology of the foothills of the Hajar Mountains provides an excellent example of what happens to rocks of the oceanic crust at an "active" plate margin - continents in collision. When Arabia, then joined with Africa, collided with southwestern Asia, oceanic crust was distorted, heated, lifted up and thrust onto the Arabian Shelf. Ophiolites, a distinctive kind of rock that formed originally as ancient oceanic crust, are now found in a broad belt from the Hajar Mountains through the Zagros Mountains of Iran to the Zagros Mountains of Turkey and are finally exposed in Cyprus. Thus, a huge amount of oceanic material that once formed the floor of a sea separating Arabia from Asia has been incorporated into the geology of many countries in the Middle East.

In the Hajar Mountains the uplift, caused by colliding continents during the Cretaceous, produced a chain of islands formed of ophiolite (the Semail ophiolite), now an unfossiliferous, reddish-black rock exposed on some jebels in the eastern mountains and especially well-exposed in Wadi Ham, emirate of Fujairah. A broad shallow and warm sea lapped against the Hajar islands and its limestones are now called the Simsima Formation. Knowledge of the palaeontology and stratigraphy of these carbonate sediments is of particular interest to ADCO, for they comprise the primary oil-bearing rocks in the Shah field, south of Liwa. The best exposures of the Simsima Formation are found at Jebel Huwayyah - known as Fossil Valley, Jebel Rawdah, Jebel Buhays and Qarn Murrah.

Around the ophiolite islands, coarse beach conglomerates and beach sands were deposited. In exposed environments with high wave activity, the pounding of the waves eroded the beach rocks to form large beds of boulders which had little in the way of marine life. In more protected bays, reefs and thickets of corals and rudist bivalves lived close to the shore while sandy bays had their own fauna of burrowing bivalves and marine snails.

CRETACEOUS FOSSILS

In the search for the hydrocarbon wealth hidden within the rocks that lie under the land and marine surface of the United Arab Emirates, essential clues are provided by the study of fossils and the sediments in which they are preserved. The fossils provide a way through which the rocks can be dated and correlated across long distances, since each set of rocks of a particular age has its own distinctive suite of fossils. Furthermore, by studying the fossils themselves, scientists can glean valuable information about the environment in which the sediments were formed millions of years ago.

Palaeontologists at the Natural History Museum, London, have identified more than 200 species of marine animals in the Simsima limestones, some new to science and one of the most diverse faunas of this age known anywhere in the world. Many of the species were previously unknown, while others show that there were strong links between the fauna of the region and those of Madagascar in the south; Iran and Pakistan to the east, and those of Saudi Arabia and Libya to the west.

Much of this ancient marine fauna of crabs, sea-urchins, bivalve shells (a new species of oyster-like bivalve *Endocostea (Selenoceramus) semaili* has been discovered), corals and sea worms would be easily recognisable to us today. However, there are also fossils from some groups of animals that have completely disappeared, having become extinct at the end of the Cretaceous period. These include the ammonites, free-swimming relatives of bivalves and sea-snails that possessed a spirally-coiled chambered shell.

Ammonites are relatively rare in the fossilised sediments of the United Arab Emirates, since they were animals of the open sea that preferred deep water and are only found as shells washed-up with sands along the shore. However, they have a crucial part to play in accurate dating of the Simsima Formation.

Another group of marine animals that no longer exists today are the rudists, a highly specialised kind of bivalve with a large, horn-shaped lower valve that rested on or in the sediment. The rudist had a cap-like upper valve that, in some groups, was covered with small perforations like a pepper pot. Through the perforations rudists filtered sea water for microscopic animals and plants for their food. A rudist found by Natural History Museum palaeontologists from Jebel Rawdah has been given the new scientific name of *Glabrobournonia arabica*.

Corals were common in these waters, sometimes forming dense bush-like thickets or patch reefs and sometimes occurring as button-like individuals (some rudists resemble these corals) scattered across the ocean floor. On the edges of the shoals, massive brain corals are to be found. Probably the most unusual of all the corals is the fan-shaped and solitary *Diploctenium*, which attached itself to the sea floor by a thin stalk. Rather delicate for potential preservation as a fossil, it is only found in rocks deposited in the more sheltered environments.

Around the coral thickets, crabs and shrimps were relatively common as were sea-urchins. These pentaradial (five rayed) animals can be found in a great diversity of forms. Some, with an abundance of strong sucking tube feet,

The Cretaceous outcrops form a series of low jebels along the eastern margin of the Hajar mountains. Here Jebel Aqabah is seen.

Left: Amongst the marine bivalves are groups of animals that became extinct at the end of the Cretaceous. One of the more important groups where the rudists, including claw-shaped forms such as this Bournonia excavata *d'Orbigny.* 49

lived within the zone of active surf on rocky bottoms. Others, with many fewer feet, lived in deeper waters below the normal base of the waves. Many other kinds of irregular echinoids lived either on or buried within the sediment. These derived their food from the sediment itself, either passing large amounts of it through their gut or using specialised tube-feet around the mouth to select organic matter from the sediment. The largest of this type of sea urchin can be fossilised in shallow-water shoals that were deposited at the base of the waves.

Of the 45 sea-urchins now known from the Simsima Formation, 14 species are new to science and some of them have been named after places where they were found or, in one instance, after a person who has helped the Natural History Museum team - *Codiopsis lehmannae*. Specimens named after places in the Emirates are *Prionocidaris? emiratus*, *Heterodiadema buhaysensis*, *Goniopygus arabicus*, *Circopeltis? emiratus*, and *Petalabrissus rawdahensis*.

This research theme shows that sea urchin species are important as indicators of the palaeoenvironment that has been established from palaeontological work in the United Arab Emirates. Equally important, is the general relevance of this research to modelling of all late Cretaceous carbonate platform sediments throughout the world. Such detailed understanding of the depositional environments of carbonate sediments will ultimately help in the search for new hydrocarbon deposits.

THE JURASSIC/CRETACEOUS SEA - 150 MILLION YEARS AGO

Hidden in deep wadi's in the Emirate of Fujairah lie outcrops of marine rocks deposited at the time that dinosaurs flourished - 150 million years ago. These limestones belong to the Musandam Group of rocks that range in time from 200 to about 97 million years. In the northern part of Musandam these limestones were deposited in a deep-water sea that shallowed towards the

south. These beds are now exposed in the vicinity of Ras al-Khaimah. Later, perhaps 70 million years ago, these limestones suffered severe tectonic events associated with mountain building in the Musandam area and were broken up into huge pieces. These pieces, some forming blocks as large as 30 metres in diameter, were incorporated into sediments of a younger age to constitute a mix of Musandam Group rocks of varying Cretacous ages.

JURASSIC/CRETACEOUS FOSSILS

Various fragments of corals can be found but most are too poorly preserved to be identified. Other fossils are fragments of sponges, algae and bivalves. Overall, this geological time period in the United Arab Emirates requires further exploration and study.

OVERVIEW

The work so far undertaken by palaeontologists in the United Arab Emirates, outlined in this chapter, has shown the Emirates to have - for its geographical size - the most diverse palaeontological heritage of any country in the Arabian Peninsula. Fossils can be found ranging in time from nearly 300 million years ago to 8 million years. In addition, modern sedimentological processes such as the development of sabkha and carbonate environments with their associated fauna and flora found along the Arabian Gulf and Indian Ocean coastlines of the United Arab Emirates are now being re-studied to provide an important example of a modern environment that, in turn, can be compared with a similar environment in the geological past. Such studies can be of importance to future hydrocarbon exploration in the United Arab Emirates.

Palaeontological studies initiated by government organisations in the United Arab Emirates, namely ADCO and the UAE Ministry for Higher Education and Scientific Research, now provide important information for international science and will be of direct benefit for the cultural heritage of the United Arab Emirates.

HABITATS AND THEIR PROTECTION

Richard Hornby

S ADLY, NOT ALL THE NATIVE DESERT plants and animals have survived. It is difficult to be specific about trends in desert plants because there is no historical data, and the appearance of annual species after the rain is notoriously variable. What we do know, however, is that the density of plant species present in any area varies greatly between different regions of the desert. It is highly probable that species have been lost from large areas of desert as a result of prolonged human impact.

THE DESERT

Few animals can tolerate the extreme heat of the desert for long so they are obliged to adopt one of a number of strategies. For many this involves burrowing, spending long periods resting in holes well below the surface, whilst others such, as the sand skink and the sand boa, move readily beneath the surface of uncompacted sand. A high proportion of species are nocturnal, coming out only at night when it is cooler, and some aestivate, i.e. spend the summer months underground in a condition of torpor similar to hibernation.

Birds cannot burrow or aestivate, but they can migrate. The number of species resident in the desert are very few, but this was probably always so. The most desert-adapted species resident in UAE are the hoopoe lark, the cream-coloured courser and the black-crowned finch-lark. The long-legged buzzard, little owl and desert eagle owl maintain small breeding populations, and the brown-necked raven is not uncommon in the desert though it is at least partially depended on man and his waste. In the cooler autumn and winter months the resident birds are joined by a range of migrants which breed in Central Asia. Birds such as various species of lark, wheatear, and warbler, not to mention the houbara bustard, have to escape the cold winters of the breeding grounds so they migrate to the deserts of Arabia and the Indian subcontinent.

There is no reliable historical data on reptile populations. In most areas of desert they are the dominant animal group, including a number of lizards, ranging from the delicate geckos to the larger and more robust dhabs, or spiny-tailed lizards, together with the giant of desert lizards, the monitor, which can be nearly a metre in length. Several species of snake occur, the commonest being the poisonous horned viper. Virtually all the reptiles burrow, mostly among the roots of perennial plants which provides a degree of mechanical support, or they excavate the sand from beneath a layer of compacted sandstone. Good holes beneath a sheet of rock can be much in demand from competing small mammals, reptiles and little owls.

In general, desert mammals have not fared as well as the birds or reptiles. Predators in particular have declined at an alarming rate. Within the last few decades the desert of UAE has experienced local extinctions of the wolf, oryx, striped hyaena, jackal and honey badger (or ratel). Two species of gazelle still survive, though both are rare and with limited ranges. The sand gazelle or rheem is present in very low numbers to the south of Liwa, and the mountain gazelle occurs in an area bordered by the major roads between Abu Dhabi, Dubai and Al Ain. The sand cat is believed to have been reduced to a seriously low level but data is lacking because this is such a shy nocturnal animal. The beautiful little Rueppell's fox and even the cape hare are said to be far less numerous than they were. The main stronghold for these species is thought to be the western part of Abu Dhabi emirate. The lesser jerboa and three species of hedgehog survive but are seldom encountered. All this desert wildlife remains under pressure from increased numbers of camels and goats whilst the *hima* system of traditional conservation and land management has been largely disbanded.

Numbers of camels and goats have increased rapidly since the 1960s. The animals are mostly managed by expatriate workers and owned by nationals who generally live in the cities but regularly travel into the desert to visit their herdsmen and animals. In this way they maintain a tangible link with their past, but without the hardship of living in the desert. The herdsmen and their animals are sustained by water which is transported to them on a regular basis in a tanker, towed by a four-wheel drive truck. Additional subsidised fodder is also taken to these 'bedu camps', permitting unnaturally high grazing densities to be maintained. Camel breeding is a high profile activity in which individual animals are often sold at much more than their value as providers of meat or milk, with a sharp eye focussed on their potential as racing camels. It could be argued that the strong interest in camel-racing is leading to subsidized camel grazing and encouraging artificially high grazing pressures in the fragile deserts of the UAE.

Another clear trend in the desert is the proliferation of vehicle tracks. This is partly a consequence of carrying animal fodder and water to bedu camps, but other factors are also involved. Many other activities are going on in the desert all the time. These include road construction, digging and use of boreholes for water, agricultural projects, drilling and other kinds of surveys used in oil and gas exploration, establishment of date palm groves at water wells, establishment and management of desert plantations maintained by drip irrigation, falconry, and recreational desert driving, the latter mostly by western expatriates. As a result few areas of desert are free from disturbance for very long. The more sensitive animals are pushed out from many places and find themselves confined to restricted areas which might be of less than optimal habitat.

Increased cultivation in the desert, creating large plantations sustained by drip irrigation, has made an impressive impact upon the landscape of the UAE and in particular of Abu Dhabi emirate where the desire of Sheikh Zayed to see the desert made green has been translated into one of the most extensive tree-planting projects in Arabia. There are both pros and cons for wildlife. Whilst many species of adaptable birds and insects may benefit, the truly desert-

Camels are well adapted for desert life. Originally part of Arabia's wild fauna, they were first domesticated in the Emirates.

transportation of water away from wells in the Western Region of Abu Dhabi Emirate. The reason for the Decree is to limit the area of desert which can be regularly grazed by camels and goats. It will make life much more difficult for the herdsmen and is likely to lead to a reduction of bedu camps and the size of the herds. It will be interesting to see the result of this imaginative action, and to consider whether it might also be benficial in other areas.

At the time of writing there are no Desert Protected Areas but this does not mean that there is no control over damaging activities. Large areas of desert are patrolled very effectively by a team of nationals employed by the ruling family of Abu Dhabi. The principal *raison d'etre* for these teams is to look out for, and to report the presence of, houbara bustard. Trackers or rangers are based in permanent desert settlements and operate in well-maintained short-wheelbase four-wheel drive vehicles, with modern radio and telephone communication equipment. They cover extensive areas, searching the ground for tracks of houbara. When enough houbara are present, usually around October or November, falconry hunting commences.

adapted indigenous wildlife probably suffers since these forms are pushed out as a result of the altered habitat conditions or through competition by more adaptable species. One obvious benefactor is the red fox, a very active predator of small mammals, reptiles, birds and their eggs. The balance of nature is clearly being altered, with some species increasing and others declining or even becoming extinct.

In 1995, a positive step was taken to reduce the impacts of grazing animals and of vehicles. This was a Royal Decree by H.H. Sheikh Khalifa Bin Zayed, the Crown Prince and Deputy Ruler of Abu Dhabi, to prohibit the

One large tract of desert is reserved for hunting, by the general public, of houbara and *karowan* (stone curlew), exclusively with the aid of falcons. This 'Public Hunting Triangle' is bounded by the Abu Dhabi - Dubai road, the Dubai - Al Ain road and the Al Hayer - Sweihan - Shahama road. Despite rather intensive use by four-wheeled drive vehicles the area still supports a rich array of wildlife. Dhabs (spiny-tailed lizards) are locally common, and a recent survey by Emirates Natural History Group revealed a significant population of mountain gazelles. Judging by their lack of timidity, they appear to be largely unmolested. Use of this area for falconry will hopefully lead to its preservation as natural desert, rather than it being zoned for development, agriculture or forestry projects.

The houbara trackers also fulfill roles as very effective wildlife rangers. Since they possess an intimate knowledge of the desert's wildlife they can report on any problems which might affect it. Federal Decree No. 9 of 1983 made it illegal to shoot birds or to hunt gazelle and hares in UAE. In the desert of Abu Dhabi this is enforced very strongly by the trackers. They have the power to impose heavy fines, and prison sentences can quickly be arranged for serious offences. These penalties are well known to most of the people living in, or visiting, the desert, so that shooting is a very rare event.

A strong case can be made for establishing Desert Protected Areas. Research needs to be carried out to ascertain what level of grazing by camels and goats is compatible with the survival of the full range of indigenous desert plants and animals. There needs to be strict control over grazing which can only be achieved by effective fencing of large protected areas, together with the capacity and political will to ensure that the fence is not breached by herdsmen or their animals. As graziers are certain to be displaced by such a move, a great deal of preparation would have to be carried out beforehand. Ideally, the graziers should themselves be involved in the establishment and management of the Protected Area.

There would be many benefits in having several Desert Protected Areas so that the full biodiversity of the desert can be represented. Vegetation would benefit through release from grazing, and within two or three years the areas would begin to take on a different aspect. Insects, small mammals and birds will respond to the increased biomass of desert plants, but it is possible that relatively simple habitat manipulation might yield yet further tangible benefits to wildlife. For example localized irrigation for a short time in the winter, in dry years only, might allow a new cohort of dormant seeds to germinate. If it appears that plant species have been lost as a result of prolonged overgrazing, it may be possible to reintroduce them, either by broadcasting seed or planting seedlings. Research is required into the most appropriate techniques for such work.

The National Avian Research Center in Abu Dhabi, which is concerned mainly with the conservation of the houbara bustard, has started a programme of research into habitat manipulation with a view to supporting the establishment of Desert Protected Areas. Protected areas would benefit their research and also provide suitable areas for release trials for captive-bred

houbara. It is likely that the reduction of grazing and enhanced plant growth would attract more migrating, birds, including wild houbara. There would be a very real possibility of being able to use Protected Areas for controlled houbara hunting, managed on an ecologically sustainable basis, and maybe only from camels and horses. Falconry has had a beneficial effect on wildlife up to now. Perhaps the desire to establish large reserves for falconry, will serve to protect and enhance a significant proportion of UAE's threatened desert ecosystem.

Houbara bustard in breeding plumage.

55

Right:

Early morning dew on Silene villosa.

Far right:

Irrigation turns desert into oasis.

Opposite page:

Rains transform this stony plateau into flowering fields.

Below:

Plantations in the sandy desert.

Sheikh Zayed's island of Sir Bani Yas has been transformed into a wildlife reserve, breeding centre, and experimental agricultural estate.

Sir Bani Yas

AN ARABIAN ARK   *Peter Vine*

First impressions of the island of the Bani Yas depend upon one's method of approach. A boat-crossing of the narrow stretch of water between it and the mainland of Abu Dhabi at Jebel Dhanna, is dominated by sight of the island's cone-shaped central 'mountains', providing an easy navigational beacon. As one sails closer, these turn out to be formed from a strange mixture of red, green and brown rock formations. Circumnavigating the island, it soon becomes apparent that there is much more to Sir Bani Yas than this unusual structure, for it is surrounded by gently sloping plains which merge with a fairly level coastal shelf. The shoreline itself ranges from mangrove covered sand-banks and hidden inlets, to buttressed foreshore and finally a well constructed small harbour at which one finally lands.

The approach by air, on helicopter or indeed fixed wing aircraft, offers an entirely different view. Surrounded by a glittering blue sea the island stands out from all around like a green emerald placed on a jewellers display cloth. First impressions are of its serried ranks of trees, which cover almost half its land area, and secondly its obvious abundance of wildlife. Large herds of gazelle skoot across the mountain side whilst over a hundred white Arabian oryx graze contentedly within their large enclosure. Close to the helicopter pad one sees more exotic wildlife: giraffe, emu and a range of African mammals. The helicopter ride itself is a noisy experience and after being deposited on firm ground, the whirling blades once more lift the craft skywards. One is gradually aware of a beautiful peace and tranquillity which acts like a balm, calming jagged nerves. Finally, with the aircraft gone, a sense of urgency builds up to explore on land everything that has just caught the eye from above.

Sir Bani Yas has attracted man for a long time. The central salt-plug of Jabal Wahid, for that is what geologists tell us forms the strange crystalline mountain, was not always surrounded by water. Towards the end of the last ice-age, around ten thousand years ago, sea-level in the Gulf was considerably lower than it is today and much of the present day seabed was above high-water mark. At that time Sir Bani Yas was part of mainland Arabia and its craggy hills rose up above a green plateau on which a wide variety of wildlife flourished. This verdant countryside, watered by ancient rivers, undoubtedly attracted fishermen, hunters and gatherers and we have firm evidence of people living here between 6,000 and 7,000 years ago. This Late Stone Age period was, in fact, quite a busy time for this region of Arabia, with its gradually emerging islands providing temporary or permanent homes for growing numbers of people.

The Abu Dhabi Islands Archaeological Survey owes its establishment to the personal enthusiasm for, and fascination with, the UAE's heritage, by the emirate's ruler and country's President, Sheikh Zayed bin Sultan Al Nahyan. Today's visitors to this unique island may well encounter the survey's team members at one of their growing list of excavations. Whether it is a Late Stone Age site at which a flint 'tile-knife' was discovered, a fisherman's midden containing the remains of dugong and turtle bones, or the pre-Islamic Nestorian church and monastery with its intricate plaster embellishments, Sir Bani Yas's past is gradually being revealed in all its varied facets.

Left:
A baby rheem gazelle on Sir Bani Yas island where a large population of gazelle have free range.

Below:
A mountain gazelle.
Gazella gazella.

*Reem gazelle on Sir
Bani Yas island.*

with his family, following an age old bedouin tradition that took advantage of the sea-breezes during otherwise hot summer weather. Away from the vast deserts, burgeoning conurbation's and affairs of state which constantly occupied Sheikh Zayed's time, Sir Bani Yas provided a place to think, and perhaps to dream of how Arabia once was. A love of wildlife and nature led Zayed to the idea of sharing his island with endangered Arabian species such as sand gazelle and oryx. Little by little, year by year, he developed the island into a special reserve where wildlife holds pride of place and where visitors are able to gain a taste of how it must have been thousands of years ago, when this landscape resembled the savannahs of Africa and shared many species with its neighbouring continent.

A brief trip around the island vividly demonstrates just how important wildlife is for the UAE's President, and what steps he is

Throughout history this fascinating island has offered challenges and opportunities for those who chose to make it their home. The Nestorian monks who lived in Arabia's most easterly monastery, undoubtedly traded with other communities further up the Gulf, but they would also have turned to the sea for their food, and probably also fed on wild birds that made the island their home during seasonal migrations. For the people of the Bani Yas tribal confederation, after whom the island is named, it offered a refuge and staging post, with a safe anchorage, good fishing and the prized Gulf pearling beds nearby.

Today the island is part of an unusual environmental and biological experiment. Initially Sheikh Zayed chose Sir Bani Yas as a place to spend time

prepared to take to ensure its survival. There are basically three kinds of 'enclosure' on the island, i.e. ones to keep animals within a defined area, ones that provide living space for humans, and finally the rest of the island in which a large number of animals roam at will. Among the latter are the Arabian or mountain gazelle (*Gazella gazella cora*), known to the locals as *dhabi*. It was this animal that gave the emirate its name since the island on which the capital city now stands is known as 'possession of the gazelle' or Abu Dhabi. Other gazelles include the more numerous rheem or sand gazelle (*Gazella subgutterosa marica*), dorcas gazelle (*Gazella dorcas*) and grant's gazelle (*Gazella granti*), an East African species.

The Arabian Oryx, brought to the verge of extinction by over-hunting, has been rescued as a viable species thanks to a number of captive breeding programmes. The oryx on Sir Bani Yas are held in a special extended enclosure where they live and breed as if in the wild.

Exotic species bred at Sir Bani Yas include, among others: top left to bottom right : common eland, defassa waterbuck, addax, blackbuck, scimitar-horned oryx and emu.

Arabian oryx *(Oryx leucoryx)*, rescued only a few decades ago from the brink of extinction, are protected within their own compound which straddles a large section of the sloping plain beneath Jabal Wahid. Here they are free to wander over several square kilometres of natural landscape and their behaviour confirms that they feel quite at home. The herd is steadily increasing in size as a result of natural breeding within the enclosure. This quietly undertaken effort, little known internationally, is testimony to Sheikh Zayed's deep seated concern for protection of Arabia's unique wildlife, so elegantly personified by the white oryx.

Also to be found wandering the open countryside, or held within other large enclosures, on this exotic island reserve are blackbuck *(Antilope cervicapra)*,

common eland *(Taurotragus oryx)*, beisa oryx *(Oryx gazella beisa)*, scimitar-horned oryx *(Oryx dammah)*, Arabian oryx *(Oryx leucoryx)*, addax *(Addax nasomaculatus)*, defassa waterbuck *(Kobus ellipsiprymnus defassa)*, fallow deer *(Dama dama)*, axis deer *(Axis axis)*, hog deer *(Cervus porcinus)*, barbary sheep *(Amnotragus lervia)*, and wild sheep or Asiatic mouflon *(Ovis ammon)*.

One experiment of wildlife management that visitors are not encouraged to observe is a breeding pen for houbara *(Chlamydotis undulata)*, members of the bustard family. These birds need to be left strictly alone if they are to to have any chance to breed successfully under wild conditions, and a large area close to the coast has been set aside just for that purpose. This island bird sanctuary is only part of the many efforts by Sheikh Zayed, and his family to revive the

Another introduced bird, but one which now breeds in the wild on Sir Bani Yas, is the Egyptian goose (*Alopochen aegyptius*), whose adults, with goslings in tow, can be seen alongside the mangrove channel close to the main residential area. Other introductions include the ground nesting grey francolin (*Francolinus pondicerianus*), black francolin (*Francolinus francolinus*), see see (*Ammoperdix griseogularis*) and chukar partridge (*Alectoris chukar*). Some other free-flying species that have begun to breed include the African crowned crane (*Balearica regulorum*), helmeted guineafowl (*Numidia meleagris*), and possibly also the common pheasant (*Phasianus colchicus*).

The success of Sir Bani Yas as a nature reserve is further underlined by the number of wild bird species that made it a temporary or permanent home. Details of sightings of around 170 species are now kept in the files of the

One important conservation project on Sir Bani Yas is the encouragement of breeding houbaras. A large fenced-off section of the island is left entirely undisturbed for these birds to nest and raise their young.

population of this bird in the wild. At the National Avian Research Centre (NARC) at Sweihan on the mainland, a highly scientific approach is taken to captive breeding, while NARC scientists are also studying the migration and breeding patterns of the houbara.

Sir Bani Yas's other birds are also impressive inhabitants of this Arabian Ark. Whilst Arabia's native sub-species of ostrich (*Struthio camelus syriacus* is now sadly extinct, a captive population of closely related African ostrich is now breeding on the island. Meanwhile successful breeding of two other flightless birds, the rhea (*Rhea americana*) and the emu (*Dromaius naavaehollandiae*) is raising the question of what to do with the rapidly increasing flocks.

This page: *The greater flamingo is present at Sir Bani Yas for most of the year. Planting of mangroves around the island's coastline has helped to create suitable shallow feeding grounds for these magnificent birds.*

Opposite page left: *Egyptian ducks have been introduced to Sir Bani Yas where they breed.*

Opposite page right: *The red cardinal is a north Amerian bird that has been introduced to Sir Bani Yas.*

Emirates Bird Records Committee. Among these, a popular favourite is the greater flamingo *(Phoenocopterus ruber)*, also known as the pink flamingo, which can be seen in shallow intertidal lagoons, protected by mangrove bushes, or at the artificial 'bird lake' where they can gather in dense flocks of over a hundred individuals.

Sheikh Zayed's success in creating a wildlife reserve has been matched by the results of field trials in which the island has been used as a testing ground for agriculture. One of the first plants that he encouraged to grow on the island was a species that has been much maligned elsewhere in the world, and which has suffered greatly at the hands of developers. Sheikh Zayed's fascination with, and respect for, the humble mangrove tree *(Avicennia marina)* is as strong today as it ever was. For someone who knows the true value of fresh-water and the real dryness of the desert, a tree that grows in sea-water creates a powerful impression. So powerful, in fact, that Sheikh Zayed has had agricultural teams planting new stands of these salt-tolerant bushes all along the coast of Abu Dhabi for the past twenty or so years, both in areas where they were previously present and in new areas, often along the edge of reclaimed land. Not only has this practice formed new stretches of coastal greenery, but it has also created important habitats for many birds, insects, fish

and marine invertebrates. Such efforts are making new nursery grounds for commercial fish, as well as aesthetically pleasing coastal features.

But the most visible achievements at Sir Bani Yas are on dry land where hundreds of acres of old or reclaimed land have been planted with literally millions of trees and shrubs. Whilst some of these are grown to provide shade and comfort for wild animals, or simply to green the landscape, some are part of food growing experiments that aim to test new ideas and to find species that show the greatest tolerance for Abu Dhabi's hot arid climate. The fact that orchards of apples, oranges and pears are now flourishing on Sir Bani Yas, not too mention olive groves, is proof that where there is a will there is a way. The island of Sir Bani Yas, so loved by the UAE's President, is a testament to the age old adage, and a monument to his sustained efforts to make the Emirates a better place for his people to live.

THE COAST

The UAE has two separate coastlines, the east-facing coast on the Gulf of Oman, and the much longer north and north-west facing coast which borders the Arabian Gulf. The former coastline typically has a narrow coastal plain between the sea and the mountains, with a similarly restricted sublittoral coastal shelf. The great majority of the Arabian Gulf coast, on the other hand, consists of an extensive area of flat coastal sabkha (or saline flat) bordered by a very shallow sea. The monotonous aspect of this coastline is relieved by a number of low rocky outcrops and by extensive stands of mangroves. There are also many islands, some near shore and others well out into the Gulf.

As we have seen in the two previous chapters, Abu Dhabi has the world's finest example of coastal sabkha, 350 km long by an average of 15 to 20 km wide. This is only very occasionally covered by high tides but it floods after heavy rain since the saturated layer of salt becomes an impermeable barrier, preventing percolation into the underlying strata. Most of this sabkha appears to be completely devoid of life, but it does support a range of specialized algae and a few invertebrates are present, at least seasonally. The sabkha's biological paucity has resulted in little interest or support for its formal protection, although one could argue clear justification for doing so on geomorphological grounds. In practice the sabkha is open territory for development with new roads, embankments, pipelines, pumping stations and powerlines being created at an impressive rate, and with levels being raised through deposition of coastal dredged marine sediments or from inland sand-mining so that plantations can be established.

Most of the Arabian Gulf coastline is actually very attractive and washed by a beautiful pale blue-green shallow sea. Variety is offered by some magnificent stands of mature mangroves and a series of inlets, or khors, which occasionally provide some freshwater input. Access is difficult in many areas, especially where there are wide expanses of intertidal mud which supports sizeable populations of wintering and passage wading birds. The khors in particular are very important in this regard. Khor Dubai is the best known and owes its protection to a Royal Decree issued by the Crown Prince of Dubai, H.H. Sheikh

Mohammed Bin Rashid Al Makhtoum. The site is well managed by the Environmental Protection Section of Dubai Municipality. It attracts significant numbers of waders, herons, wildfowl and flamingos.

Mangroves are of great importance in several respects. In addition to their aesthetic appeal, they are valuable havens for birds and provide spawning and nursery ground for a host of different species of fish, many of them of commercial importance. The fall of leaves and twigs from the mangroves supports a range of invertebrates at the base of a complex food chain. The overall productivity of coastal areas with mangroves is very much higher than that of adjacent coasts without mangroves.

One of the finest and most admired areas of mangrove is in the Eastern Lagoon of Abu Dhabi. This is a large area with many islands of mangrove separated by shallow channels. Boating is strictly limited and fishing is prohibited. Other fine stands are in the Western Lagoon, Futaisi Island, the Dhabbiyah peninsular, and the islands of Ras Ghanada, Abu Al Abyadh and

Merawah. In several of these sites steps are being taken to extend the area of mangrove by lowering the level of adjacent areas and planting cuttings. The technique is successful but mangroves are naturally slow to grow, so some patience is required.

Further north, there are two particularly fine areas of mangrove. One is in Ras al-Khaimah emirate, north of the village of Rams, inland of the long island of Hulaylah. This area is unique in UAE because of the extensive stand of rushes, whose survival depends upon freshwater input from the nearby mountains. The combination of rush marsh and mangrove provides habitat suitable for birds such as little bittern, grey heron and moorhen, in addition to many crabs and mudskippers.

The other truly remarkable area of mangrove is at Khor Kalba, to the south of Fujairah, but actually in the emirate of Sharjah. This area, again with freshwater input from the mountains, supports the largest and oldest mangroves in the country, and is home to two bird species found nowhere else in UAE. These are the booted warbler and a race of the white-collared kingfisher known as *kalbensis*, after the name of this location. With only about fifty breeding pairs, and very few seen outside this area, this is one of the rarest birds in the world.

Statutory protection has been granted to three Marine Reserves in the emirate of Fujairah: at Al Faqit, Dhadnah and Al Aqqa, where the reserves have been established to protect the valuable coral reef communities. Whilst fishing and coral or shell collecting are prohibited within the reserves, there is room for improvement with regard to enforcement and base-line field studies would also provide a useful management guide. There is also a case to be made for establishment of a large Marine Reserve to protect the coral reefs and shallow sea around the islands of Merawah, Butinah and Bazam Al Gharbi,

Left:
Mangrove swamps at the Abu Dhabian island of Merawah create important habitats for bird and marine life.

Opposite Page:
Along the Indian Ocean coast white beaches lie hidden between rock promontories.

*Offshore islands form
natural sanctuaries
for birds such as the
osprey seen on the
opposite page..*

believed to be the UAE's most important area for marine conservation. In this area extensive seagrass beds support a feeding population of at least 3000 green turtles. In view of the relatively low number of turtle nesting beaches in UAE it seems likely that these turtles must migrate out of the Gulf to breed on the coast of Oman, or even further afield. The fertile seagrass beds in warm, shallow and productive waters are essential habitats for the turtles, providing rich feeding during the prolonged process of maturation, which may last as long as fifty or more years.

Another threatened species which lives here is the dugong, or sea cow. This large, herbivorous, marine mammal is present in large numbers in the Merewah - Butinah area, at least for part of the year. Their movements and life history are still poorly understood and it remains a mystery as to whether these are part of the same group of dugongs which are regularly seen around the Hawar Islands of Bahrain. The dugong is regarded as a globally endangered species and the Gulf supports the world's second largest population; the largest being off north-eastern Australia. A large and well protected marine reserve to protect the coral reefs and seagrass beds around Merawah, Butinah and Bazam Al Gharbi would make a significant contribution to nature conservation in the UAE. In addition to dugongs and turtles, the area supports a large number of fish species together with important populations of cetaceans.

There are numerous islands within Abu Dhabi's territorial waters. Whilst a few of these are associated with the oil industry and have significant human settlements, many are free from large-scale development and are effectively private nature reserves. In some cases great care is taken to ensure that no harm comes to the very important seabird colonies. The islands vary in size from the massive Abu al Abyadh which is more than 300 square kilometres to tiny exposed islets of sand or mangroves. Abu al Abyadh has a large population of introduced gazelles and is an important site for birds. Huge numbers of migrant waders feed on the extensive intertidal mudflats and the island supports an important breeding colony of crab plovers, the largest known anywhere in the Arabian Gulf. This extraordinary wader excavates a

tunnel in sand, generally 1.5 to 2 metres long, and lays a single egg at the end. The dome of sand holding the colony of about 300 pairs is not much larger than a football field. It is adjacent to a channel with extensive fringing mangroves where the healthy crab population provides the principle diet for this very specialized bird. The colony has been thoughtfully protected by a fence and a moat excavated around the colony. This small but significant action is typical of the important steps often taken in the UAE to protect nature, in a low-key, non-statutory manner, with little or no publicity.

The island of Sir Bani Yas is haven to more species than those that occur naturally in Arabia. Its southern part has been transformed into a green oasis of trees, shrubs and flowers, together with a remarkable collection of animals. Large paddocks support healthy populations of gazelles, oryx, ostrich, emu, zebra and giraffe, while several artificial lakes attract significant numbers of ducks, geese, swans and other birds. The rest of the extensive island is an undisturbed haven for several thousand gazelles which are provided with fodder but are free to roam where they like.

Abu Dhabi's islands support internationally important populations of five species of tern, namely Saunders' little, white-cheeked, swift, lesser crested and bridled. They thrive on the fish in the shallow productive waters of the Gulf. A dozen islands support breeding colonies of several thousand pairs. The colonies of swift and lesser crested terns are so dense that there is only about one square foot per pair, i.e. they are spaced at pecking distance. This is an adaptation to afford protection from predators but it makes the colony very susceptible to human disturbance and development.

Other internationally important breeding seabirds include the sooty gull and the beautiful but enigmatic red-billed tropicbird. It remains a mystery where in the oceans these graceful, night-feeding, long-tailed wanderers go to when they leave their rock crevices. Only one colony, on the island of Qarnein, appears to be secure and well established. Other islands would be suitable but it is believed that the birds are deterred from nesting by the presence of feral cats, which sadly are to be found on many islands. Even ospreys appear to shun islands with cats. This antipathy towards cats might be the reason why so very few ospreys breed anywhere on the mainland. They use the same nest site year after year, steadily adding to the pile of sticks and miscellaneous flotsam and jetsam. Some of the nests are huge mounds approaching two metres in height.

Smaller islands in the west of Abu Dhabi emirate support a few pairs of sooty falcons, which are diminutive, fast-flying, blue/grey falcons with bright yellow eyes. They breed late in the year so that they can feed their young on small birds migrating south for the northern winter. Sooty falcons breed only around the coast of Arabia and north-east Africa, and they spend the winter in Madagascar. This is another species which is very intolerant of man and whose breeding sites need to be afforded formal protection.

One of the most spectacular sites in the Gulf is the massive flocks of Socotra cormorant which move around *en masse*, presumably in search of large shoals of fish. When one sees the huge size of these rafts of cormorants it is difficult to comprehend that the species is globally endangered. It has a restricted world range and has already suffered a great decline. Breeding colonies occur on just a handful of islands in the Arabian Gulf and off Oman and there is a strong case for its protection. Unfortunately cormorants are unpopular since they are perceived by fishermen to be serious competitors, and also because of the

Ospreys fish on the east coast.

unpleasant smell associated with the breeding colonies. Several traditional nesting sites have been abandoned as a result of development on the islands, or through other forms of interference. In recent years the largest colony in UAE has been on Sinaiya Island, Umm Al Quwain, but no breeding took place here in 1995, probably because of the use of four-wheel drive vehicles on the island at the time when the birds would have been returning. Improved protection will be required if the population decline is to be arrested.

69

Khor Kalba

The most southern tip of the UAE's Indian Ocean coastline ends in an extensive mangrove marsh. The dark green belt of almost impenetrable ancient mangrove contrasts strongly with the brown and purple rocky mountains and the sparkling blue water. Young seedlings surrounded by air roots signal a healthy environment. The mud at low tide reveals myriads of pretty crabs, while in the shady canopy of the trees a unique small bird makes its home. The white-collared kingfisher is a breeding resident here - and only here. Many other birds like reef herons and booted warblers also nest here. Khor Kalba is a magical place, a place of exquisite beauty, a place worthy of protection.

THE MOUNTAINS

The cooler and wetter climate high in the mountains attracted people to grow a few crops and keep goats. The high villages may have been deserted during late summer and early winter before the rains returned, but essentially the settlements, of varying levels of sophistication, provided a base from which to run a herd of goats. Today goats appear to wander freely throughout the mountains but the herdsmen have stronger links with communities on the lower ground and they use the mountain wadis rather than living a life of rugged isolation high in the hills.

Not surprisingly the mountain farmers did not take kindly to their goats being killed by wild predators, and they would miss no opportunity to shoot, trap or poison any such animal. The predators comprised the Arabian leopard, the caracal lynx, the Arabian wolf, the striped hyaena and various eagles. All were persecuted and all declined, to the point of extinction in the case of the wolf and the hyaena. The wild mammalian herbivores, which may never have been numerous, were also killed but competition from goats was probably a more important factor in their decline. Populations of ibex, wild goat, mountain gazelle, Arabian tahr and rock hyrax were all decimated and today it is believed that only a very few tahr and mountain gazelle still survive.

It seems truly incredible that the Arabian leopard has survived despite all the efforts of man to eradicate the species. Ironically, their survival into the 1990s was tracked primarily by news of leopards having been killed. Determined efforts to find leopards in the mountains of UAE have produced relatively few positive signs, such as footprints, scrapings and droppings. There can be little doubt that they do survive but in precariously low numbers and it is possible that nothing that can be done will save them from extinction in the wild. Thankfully, the Arabian leopard still survives in healthy numbers in part of northern Yemen and it is hoped that steps can be taken to maintain the whole ecosystem in this important area.

Meanwhile what can be done to try to maintain biodiversity in the mountains of UAE? The Arabian Leopard Trust was formed to promote conservation of wildlife in the mountains, using the Arabian leopard as a

Opposite Page: *The steep-walled wadis of the high mountains make this area almost inaccessible.*

Left: *High mountain village on the Ru'us al-Jibal.*

Below: *Jebel Hafit, near Al Ain, is a recent habitat of the Arabian tahr.*

flagship species. The Trust's volunteer naturalists and professional biologists have been investigating the daily life patterns and attitudes of the farmers and making efforts to raise their awareness about the importance of the indigenous wildlife. One of the principal approaches has been through the children whose responses have been most encouraging.

Ecotourism may help to provide an alternative source of employment, turning mountain farmers into mountain guides, porters and rangers whose task would be to prevent encroachment of grazing stock from adjacent areas. Tourists will come to the area for the spectacular scenery and the prospect of seeing rare wild birds and mammals. Hotels already established in Ras Al Khaimah, Khorfakkan and Dibba, would make very suitable bases for trips into the mountains.

The first step must be to reduce the numbers of goats and donkeys, so that the vegetation and the associated indigenous animal life can recover. This should allow the tahr and gazelles to increase, and one can consider the possibility of reintroducing ibex, wild goat would then provide the prey base for the caracal, hopefully the leopard and possibly even the wolf, which survives in Oman. Provision of freshly killed goats in high remote areas would help the predators as well as scavengers such as eagles. In such a scenario the magnificent lappet-faced vulture and the smaller Egyptian vulture might re-establish themselves as breeding residents.

Another serious problem in the mountains is the increasing amount of settlement in the wadis. This is mostly recreational in nature resulting from the desire of nationals from the coastal towns and cities to maintain links with their past. Many of them have built simple holiday homes in

Left and right:
*The UAE is a land of
contrasts, both in
terms of physical
terrain and climate.
Whilst encompassing
some of the most arid
habitats on our
planet, it also
possesses mountain
streams and moist
habitats where water-
loving plants,
freshwater fish and
amphibians flourish.*

mountain wadis where they establish gardens and grow a few crops and palm trees. Apart from the direct impact, the diversion of water into the cultivations causes problems as it deprives the pools downstream. This is happening in many mountain areas, to the detriment of the specialized and sensitive freshwater ecosystem. There are two species of toad, at least two species of fish (probably of endemic subspecies), several species of dragonfly and many other invertebrates. These are under threat from the reduction in quantity and quality of water in the mountain streams. The impact of pesticides and fertilizers is unknown but requires investigation.

The Federal Environmental Agency (FEA) was established by Royal Decree in September 1993, with statutory duties covering environmental assessment, monitoring and advice, together with an obligation to produce legislation and to promote collaboration between the various official bodies for the enhancement of the environment. In the spring of 1996 Bye-laws for the FEA were approved by the Cabinet, enabling them to employ their own staff. The scope of work facing the FEA is enormous, covering marine pollution, gaseous emissions, water and soil contamination, groundwater resources, biodiversity and public awareness.

Draft federal environmental legislation has been produced and efforts are being taken to make it as useful as possible, as well as acceptable to all parties. The draft legislation includes a section on National Parks or protectorates and upon its enactment FEA will have power to exert effective control to protect nationally important areas. Progress in this area will not happen overnight

however and, in the meantime, in order to promote exchange of information and ideas, the FEA has established a Biodiversity Conservation Committee for UAE, following guidelines produced by IUCN the World Conservation Union. This Committee includes specialists with expertise in most groups of plants and animals, and has representatives from several government Ministries and Municipalities. To date the Committee has reviewed the extent of knowledge of biodiversity, assessed survey requirements, and drawn up provisional priorities for Protected Area status.

A major role of the FEA is to ensure that the relevant bodies have a good understanding of national issues and priorities, and to help them to implement a national Action Plan. A crucial part of this must be to promote environmental education and greater awareness of nature conservation issues. Pending federal action there is an effective procedure for affording statutory protection to a nature conservation area in the form of a Royal Decree, which can be made, with a minimum of consultation or bureaucracy, by the ruler of each Emirate. This mechanism may be put into effect to protect some large areas of desert, coral reefs, seagrass beds and several of the critically important islands. Mountain areas can be protected by the same means but it is to be hoped that larger federal Protected Areas can be established in due course, covering several emirates. In fact success in the mountains will only happen if there is a commitment to take on a regional approach, incorporating several emirates, together with close cooperation with the Sultanate of Oman, so that joint action programmes, involving trans-boundary mountain ranges, can be established.

THE SEA SHORE

Robert Baldwin

Much of the UAE coast is lined with gently sloping sandy beaches offering hours of interesting and quite unique beach-combing. Shores composed almost solely of coral and shell fragments generated by years of wave action and natural biological processes create endless white beaches

Beach at sunset.

fringed by inviting turquoise shallows. Beach-combing along these shores can be relaxing and enjoyable. The vast variety of material that you will find cast ashore or living on the beach can reveal almost all there is to know about the UAE's shallow seas. Among the marine debris are exquisite shells in a variety of shapes, sizes and colours, bleached coral skeletons of intricate design, delicate starfish, sea urchins, sand dollars and bryozoans, chalky white cuttlefish bones, tree-like gorgonians, multi-coloured jellyfish and seaslugs, carapaces of outlandish crustacea, bright green seagrasses, peacock's tail algae, bones and skulls of dolphins, whales, turtles, birds and fishes, and jetsam and flotsam from near and far, including driftwood smoothed and shaped into impossible twists by years of scouring sand, waves and the effects of salt water and a harsh sun. Identification of some of the animals and plants that you will find, living or dead, will challenge even experts in their field and still others may defy identification entirely, requiring fresh description for the scientific literature.

The variety and sheer abundance of shells in UAE waters coupled with the fact that relatively few people regularly beach comb can lead to some exciting finds. Consult the tide tables before you set out and try to plan a search at low spring tide when the largest area of beach is exposed. Search also along the high tide line, marked by a clear line of beached material at the furthest reach of the waves at high tide, and along the more pronounced storm berm, often marked by a bank of sand with beached material deposited on top. Beaches facing north are often best and accumulate most material, although more delicate shells can be found intact in sheltered coves or on leeward island beaches. Never collect live shells as you may take something rare or endangered or pick up a species that is dangerous itself, like the venomous cone shells. The variety of shells that you are likely to find on a particular stretch of beach is mostly determined by the local conditions and hence the distribution of the living animals that have created the shell. Many live in the sand of the beach itself, others live below the low tide mark, or on reefs, amongst algal or seagrass beds, or are pelagic, spending their lives in the open ocean. All shells are made by molluscs that secrete a calcium carbonate shelter in which to live. When the animal dies, the empty shells are often washed up onto beaches, unless a hermit crab has chosen one as a home. There are far too many species of shell to mention all of them here. In fact, the phylum Mollusca, to which all shells belong, is the second largest in the animal kingdom and beachcombers will be amazed at the diversity of shells in the UAE.

Exposed sandy shores are home to burrowing gastropods and bivalves. Gastropods are more numerous and some species like the top shell, *Umbonium vestiarium* can be found in their thousands, scattered along the tide lines. Their loosely whorled, small, smooth shells come in whites, pinks, greys, browns and purples, patterned with chevrons, streaks and spiral bands. Look carefully and you may find turban, button, bubble, and abundant olive shells, pheasant shells, glossy dove shells, nerites, mitres and mud creepers like *Cerithidea*. Less conspicuous shells include finely curved, hollow white shells, aptly named tusk shells. Larger and more obvious are the many species of strikingly coloured cowries and cones. If you are fortunate you may find the exquisite and rarely collected wentletrap, its high spire multiple whorled and buttressed by thick ribs, the whole shell creamy in colour and partially translucent. Near mangroves you may pick up winkles and the heavy shell of *Terebralia palustris*, once a favoured item on the menu of ancient man and often found buried, along with the murex *Hexaplex kuesterianus*, in shell middens.

Rocky shores have their share of gastropods too, like limpets, false limpets and keyhole limpets and there is a range of bivalves including mussels, and the once prized pearl oysters, as well as wing and hammer oysters, thorn oysters, saddle oysters and true oysters. Jewel box clams attach themselves to rocks, corals or even other shells, meanwhile scallops and cockles often wash up on sandy shores along with elongate razor clams, and the occasional large and brittle fan or file shell. The UAE's Gulf beaches are also littered with tens of thousands of chalky white cuttle bones, the internal shells of the cuttlefish. Some bear tooth marks, often made by bottlenose dolphins that feed upon the live animal.

Another animal that secretes calcium carbonate is the coral. Patterns on the surface of the coral skeleton can be ornate and pronounced, such as the meandering channels of the lesser brain coral (*Platygyra),* or the

Cistanche tubulosa, *the desert hyacinth is a parasitic plant that usually grows in association with the roots of the salt-tolerant* Zygophyllum.

striking star-like calyces of the starburst coral (*Galaxea*). Some coral skeletons have a less clear pattern, but look closely and you will see the individual cup-like depressions, or calyces, that house each coral animal. These can be small, as in the case of the boulder coral (*Porites*) which has calyces just 2-3mm in diameter, or they can be large, for example in the greater brain coral (*Symphyllia*) and the starry cup coral (*Acanthastrea*) in which the calyces may be 2-3cm in diameter. Some corals can be difficult to distinguish and only detailed examination can reveal the answers, such as the number and arrangement of the rib like septa that radiate from the mouth in the centre of the calyx. It is also such features that allow coral skeletons to be easily distinguished from other superficially similar looking structures, such as stone-like bryozoans and encrusting pink coralline algae.

Some of the branching corals, like bush and table coral (*Acropora*), hood coral (*Stylophora*) and cauliflower coral (*Pocillopora*) may break in storms before they reach the beach. Similarly, the delicate, leafy, or foliose, corals such as cabbage coral (*Montipora*), leaf coral (*Pavona*) and vase coral (*Turbinaria*) are unlikely to be found as complete skeletons. Others are robust and will survive intact through even the most ferocious storm. It is easy to become enthralled by the lives of these simple and yet important components of the marine ecosystem and much can be learnt from their remarkable skeletons. In the UAE relatively little study has been conducted on corals and the keen eyed naturalist may be rewarded with new records of their occurrence in the country, simply by collecting bleached, beach specimens.

Whorled necklaces of compressed, flattened sand often lie near the low tide line of the beach with no obvious clue as to what they are, or what has made them. They are in fact, made by the moon snail, which secretes mucus to bind together mud and sand from the seabed, before laying its eggs amongst this elaborate structure. Another odd-looking find is the sand dollar; a brittle disk, often covered in tiny spines with a clear star-shaped pattern that appears to have been etched in the centre. The five arms of the star pattern give away this animal's identity, as only echinoderms show this kind of radial symmetry. The sand dollar is simply a flattened sea urchin.

Greater flamingoes on a beach at Sir Bani Yas island.

Conspicuous pyramid like mounds that often tower above the sand's surface can be seen under construction if the patient observer sits for long enough for their maker, the ghost crab, to overcome its wariness of potential danger and continue in its chore of tunnel digging.

Among the variety of seeds and other vegetation washed up on beaches are those of the mangrove. A trip into a mangrove forest will help to confirm the identity of their sporelings, that have almost opaque, stringy roots and a winged pair of tough fibrous leaves that may allow them to drift on surface currents for many kilometres before settling on a beach and attempting to grow.

Not all of the material to be found on a beach is necessarily pleasant. UAE beaches are often strewn with litter thrown from passing ships and may also be covered in tar. Banked masses of discoloured seagrasses, like discarded lawn mower cuttings, house sandhoppers, or sand fleas, that have an irritating bite. The seagrasses tend to turn from green to brown to opaque and as they do so, can give off a rotten smell. Also emitting an unpleasant odour are the carcasses of dead fish and other animals. Over 80% of our knowledge of marine mammals comes from the study of beached remains and fishermen's catch or by-catch. Researchers spend hours combing

beaches investigating and collecting remains of dead animals, furthering science in the process. It is remarkable that even today, in a world of high technology and advanced research methodology, some species of whales, such as the shy beaked whale *Indopacetus pacificus*, are known only from a few bones washed ashore and apparently no-one has seen them alive. There are many examples of whales and dolphins and one species of turtle in the UAE whose presence in local waters has only been confirmed from their remains found on beaches, rather than by sight of live animals. In addition to providing clues as to the whereabouts of the living creatures, their remains also tell us something about seasonal abundance and can offer substantial insight into feeding, breeding, familial relations, genetic lineage, numerous biological functions, even social behaviour and environmental factors.

Measurements of skeletal remains, such as skulls, allow scientists to accurately compare populations of animals in different geographic locations. In the UAE, for example, bottlenose dolphins tend to have longer snouts and comparatively more teeth compared to those in many other countries. Common dolphins in the UAE, on the other hand, judging by the very few skulls that have been collected, have relatively few teeth, despite their elongate beaks. Coupled with DNA analysis of fragments taken from skin, bone, flesh or teeth, it is gradually becoming possible to establish relationships between separate populations and even to stumble across isolated gene pools that deserve merit as distinct races or sub-species. It has been suggested that the UAE hosts a race of dolphin unique to science, though this has yet to be proven.

Dolphins are especially good indicators of pollution. As top predators and with a naturally high fat content, hydrocarbon (oil) pollutants accumulate in the blubber. Blubber samples from dead dolphins can be analysed and levels of pollution determined. Using information gained from analysis such as this, conservationists are currently investigating ideas that dolphins could act as early warning indicators of potential damage to the environment by oil pollutants, including effects on commercial fish stocks.

The long sweeping bay at Khor Fakkan on the east coast.

79

Although pollution may be responsible for the death of many marine animals, there are numerous other possible causes for their deaths. Most of these can be determined by careful inspection and can further add to our knowledge of the live animals, as well as aiding in their conservation. Dolphins, for example, are now known to die of diseases such as pneumonia and to suffer from arthritis and other afflictions. Frequently, scars on the skin of cetaceans, dugongs and turtles in the UAE indicate that individuals have become caught in fishing nets, or struck by boat engine propellers, probably leading to death in most cases. Armed with the knowledge of the percentage of animals that die in this way, conservationists can suggest actions that could be taken by relevant authorities in order to protect animals, particularly those that are in danger of local or even global extinction.

One of the best ways to discover what whales and dolphins inhabit a particular region is to study the remains of washed up animals. These may have died as a result of perfectly natural causes, or become victims of a variety of environmental impacts.

The most comprehensive information on the feeding habitats of many marine animals comes from the collection and inspection of the stomach contents of those that have died. It has been found, for example, that dugongs feed almost exclusively on seagrasses; fragments of algae and other matter only appearing in the stomach at times when seagrasses are unavailable or scarce. This is also true of green turtles. In some cases, samples from hundreds of dead dolphins have shown interesting trends. Weaned dolphin calves have stomach contents closely matching adult females, suggesting, as expected, that mothers and calves are feeding together. Slightly older juveniles, however, have stomach contents similar to the group's oldest females that are no longer capable of reproducing. This suggests that older females may be acting as surrogate mothers within a pod of dolphins. While reproductive females continue to look after the very young, their offspring of previous years appear to be cared for by the group's aunts and grandmothers. This interpretation of social interaction is supported by observations of live animals.

Research of dead animals continues to provide information that simply cannot be obtained from live animals. It is worth reporting carcasses lying on a beach or caught in a fishing net to a local natural history group or museum. The carcass may hold invaluable secrets whose unravelling may help to save other members of the species from a similar fate.

Beaches are a natural interface between the land and the sea and as such are a crucial component of the coastal zone. Like all coastal features, however, beaches require careful management directed at sustainable utilisation. Examples of conflicting uses of beaches in the UAE are not hard to find. Obstructions, such as jetties and breakwaters frequently cause altered patterns of erosion at locations further along the coast, sometimes leading to recreational beaches disappearing altogether. Litter frequently blocks the path of nesting turtles. Sand extraction leads to a loss of dune vegetation. Planning and foresight are required for the careful management of beaches that used properly can yield a wealth of information, create a basis for substantial economic profit, and remain a stable and healthy home for the organisms that live around and within them.

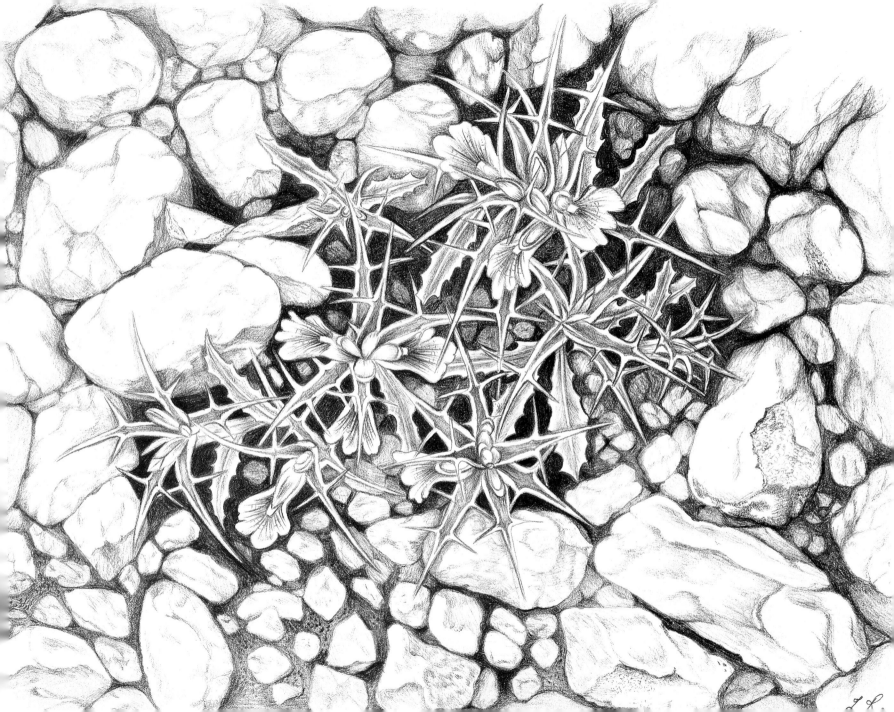

Plant Life

Marijcke Jongbloed

Considering its size the UAE has a wide variety of natural habitats and for our chapter on plants in this general wildlife book we shall take a look at communities within these habitats, rather than present a taxonomic treatise or *flora*, a task better left to the professionals. As we undertake this floristic escapade, briefly exploring their plants within different communities, I shall guide you, not as a trained botanist, but rather as an enthusiastic plant collector and observer. In nearly thirteen years of enjoying the deserts of the UAE, I have been amazed at the diversity of its plant life and the wonderful adaptations that have evolved to cope with the harsh living conditions.

On a four-hour drive along the western coast going from south to north, you will see the saline sabkha flats of Abu Dhabi turn into sandy plains dotted with halophyte vegetation like *Salsola imbricata* and *Zygophyllum mandavillei* with a few stunted *Tamarix*. All these halophytic plants have their methods of dealing with the high levels of salt in the soil. The tamarix excretes the salt on its needlelike leaves whilst the succulents store it in the fluids of their globular leaves. In sheltered lagoons along much of the Gulf coast mangroves (*Avicennia marina*) are home to many species of birds and fishes.

Where low sandy hillocks start to appear, grasses like *Panicum turgidum* and *Pennisetum divisum* become abundant, while *Haloxylon salicornicum* is present throughout most of the coastal (and also the inland) sandy plains. The delicate fruitwings of this plant, which appear in December, can turn the roadside into a feast of translucent whites, pinks and purples. In some places the sabkhas have dense vegetation where grey-leaved *Atriplex leucoclada* sets off the intricate yellow branches of *Halocnemum strobilaceum*, the white-flowering *Heliotropium kotschyi* and the maroon globular leaves of *Halopeplis perfoliata*. The fragile plumes of *Sporobolus arabicus* and the purple sprays of *Limonium axillare* complete a master's palette of colours and textures. In spring the multi-coloured flowers of *Moltkiopsis ciliata*, the maroon seedheads of *Cyperus arenarius* and the yellow daisies *Senecio glaucus* form a continuous ground cover as far as the eye can see.

Mangrove with pneumatophores.   *Ghaf tree, browsed by camels.*

We are coming close to Dubai, and the sand is now more obvious, shimmering white between bushes of *Cornulaca monacantha, Crotalaria persica, Calotropis procera* and *Taverniera spartea*. Two of the three parasitic plants of the UAE are abundant in these sandy coastal strips: the pretty yellow/maroon desert hyacinth (*Cistanche tubulosa*) and the red thumb (*Cynomorium coccineum*), which the bedu like to eat. One of the most important plants in bedu folklore, *arta or Calligonum comosum*, is at home here - but it is under threat of local extinction in areas of intense grazing. Along the main highways strips of about ten metres wide have been protected from grazing by came lfences, placed there to prevent collision between the animals and speeding cars. Wherever the fences are intact, the *arta* thrives, showing off its brilliant red seedpod lanterns in early spring. But outside the fences hardly a live plant can be found, having been browsed to death by domestic stock. With the disappearance of the *arta* several species of nocturnal moths, whose larvae feed on it, are threatened. The importance of these moths to the pollination of desert flora is not yet understood, and it could be that the impact of their loss of food source will lead to a population crash with a much more far reaching impact upon desert flora throughout the region.

Cistanche tubulosa is a parasite of salt-tolerant plants.
Top right: *The edible mushroom, faqah.*

Tidal creeks cut into the coastline from Sharjah northwards. Mangroves are abundant, but low, and the landspits in between the creeks are covered with the same grasses and halophytes, that occur all along the coast. But these areas are also the last places where an abundance of the edible mushroom *faqah* still occurs. These fungi live in symbiosis with the small woody perennial shrub *Helianthemum lippii*. The extremely wet spring of 1995-1996 brought out the mushrooms in great multitudes - and local people in droves to collect them! Nearer to Ras al-Khaimah high sand-dunes with impressive ghaf (*Prosopis cinerea*) forests come close to the coast. In the springtime these dunes are covered with the lovely ephemerals, *Eremobium aegyptiacum, Silene villosa, Senecio glaucus, Malva parviflora* and several *Launaea* species. A narrow gravel plain leads north of Ras al-Khaimah to the point where the high Musandam mountains descend straight into the sea.

The plains around Ras al-Khaimah are among the most fertile of the country and plantations prosper. Abandoned fields in the springtime have a special fascination for plant lovers. There are all the common favourites like *Anagallis arvensis, Aerva javanica, Astragalus* species, *Lotus halophilus, Monsonia nivea* and the bindweed *Convolvulus arvensis*. *Aloe vera* is an introduced species that has established itself as a 'feral' plant.

The high mountains have temperate climate flora, like the blue mountain lily, Ixiolirion tataricum.

Towards the mountains the gravel plains are thick with stands of *Prosopis juliflora*, the indestructible mesquite, probably imported into the country in times long gone by. Starting from these plains, another four-hour drive leads through boulder-strewn Wadi Bih to a high pass, where some of the original montane flora can be found in those places where fences protect it against the voracious appetite of goats and donkeys. Dark purple *Ixiolirion tataricum* lilies, and bright blue irises vie for attention with the showy pink *Gladiolus italicus* and the strange *Muscaris longipes*. Smaller weeds, more commonly found in European meadows, also occur, including *Vicia sativa*, *Galium setaceum*, and strong-smelling herbs like *Salvia aegyptiaca*. Under overhanging large boulders tiny plants like the yellow *Vicoa pentanema* and the starry *Spergula fallax* stand side by side with the small white daisies of *Anthemis odontostephana* and the yellow globes of *Matricaria aurea*. The most conspicuous plants of these high plains are the thorny *Astragalus spinosus* bushes, the arabian almond *Amygdalus arabicus* and the graceful pink-flowering *Moringa peregrina* trees. A hairpin track with magnificent views zig-zags down into the steep-sided canyon of Wadi Khabb Shamsi, one of the sites of the strange *Periploca aphylla*, and leads into the Dibba gravel plains, where *Acacia tortilis* trees spread their flat-topped umbrellas. I have noticed a sort of symbiosis between this Acacia and *Lycium shawii*, the desert thorn. The latter, wherever it grows by itself, is often cropped

87

into stunted shapes by domestic animals, and the only specimens that manage to thrive are those that grow between the protecting branches of the *Acacia*. The *Acacia* itself often shows a double umbrella: most of the tree, which is browsed by camels remains low and shrublike, but in the middle, where camels cannot reach, some branches have managed to grow out and reach their proper height to form the second umbrella.

The east coast road affords different views every few minutes. In some places the Hajjar mountains reach to the sea, while in other places extensive palm groves hide white-washed villages. The plantations are often bordered with lush vegetation including *Abutilon pannosum*, *Pergularia tomentosa* and *Vernonia arabica*, while the rocky passes in between have stands of the very common red-flowering *Tephrosia apollinea*, with here and there a bright yellow patch of the foul-smelling *Haplophyllum tuberculatum* and the inconspicuous *Pulicaria arabica*.

Tidal marshes extend inland from the main road in places just north of Fujairah, which lies in the widest stretch of gravel plain. In the south the coast road ends in one of the largest mangrove forests of southwestern Arabia, Khor Kalba, earmarked to become a nature reserve.

The next four hours of driving are along a brand new road that leads west again through a few large wadis to the central Hajjar mountains near Hatta. The wadis in the whole mountain range are extremely interesting botanically. Permanent pools and dripping aquifers provide habitats for fragile ferns like *Adiantum capillus-veneris* which occurs in close conjunction with the only UAE orchid *Epipactis veratrifolia*. These moist places also harbour *Lippia nodiflora*, *Centaurium pulchella*, *Bacopa monnieri* and *Sida urens*. Impressive stands of *Phragmites australis*, *Imperata cylindrica* and *Typha domingensis*, with

colour added by the wild oleander *Nerium mascatense* make you forget you are in a desert country. The rocky wadibanks are equally fascinating with the pink clouds of *Boerhaavia elegans*, the fine sprays of *Launaea massauensis*, the pink pea *Argyrolobium roseum*, the delicate grey violets *Viola cinerea*, the stork's bill *Erodium laciniatum* and the tiny blue borages *Paracaryum intermedium* and *Gastrocotyle hispida*. In some good springs, you can find the tiny-flowered weeds like the poppy *Papaver dubium*, the yellow flax *Linum corymbulosum*, the snapdragon *Misopates orontium*, *Euphorbia prostrata*, *Kickxia hastata* and the carnation *Dianthus cyri*. To find these takes footwork, while bigger plants with showy flowers like *Capparis spinosa*, *Leucas inflata*, *Reseda aucheri*, *Cleome rupicola*, *Physorrhynchus chaemarapistrum*, *Salvia spinosa* and *Hyoscyamus muticus* can be identified from the car.

Left: Cleome rupicola *turns its face towards the sun.* Opposite page: *A field of* Gladiolus italicus, Ixiolirion tataricum *and* Muscaris longipes. Below: Calligonum comosum *showing off its brilliant seed capsules.*

Papery balloons carry the seeds of the "popcorn" plant, Pseudogaillonia hymenostephana.

The higher slopes of the mountains must be climbed in order to see the plants that occur there. *Hibiscus micranthus*, aptly named for its 2 mm diameter flower, *Euphorbia larica*, *Teucrium stocksianum* and the *Caralluma* species, both the maroon fringed-petalled common one and the rare yellow *Caralluma flava* all occur here. I have my personal list of favourites from this cooler mountain habitat: firstly the popcorn plant with its unpronounceable name *Pseudogaillonia hymenostephana*- its tiny white trumpet flowers sit on velvety pink calyces, which start to become larger, whiter and papery thin with age, until the wind can blow these seed-carrying ballooons all over the place; secondly *Blepharis ciliaris*, the eyelash plant with its single blue petalled flower,

the seeds of this plant remain with the mother plant until a heavy rainfall drenches the plant and hygroscopic mechanisms come into action to shoot the seeds over long distance away from their source; thirdly *Asteriscus pygmaeus*, a small yellow composite, that dries up into a tight woody bud, that shelters the seeds, drenched by a downpour (or by water from my waterbottle) the petals of this seedhead unfold and the seeds can drop out; and finally the 'Hand of Miriam' *Anastatica hierochuntica*, which folds up all its branches to form a clenched fist, that only unclenches to release the seeds during heavy rain. In spring, the relatively level plateaus between the mountains are carpeted with *Erucaria hispanica*, *Diplotaxis harra* and *Asphodelus tenuifolius*.

such large bushes could have escaped my attention earlier. I was even more amazed the next spring when just south of this location many dozens of bushes had sprung up. That spring several valuable racing camels died after browsing the succulent leaves. Analysis showed that the leaves contained powerful poisons, called sesquiterpenlactones (Prof.U.Wernery, Central Veterinary Research Laboratorium Dubai). Orders were given for the plant to be destroyed, but this is an impossible task when it concerns a composite. Nowadays the first fifteen kilometres on either side of the road leading from Hatta to Mahda is permanently green with *Iphiona* foliage and the camels have learned to avoid it! The intriguing question is: what happened to this plant between 1983 and 1990, when I never found it during my weekly desert trips?

Near Buraimi the mountains give way to large sandy plains separated by low fossil bearing ridges. If it is still early in the day, large bushes of *Convolvulus deserti* can be found showing off its white flowers. The extended palm groves of Buraimi and Al Ain nestle at the foot of the 1000 m high Jebel Hafeet, an imposing piece of rock, that rises from the plains like the back of a beached whale, as Thesiger wrote when he first saw it. The mountain is not as empty as its name indicates, but one needs mountaineering skills in order to

Of the two species of Capparis, C. cartilaginea *grows at lower altitudes.*

On the southward trip from Hatta to Al Ain the plant communities change continuously, even though the landscape seems to be more or less the same. Areas dominated by the very poisonous *Iphiona aucheri* give way to others where *Fagonia indica* and *Pulicaria glutinosa* reign supreme. Then follow stretches where the only perennial visible is the shrub *Jaubertia aucheri*. Further south *Tephrosia apollinea* is the main plant, with smaller stretches covered with *Schweinfurthia papilloniacea* and *Rhazya stricta*.

Anvillea garcinii is *known from only one location at the foot of* Jebel Hafit.

There is a story concerning *Iphiona aucheri*: When I arrived here in 1983, I took only pictures of plants. I was taught to take specimens after my first visit to Edinburgh botanical gardens. One of the photos that I showed in Edinburgh was of a stem with leaves and a seedhead of *Iphiona aucheri*, taken on Jebel Qatar near Al Ain. I never saw the plant again until 1990, when I noticed two lush shrubs along the Madam-Hatta road. At the time I wondered how two

find all the species of plants that grow on its craggy flanks. However, since a road has been constructed a good way up the mountain it is now relatively easy to reach the summit, and although much of the natural plantlife was destroyed during the construction work, some has made a come-back. It is the easiest place to see *Capparis cartilaginea. Echiochilon thesigeri, Salsola rubescens, Launaea spinosa, Farsetia aegyptiaca, Helichrysum somalense* and *Gymnarrhena micranthus* are but a few of the many species that occur along the top ridges.

At the foot of the mountain a sandy plain is the only location, that I know of, where *Anvillea garcinii*, a crinkly-grey-leaved woody perennial, occurs. The area where the plant thrives is only a few hundred metres square and road construction is likely to destroy the site.

From Al Ain a tarmac road leads to Al-Wigan at the edge of the empty quarters. Row upon row of red sand-dunes are the waves of an endless sea of sand. But again, the sands are not completely empty. Between the dunes are salt plains with bright green *Zygophyllum* bushes as the dominant species, while sedges are the main vegetation on the dunes themselves. From Al-Wigan there are tracks across the dunes, that become higher and more forbidding as you go on. Only seasoned drivers venture across these drifting dunes, and it is a relief to reach one of the vast sandy saline plains that lie in an east-west

direction and are used as the main roads for travelling here. It takes far more than four hours to do the circuit from Al-Wigan to either the Liwa oasis in the middle of Abu Dhabi's western region, or the main road leading to the north from Liwa to Tarif.

One of the finest surprises of travelling in the dune habitat is to encounter a stand of *Tribulus omanense*, the flower that gave its name to the Emirates Natural History Group magazine, and which should be a major contender as the still to be declared national flower of the UAE. The beauty of the yellow flower on a plant that manages to survive the extremes of heat and drought and provides a favourite fodder for the gazelles and oryx that (used to) live here, symbolizes, for myself at least, the very essence of the desert.

Driving north from the Empty Quarter back to the coast road where we started the trip, leads us through the central desert area, where we can find patches of the desert squash *Citrullus colocynthis*, the spreading bush *Tribulus*

A typical example of convergent evolution - a Euphorbia that looks like a cactus (Caralluma sp.)

All Tribulus spp. *are good fodder plants for wild and domestic ungulates.*

not so. It was more a case of every plant being present in great abundance. Surprisingly, plants came up in places where I did not expect them: violets on dry mountain tops, *Calendula arvensis* at low altitudes and the parasite *Orobanche cernua* away from its usual hosts; in addition normally rare plants such as *Silene linearis*, *Cleome scaposa* and *Ophioglossum polyphyllum* were suddenly locally abundant. This unexpected profusion vividly demonstrated that thousands of seeds lie dormant for many, many years without germinating, waiting for that one season with unusual rainfall.

But not every plant thrived during these wet months. *Bleparis ciliaris* was either completely vegetative or it died, *Rhynchosia minima* bushes looked lush but lacked flowers. I searched in vain for *Cleome pruinosa*, and saw only a few bushes of the otherwise relatively common *Taverniera glabra*. It was particularly impressive to observe the huge quantities of seeds being produced. I also noticed that many plants went through the whole cycle of germination, flowering and seeding twice in a single season. The desert flora has given me countless hours of pleasure and offered many challenges. Among these is the rediscovery of the lovely *Scrophulariacea*, of which I only ever found one specimen.

Ophioglossum polyphyllum is an edible fern, found mainly in coastal sabkhas.

Unidentified beauty from the foothills of the Hajar mountains.

megistopterus and the greygreen bushes of *Indigofera intricata*, as well as the high broomlike shrubs of *Leptadenia pyrotechnica*, that often provide a shady lair for the delicate gazelles. Spring rains herald the appearance of endless fields of grasses like *Stipagrostis plumosa*, *Coelachyrum piercei*, *Setaria verticillata* and *Cenchrus pennisetiformis* as well as the popular fodder grasses *Pennisetum divisum* and *Panicum turgidum*.

Since 1980 there have been years of drought interspersed with good rains in the winters of 1982, 1987 and 1988; but the rains of 1996 were the most copious since 1962, according to local farmers. Many people remarked that these rains must have brought out many plants, which were unknown to me. But this was

INSECTS

Mike Gillett

DESERT HABITATS SUCH AS THOSE that dominate the territory of the United Arab Emirates, although not so rich in insect species as most tropical and temperate regions, still manage to support a remarkable variety of insect life. The observant first time visitor to this land is usually amazed at this variety and does not expect to see for example, delicately coloured dragonflies patrolling the sparse vegetation along the sides of sand dunes or clouds of butterflies swirling like a snow storm around the crown of a flowering *Acacia*

Blue Pansy, Precis orithya.

tree. A nocturnal excursion to the desert can produce enormous numbers of insect visitors at even the smallest lantern. These include numerous beetles, grasshoppers and wasps as well as the inevitable moths. However, perhaps the most interesting and unusual insects attracted to artificial light are the lacewings and antlions that belong to the nerve-winged insects (Neuroptera). Some of these are delicate insects with long streamers replacing the hind wings, but others are amongst the giants of the UAE insect world with wingspans of 10 cm or more. Such sights, whether during the day or at night, quickly dispel any preconceived idea that desert insects equate to swarms of obnoxious flies buzzing around one's head, plus the occasional ugly black beetle seen crawling across the sand. Pestiferous flies there are in the UAE, black beetles too, but as we shall see, there is much more besides.

That desert environments such as those in the UAE are able to support a rich and varied insect fauna should not really come as any surprise. Insects represent, at least in terms of numbers of species, the most successful life forms presently inhabiting our planet. Throughout more than three hundred million years of evolution, they have adapted to all terrestrial and fresh water environments, from the low water mark of marine beaches to the snowline on mountains.

INSECTS AND MAN IN THE UAE

Despite their numbers of species and of individuals, the majority of UAE insects probably go largely unnoticed by late twentieth century man. This may be because of their small size, their mainly nocturnal lifestyle or simply because they have no direct impact on mankind. There are of course important exceptions and few inhabitants of even the large modern cities in the UAE will be totally unaware of at least some of the insect productions of the country. They will have seen large showy butterflies such as the Lime Butterfly [*Papilio demoleus*] or the Plain Tiger [*Danaeus chrysippus*] gliding around flower beds in gardens and city parks and at favourable times, these resident species may be joined by equally conspicuous migrants such as the Diadem [*Hyplimnas misippus*] and the African Emigrant [*Catopsilla florella*]. Another group of insects that make themselves well known, although they may never be seen, are those with vocal ability. In the UAE, two insects stand out in this category. The common Arabian Cicada [*Platypleura arabica*] occurs during summer in almost every tree and bush in the country and the loud continuous 'singing' of the male insects is well known. Taking over from the cicadas at night time are crickets. The House Cricket [*Acheta domestica*], a native UAE species, produces a particularly loud chirruping that few people would fail to recognise.

Whether or not we are aware of them, a significant minority of UAE insects do impact human activities. This may be beneficial or detrimental depending upon the species of insect. Some like the blister beetles, *Epicauta*, fit into both categories, the larvae being ectoparasites of locust egg pods and the adults, leaf-eating pests of market garden crops.

chance encounters with insects, but is always carried out manually. Another invisible beneficial effect of insects is their predation of insects pests of crops and forage plants. Beetles, wasps, ants, bugs, preying mantises and flies are particularly important in this respect. Examples of such predators are the ladybirds which feed on aphids and the ground beetle *Calasoma imbricatum* which specialises in hunting caterpillars, as do potter wasps of the genus *Delta*. Some UAE insects play important roles in cleansing the environment of waste products. Scarab beetles bury and recycle dung, an activity which can limit the breeding of other insect pests and the spread of disease-causing micro-organisms, and can also improve the quality of range land. Scavenger beetles are equally important in the disposal of animal remains.

Detrimental insects in the UAE are quite diverse. Many attack crops and ornamental plants, including many species of caterpillars which feed on leaves, flowers and fruits as do grasshoppers. Other insects, including beetles and

Cueta lineosa, the ant-lion.

Gangling grasshopper Truxalis procera.

In the UAE, insects have traditionally contributed towards human nutrition; honey is still a common ingredient of the local diet, but the practise of eating locusts and grasshoppers, important traditional food items in the past, has largely died out. Insects in large numbers and in great variety (beetles, wasps, flies, butterflies and moths as well as bees) play an important role in pollination, not just of the indigenous UAE flora, but also of crops. Ironically, pollination of that most important UAE food plant, the date palm, is not left to

Plain Tiger,
Danaus chrysippus.

mole crickets, attack the roots of the same plants. Stored products such as grains and pulses, animal skins and woollen goods attract the attentions of other pestiferous insects including grain beetles, bean weevils, carpet beetles and clothes moths. Many of these pests are introductions, imported into the UAE in consignments of foodstuffs and other products. Soil-dwelling termites occur in the UAE and cause serious problems when they attack structural timbers in buildings or furniture.

A few UAE insects are of medical or veterinary importance either because they assist in the spread of disease or because they are venomous or poisonous. General nuisance species include the cockroaches, filth flies and flesh flies, common to most of the warmer regions of the world, whose activities lead to the spoiling of food and the transfer of diarrhoea-causing infections. Camel trypanosomiasis or 'surra' is a disease caused by protozoans that are transferred mechanically by haematophagous flies and an important cause of morbidity and mortality in camels and other livestock. It is not infectious towards man, but historically, two other protozoans spread by insects, have been important causes of human disease in the region. These are malaria, transmitted by anopholine mosquitoes, and cutaneous leishmaniasis (oriental

sore) spread by the bites of infected sandflies. The modernization of the UAE has led to a remarkable decline in their incidence.

Venomous insects in the UAE include bees, wasps and ants. Honeybees have potent stings which can be dangerous to susceptible individuals. The Oriental Hornet [*Vespa orientalis*] is a common wasp in the UAE which stings both humans and domestic animals. It preys heavily on Honey Bees and it is not unknown for hives to be completely taken over by it. Many other insects, both harmless and venomous, mimic this hornet. Another venomous UAE insect worthy of note is the Samsum Ant [*Pachycondyla sennaarensis*] which may occur in houses and is known to have caused several deaths.

Amongst the poisonous insects are many whose poisons serve to deter the attacks of both invertebrate and vertebrate predators, but which pose no danger to man. These include such insects as ladybirds, other beetles, bugs and some butterflies and moths, including both the Plain Tiger and Lime Butterflies. However, a few beetles are severely poisonous and capable of inflicting injuries to man. Two groups are represented in the UAE, the oil or blister beetles of the family Meloidae with twenty or so species and the staphylinid or rove beetles of the subfamily Paederinae. The UAE oil beetles are usually brightly coloured insects, red, orange or yellow with contrasting

Wasp Oil Beetle,
Croscherichia
richteri.

black spots and stripes, designs which, as in ladybirds, hornets and other insects, act as warnings to potential predators. The soft tissues and haemolymph of oil beetles contain cantharidin which is a powerful vesicant or blistering agent. If the insects are handled or accidentally crushed when in contact with human skin, cantharidin is released and painful, slow-healing blisters result. An extract of oil beetles known as cantharides was once used in Western medicine to treat a whole range of maladies, but is now discredited although still prescribed in Oriental medicine. Oil beetle extracts were used as poisons in medieval times and in some parts of the world continue to be used illegally as abortificants and aphrodisiacs. These practices regularly cause human deaths, although there are no records of such abuse in the UAE. The less widespread paederine rove beetles such as *Paederus fuscipes* contain the poisons pederine and pseudopederin which have similar effects to cantharidin on human skin and can cause serious eye injuries. Other medically harmful beetles, common in the UAE, are the hide and carpet beetles (Dermestidae) such as *Dermestes frischii*. As indicated by their common names, they live in dried animal remains, hides and woollen and silk rugs. Whilst not poisonous, their larvae are equipped with irritating, detachable hairs, contact with which can cause dermatitis and dyspnoea, although the beetles and their larvae are probably more feared for their destruction of expensive oriental rugs.

INSECTS OF THE UAE

Twenty one orders of insects are known to be represented in the UAE; some others will undoubtedly be found as a result of further studies whilst some are not likely to occur because they contain only rare species adapted to climates and habitats quite unlike those available in the UAE. The orders known from the UAE are listed in the table below, together with the common names of the insects which they contain. Orders which are well represented in the UAE and which can be considered as major orders in the country's fauna are indicated with bold-faced type. The other orders, with fewer than a dozen UAE representatives, are considered as minor orders.

SUBCLASS/DIVISION	
Order	Common name(s)
APTERYGOTA	
Thysanura	Silverfish & Bristletails
Collembola	Springtails
PTERYGOTA/EXOPTERYGOTA	
Ephemeroptera	Mayflies
Odonata	**Dragonflies & Damselflies**
Orthoptera	**Crickets & Grasshoppers**
Phasmida	Stick insects
Dermaptera	Earwigs
Embioptera	Web-spinners
Dictyoptera	**Cockroaches & Preying mantises**
Isoptera	Termites
Anopleura	
Mallophaga	Sucking lice
Biting lice	
Hemiptera	**Aphids, Cicadas & True bugs**
Thysanoptera	Thrips
PTERYGOTA/ENDOPTERYGOTA	
Neuroptera	**Antlions & Lacewings**
Lepidoptera	
Trichoptera	**Butterflies & Moths**
Caddisflies	
Diptera	**True or Two-winged flies**
Siphonaptera	Fleas
Hymenoptera	**Bees, Wasps & Ants**
Coleoptera	**Beetles**

Oleander Hawkmoth, Daphnis nerii.

Just as the UAE does not have representatives from some orders, so too, many of the lower insect groupings, such as families and genera, are also absent. Current knowledge is insufficient to say exactly how many of the world's one million or so species are found in the UAE. A provisional and probably conservative estimate for the number of UAE insect species is between 5,000 and 10,000. The majority are beetles, true flies, ants, wasps and bees, but butterflies and moths, grasshoppers, crickets, bugs, neuropterans, cockroaches and preying mantises also contribute numbers of species, with the smaller orders making up the rest. It should, however, be emphasised that this is a crude estimate and unlikely to be substantiated in the near future by a complete listing of UAE species.

PRIMITIVE WINGLESS INSECTS (APTERYGOTA)

Lesser Emperor, Anax parthenope.

These tiny insects are of little interest to naturalists and the number of species occurring in the UAE is not great. The order Thysanura includes several species of bristletails including, *Lepisma saccharina* (Linnaeus) and *Ctenolepisma ciliata* (Dufour) and the Firebrat [*Thermobia domestica* (Packard)]. Some of which have become cosmopolitan and are minor household pests, but in the UAE they appear to be native and are found outdoors even in remote areas. Springtails (Collombola) from the UAE have been little studied, but several minute species occur in permanently damp areas in oases and in the mountains.

INSECTS WITH INCOMPLETE METAMORPHOSIS (EXOPTERYGOTA)

This subclass is represented by a dozen orders in the UAE. Many are little known and because they contain just a few small species, they rarely come to the attention of the general naturalist. Nevertheless, some are economically or medically important. Amongst the former may be mentioned the thrips (Thysanoptera) which are minor pests of flowers and horticultural crops, as well as the termites (Isoptera) which are well known for their destructive activities. A common termite in the UAE is *Anacanthotermes ochraceous* (Burmeister). The medically important insects in this subclass include the sucking lice (Anapleura) of which three species that attack humans are well

Striped Mantis,
Blepharopsis
mendica.

Bug (Anoplocnemis
curvipes) - *a*
common and
gregarious
Afrotropical species
found in oases.

known cosmopolites and the biting lice (Mallophaga) which may be serious pests of livestock, but are also found on native birds and mammals. Of less importance to man are the mayflies (Ephemeroptera), a few species from the families Baetidae and Caenidae occurring in the UAE mountains and oases. The webspinners (Embioptera) include some truly native species elsewhere in Arabia, but in the UAE, they seem to be represented only by the 'weed' species *Parembia persica* (McLachan). This insect has been spread by commerce and is a common, if largely unseen, inhabitant of suburban gardens where it constructs silken tunnels amongst fallen leaves. The earwigs (Dermaptera) are represented in the UAE by only a few species and again they are little seen.

The commonest example is the widespread *Labidura riparia* (Pallas), which is typical of the order and found in damp places. The Phasmida is another minor order in this subclass and, in the UAE, is represented by a few species of stick insects that are seldom seen because of their excellent twig-like camouflage. The remaining four orders all contain bigger numbers of insects, including some of large size.

Mediterranean Pierrot, Tarucus rosaceus.

INSECTS WITH COMPLETE METAMORPHOSIS (ENDOPTERYGOTA)

Of the seven orders in this subclass found in the UAE, five are major orders and contain large numbers of often big and conspicuous insects. Of the remaining orders, the Trichoptera or caddisflies are uncommon insects in the Arabian Peninsular. In the UAE, the few species known are restricted to mountain wadis with permanent flowing water, in which their case-carrying larvae live. They include *Setodes sugdeni* Malicky first described from Wadi Madha in Fujairah and *Cheumatopsyche capitella* Martynov. The Siphonaptera include the fleas, with over 120 species recorded from Arabia. Some are hosted by man and domestic animals, but most are associated with native birds and mammals, especially rodents. Providing that the hosts occur in the UAE, most of the fleas known from Arabia will probably be found there, but no systematic studies are available.

Caterpillar of Striped Hawkmoth, Hyles lineata.

CONSERVATION OF THE INSECT FAUNA OF THE UAE

Given the incomplete state of knowledge about the insect fauna of the UAE, it is very difficult to decide whether insects as a group or as individual species are under threat. Indeed the problem of conservation of insects is somewhat different from that relating to conservation of other groups such as vertebrate animals or vascular plants where the species are generally well known and the

Eastern Deathshead Hawkmoth (Acherontia styx) - *beautifully camouflaged caterpillars feeding on garden jasmin.*

threats much easier to evaluate. Insects populations tend to fluctuate widely in numbers and as a group, insects are well able to build up their numbers very quickly as conditions improve after a period of adversity. Many of the more obvious UAE insects are migratory. Some of these are not truly adapted to the desert environment, but are able to colonise areas of the UAE when conditions permit. After one or more seasons, such colonies may die out as conditions deteriorate, as for example in a year when little rainfall occurs. However, as conditions once more improve, new colonies may be established by insects flying out of their strongholds in areas such as Oman where they are permanently present. This natural decline of insect colonies must not be confused with threats that may occur as a result of pollution, altered land use or any other result of man's activities in the UAE. Clearly concerns can be expressed about some activities, such as indiscriminate spraying of insecticides over farmland adjoining desert and oasis habitats, but it is by no means clear at the moment whether such practises constitute a real threat to the continued survival of any given species of insect in the UAE. Similarly, however much one might lament the use of the desert as a dumping ground for all types of refuse, it is not easy to assess the risks to insect populations that such practices entail. However, a single motor car tyre dumped in the desert may cause the deaths of several thousand insects, particularly beetles, that clamber over the sides and cannot climb back out again until the accumulated dead bodies reach the rim! Obviously any efforts to stop such dumping and to remove rubbish from the desert may help to strengthen local insect populations, but any such action is likely to be taken as a general measure for conserving the environment rather than as a specific one for protecting insects. Indeed in general it would be logical to assume that any measures specifically

Jewel Beetle (Julodis euphratica) - *Adult female on a plant of* Clitoria *in a garden.*

aimed at conservation of other wildlife, especially plants, are also likely to benefit the diverse species of insects found in the same habitats. It, therefore, seems likely that the biodiversity of the UAE insect fauna will be safeguarded for future generations, if sufficient good examples of different UAE habitat types are taken under effective conservation management.

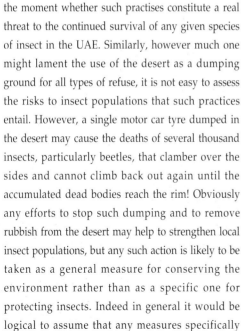

members are dependent upon the ants. The future of the butterfly could, however, be safeguarded if colonies of the butterfly are pinpointed and steps taken to ensure that old palms with *Crematogaster* nests are left in place. The Desert Leopard Butterfly is a true desert species and lives in the Rhub al-Khali desert including those parts of it that fall within UAE territory. The butterfly has seldom been seen and its habits are by no means well known. However, like the Leopard it probably lives in small colonies and is dependent upon one or other species of ant. Access to the Rhub al-Khali for man and his domestic animals has increased dramatically in modern times due to the introduction of all-wheel drive vehicles. This, combined with the utilisation of subterranean water to improve pasture in remote areas of this desert could conceivably put pressure on isolated colonies of insects, such as the Desert Leopard, and threaten their survival. There may,

Nevertheless, it seems necessary to qualify this general statement by providing a few exceptions and examples where specific measures may be appropriate for the conservation of what might turn out to be particularly vulnerable species. Two of Arabia's least known butterflies, the Leopard and the Desert Leopard, occur in small isolated colonies and are non-migratory and, therefore, lack the ability to quickly disperse to new breeding grounds. The Indian subspecies of the Leopard Butterfly is found in the UAE under oasis conditions and is dependent for its survival on ants of the genus *Crematogaster*. The caterpillars of this butterfly are found in the ant nests where their presence is tolerated, despite the fact that they feed on ant larvae, since they produce a sweet secretion on which the ants also feed. *Crematogaster* ants make their nests in the cavities eaten into old date palm trunks by the larvae of rhinoceros beetles. Often the ants are restricted to a few particular palms which may be old and unproductive. Removal of such trees to allow replanting would seriously compromise the future of any Leopard Butterfly colony whose

Preying Mantis
(Mantis religiosa) -
*a mating pair beneath
a flower of cultivated
onion.*

105

Beetle wasp, Scolia sp.

detailed scientific knowledge. Similarly there is also a need for more information about the beautiful tiger beetles of the UAE, many of which seem to be very local if not actually rare.

Summarising the situation regarding the conservation of the UAE insect fauna, it appears that measures being considered to safeguard the country's other faunal groups and flora should serve in the interim to protect many, if not most, of the country's insect species. There may be a few exceptions to this, some of which have been duly noted, but in general before any more specific conservation measures can be proposed, there has to be a period during which active research of the insect fauna needs to be undertaken in order to build up our database from its present rather meagre level. In effect, without a thorough working knowledge of the UAE insects, we are powerless to discuss their conservation needs.

ACKNOWLEDGEMENTS

Editor's Note: *This chapter is a considerably abbreviated version of Dr. Gillett's submitted work on the UAE's insects. The publishers intend to produce the full length chapter in the form of a separate booklet.*

therefore, be a need to locate colonies of this butterfly, assess whether they are under threat and evaluate what active measures might be required to conserve them, perhaps by preventing access for livestock to key areas.

Similarly other insects that appear to be of rare occurrence in the UAE need to be evaluated in case conservation measures should become necessary at some future date. Into this category, one could assign several other butterflies such as the Green Striped White, Desert Black Tip, Baluchi Ringlet and the Diadem, although the latter is a well known migrant and probably comes and goes in the UAE according to climatic conditions. There are other insects too that might be included; the small scarab *Apsteiniella naviauxi* Baroud is known to science from only three specimens found singly in Iraq, Saudi Arabia and more recently near to Al Ain. Its apparent rarity suggests that some research might be undertaken to assess the situation with regard to this beetle in the UAE, so that any future threats to its habitat could be considered in the light of

Shortly before I left the UK to join the UAE University in Al Ain, I purchased a copy of a little book on Arabian insects, thinking that it might be a useful way of getting to know the orders other than Coleoptera which is my main interest. The Insects of Eastern Arabia by D.H. Walker and A.R. Pittaway, illustrated by A.J. Walker and published by Macmillan, London (1987) proved to be a very shrewd buy. Unbelievably, for such a small book, it seemed to cover exactly the insects that I came across during my leisure trips to mountains wadis and deserts. I gratefully acknowledge the help and insight that this publication has provided over the last five years. I would also like to thank my wife Antoniêta, who for the last few months has had to live with a collection of insects in the deep freeze, in the spare bedroom and spread across the dining table and any other bit of flat space at hand. My children, Conrad, James and Caroline also deserve credit since they have all accompanied me on collecting trips and have made many interesting discoveries. Finally, I would like to acknowledge the encouragement and support that I have received from the head of my Department, Professor Bill Montague, currently Acting Dean of the Faculty of Medicine and Health Sciences.

TERRESTRIAL ARTHROPODS (excluding insects)

Barbara Tigar

THE FLORA AND FAUNA OF THE UAE contain a mixture of elements from three major biogeographic zones: the Northern Palaearctic, Africa and Asia. This, in combination with an extremely dry climate, results in a characteristic invertebrate fauna with typical arid-zone species, such as camel spiders and scorpions, being relatively abundant. Legends and tales of the terrible scourge that these creatures cause abound. Indeed, on first sight they look like products of an arachnaphobe's nightmare. In this chapter I hope to dispel such myths and show the important roles these animals play in their environment. I also explain how, through their biology and ecology, invertebrates are well adapted to one of the most inhospitable parts of the world: while most humans venture only briefly from the comfort and safety of their air-conditioned, four-wheel drive vehicles, the arthropods take the desert in their stride, albeit using many legs!

Argiope, the orb or signature spider, packaging its prey. The zigzag anchoring chords may serve to draw the attention of a potential victim away from the web which captures it.

HISTORICAL RECORDS OF TERRESTRIAL ARTHROPODS

Invertebrates of the Arabian region as a whole remained poorly studied until the late 1970's, and the UAE still has far fewer records than neighbouring Saudi Arabia and Oman (see the Fauna of Saudi Arabia series and the Journal of Oman studies for further details). This is mainly due to the lack of collectors and records rather than a paucity of fauna, although the other two countries are larger with greater climatic and biological diversity. In this chapter I have gathered together all published records and some of my own unpublished findings of terrestrial arthropods in UAE. I have also added information on arthropod groups which have not been found in the Emirates but which probably do occur on the basis of records from neighbouring countries and similar climatic regions elsewhere. Wherever possible I have included information on first aid for bites and stings.

AN INTRODUCTION TO THE ARTHROPODS

The arthropods form a major taxonomic division, also known as a phylum, which consists of invertebrates (animals without backbones) that possess jointed bodies and limbs, and an exoskeleton. For more detailed information on arthropod biology and phylogeny see Barnes (1987), Manton, (1977) or Meglitsch (1967). The exoskeleton or cuticle can either be thin and flexible forming the joints, or deposited in thick, stiff plates called sclerites which function like armour. Crack open the claws of crabs or lobsters and you will know just how strong the sclerites can be. The cuticle also acts as a barrier against water loss and therefore helps arthropods to survive in arid environments. Arthropods are further classified according to the similarity of their body structure, in particular the shape of their mouthparts which reflects the range of diets and feeding habits.

Five sub-phyla are recognised of which three, the Crustacea, the Insecta-Myriapoda and the Chelicerata, occur in UAE. The vast majority are insects, which differ from other arthropods by having specialised antennae, two pairs of wings, six pairs of legs and compound eyes. The insects are described in a separate chapter of this book. Here I shall consider the remaining terrestrial arthropods which are more diverse although they tend to be either predatory or parasitic animals.

There are few species of terrestrial Crustacea (crustaceans) in UAE although they are more common than might be expected of these generally mesic (ie moderate moisture) creatures. Besides the vast array of insects, several other groups belonging to the Insecta-Myriapoda frequently occur in arid-zones like the Emirates, particularly the Scolopendrida or centipedes. By contrast, the Chelicerata (chelicerates) are very well-represented by various members of the class Arachnida which again can be divided into 11 sub-classes. Of these sub-classes, nine are likely to occur in UAE. They are the scorpions (Scorpiones), pseudoscorpions (Pseudoscorpiones), solifugids or camel spiders (Solifugidae), whip scorpions (Schizopeltida and Thelyphonida), tail-less whip scorpions (Amblypygi), spiders (Araneae), harvestmen (Opiliones) and mites and ticks (Acari). In terms of biodiversity and biomass, or the amount of biological material determined by body size and relative numbers, the scorpions and solifugids are the dominant groups in UAE. Some of these animals are predatory and a few are venomous, but they are not generally aggressive towards humans and only use their poison to kill and capture their prey or as defensive weapons. Most stings or bites only occur when these animals come into accidental contact with man.

All invertebrates are poikilothermic, or cold-blooded, so their body temperature is dependant on that of their environment. Activity therefore is often directly related to temperature and there are noticeable differences in activity levels between day and night, and the summer and winter months. Indeed, during the day, deserts appear devoid of animal life and it is not until dusk that their many arthropodian inhabitants become apparent. Conversely, during the winter, if the ambient temperature is too low for their basal metabolic rate or that of their prey, invertebrates remain inactive and will rarely be seen.

Although most arthropods have a relatively small body-size, their biology is quite varied and many species show a high degree of specialisation. Everything from parental care through to complex behaviour and adaptation to environment are exhibited. In some arthropods, the juvenile stages are exact miniatures of the adults while in others they not only look very different, but also have totally different habitats and diets. In order to grow most arthropods have to moult, known as ecdysis, before they can increase in size. During this time they are very vulnerable until the new cuticle has hardened.

In terms of classification, I have tried to follow Sheals (1973) and Sheals & Rice (1973), but there is considerable disagreement in the scientific literature about how closely related some of the arthropods are to one another. Indeed, it is not always clear at what level they should be split and whether they are separate phyla, classes or orders. By keeping to one system of classification I hope to simplify matters and avoid confusion. I shall therefore start by introducing the various groups, then deal with each in turn by describing their general appearance, biology, ecology and natural history. Finally, for each taxa, I shall list those species known to occur in UAE. In most cases this consists of a scientific name because they have no known common name.

SUB-PHYLUM CRUSTACEA

The crustaceans are a very diverse group dominated by marine and aquatic species. In many deserts, numerous tiny brine shrimps are found in temporary pools following the rains. These creatures are able to withstand immense periods of desiccation and reproduce very rapidly to ensure the continual survival of their kind. Such pools have not been studied in UAE but it is possible that ephemeral crustaceans do occur. The only terrestrial crustacea are the sub-class or class isopoda.

CRUSTACEA
ISOPODA

Since most isopods are either aquatic or associated with very humid environments, it is perhaps surprising that the family Porcellionidae or woodlice is common in desert areas. These creatures have small, ovoid bodies up to about 6mm in length, with two long antennae and a shorter pair of antennules at the front of the head, and a thorax divided into seven segments.

They are detritivores and survive by remaining in the humid micro-climate of burrows at the base of desert shrubs and only emerge to feed at night. They are probably relics of a more moist environment.

TERRESTRIAL ISOPODS IN UAE

Ferrara & Taiti (1985) and Taiti & Ferrara (1989, 1991) list 20 species of woodlice which occur on the Arabian peninsula. Of these there are two species introduced by man (*Porcellionides pruninosus* and *Protracheoneonisus inexpectatus*) and three cosmopolitan species (*Porcellio assimilis*, *Porcellio evansis* and *Koweitoniscus tamei*). All of these are likely to be found in the Emirates. Taiti & Ferrara (1991) also describe a new species *Littrorophiloscia stronhali* which was first discovered in Sharjah along with another isopod *Somalodillo paeninsulae*. Isopods remain a relatively poorly known group in UAE.

SUB-PHYLUM CHELICERATA
CLASS ARACHNIDA

Most chelicerate arthropods belong to the class Arachnida and include some of the most typical arid-zone animals. All arachnids have a pair of feeding organs called chelicerae, a pair of pedipalps and four pairs of walking legs. The chelicerae and pedipalps are variously modified according to biology, usually reflecting diet. In structure the chelicerae resemble a pair of pincers with teeth along their inner edge. The arachnid body is divided into two regions: the anterior prosoma or cephalothorax and the posterior opithosoma or abdomen. However, in the Acari and Opliones, the prosoma and opithosoma are not clearly differentiated. Arachnids are nearly all terrestrial predators of other arthropods. For further information on Arachnids see Savory (1964 & 1977) and Cloudsley Thompson (1958).

CHELICERATA
ARACHNIDA
SCORPIONES (SCORPIONS)

Almost everybody knows what a scorpion looks like even if they have never actually seen one. The image of their body-shape is ingrained in our minds from earliest times, and myth and superstition surround them. Many people fear and loath scorpions but in common with other venomous animals they normally avoid humans and will only sting when threatened. Most stings occur when people inadvertently come into contact with scorpions, particularly during camping trips, when they are found hiding under rocks, stones, tents, clothing, debris and rubbish.

The scorpions are structurally a very homologous group and have been highly successful for over 450 million years. They can be relatively large although some are only 9mm long. Their bodies are heavily sclerotized with a thick cuticle forming a compact shield or carapace over the prosoma. They have one pair of median eyes and from two to five smaller simple eyes or ocelli. Their chelate-pedipalps or pincers are massive and powerful and are used to grasp and manipulate prey. They have four pairs of walking legs, and the basal segments of the first two pairs are modified for chewing. Their opithosoma is broad and made up of a seven-segmented pre-abdomen and a five-segmented tail or post-abdomen with a sting at the tip. On their ventral side is a pair of delicate comb-like organs known as pectines which are thought to be sensory in function.

Of the various species of scorpions, that occur in the UAE, the small yellow Buthacus yotvatensis nigroaculeatus is the most poisonous.

Scorpions prey on other arthropods, particularly insects and arachnids but may also feed on small vertebrates. Scorpions that have very large pincers do not always use their sting to kill prey, but may simply rely on the crushing power of their claws. The chelicerae are used to tear-up the prey and digestion actually starts outside the mouth. They have a long gestation period and surprisingly are viviparous, meaning that they give birth to live young. Young scorpions are smaller versions of their parents. Maternal care of the young ranges from a few days to several months and can include complex behaviour such as co-operative feeding and burrow building. The lifespan of most scorpions is from two to five years but in at least one species it exceeds 25 years! To find out more about scorpions I thoroughly recommend an excellent book edited by Gary Polis (1990).

A. crassicauda *is one of the largest UAE scorpions.*

An interesting phenomenon concerning scorpions is the fact that they fluoresce when exposed to ultra violet (UV) light. No-one knows why this happens; it is just a natural property of the cuticle. However, it provides an easy way of detecting scorpions and is used by biologists to estimate their numbers without having to capture them. It is also an effective way of avoiding scorpions when camping, although in some desert locations it is alarming to see just how many the UV light reveals!

SCORPIONS IN UAE

Vachon (1989) lists 14 species or sub-species of scorpions from the Arabian peninsula. They belong to two families; the Buthidae and the Scorpionidae.

There are eight genera of buthids: *Androctonus, Apistobuthus, Buthus, Compsobuthus, Leirus, Orthochirus, Parabuthus* and *Vachoniolus*, but only two genera of scorpionids: *Hemiscorpius* and *Scorpio*. To date only buthids have been found in the Emirates. They are *Androctonus crassicauda, Apithobuthus pterygocercus, Buthacus yotvatensis nigroaculeatus, Compsobuthis arabicus, Parabuthus liosoma, Vachoniolus minipectibinus* and possibly *Vachoniolus globimanus*, although it is not clear whether the latter are two separate species, or male and female of a single species. There may well be further scorpions awaiting discovery in the Hajar mountains.

A.crassicauda and *A.pterygocercus* are the two largest scorpions in UAE. Adults of both species can measure up to 150mm from their head to the tip of their sting and they can occur near human habitation. They are quite different in appearance. *A.crassicauda* is black with very chunky claws and a highly

111

sculptured tail, while *A.pterygocercus* is pale-yellow with very long, slender pincers and a swollen disc-shaped second segment on the tail.

The most common species in sandy areas is *B.y.nigroaculeatus* which is mostly yellow, but is black on the last segment of tail and sting. Adults can reach up to about 75mm in length. The *Vachoniolus spp.* are slightly smaller and also yellow with a darker-coloured tip to their sting. The first *Vachoniolus spp* ever collected were from Bada Haza, Abu Dhabi. Both *C.arabicus* and *P.liosoma* are smaller and only reach about 25mm in length. The former is all yellow, while the latter is mainly pink, except for the last two segments of the tail and sting which are brown. I have also found a fragment from the tail of another scorpion, possibly *Orthochirus innesi*, which is awaiting confirmation.

SCORPION VENOM AND STINGS

In recent years there has been much interest in the biology of scorpions, particularly their venom which is a mixture of some of the most potent and biologically active compounds in the animal kingdom. The venom of all buthid species contains powerful and dangerous neurotoxins. Of the buthids, *Androctonus australis* is considered to be very venomous and symptoms of its sting resemble strychnine poisoning. Its close relative, *A.crassicauda*. occurs in the Emirates and should be treated with caution. Victims of stings feel a sharp pain followed by numbness, drowsiness and an itching of the throat. This can be accompanied by excessive saliva and the tongue becomes sluggish with the jaw muscles contracted. If large amounts of venom have entered the blood system, difficulties in co-ordination arise and body temperature increases while the production of saliva and urine are reduced. Touch and sight can be affected, with sensitivity to strong light. There may also be haemorrhages and convulsions with increasing severity. Most victims are normally out of danger within three hours but they should receive medical supervision for at least eight hours.

Primary first aid for scorpion stings is to reassure the victim who will be suffering from shock. Clean the wound and then try to isolate it by immobilising the sight of the sting. Use a firm supporting bandage but not a tourniquet, and hold the limb up to avoid the venom going directly to the heart. If possible keep the site of the sting cold by placing it in iced water. Although fatalities are very rare, do seek medical help, particularly in the case of small children and invalids who are most at risk. In some cases, an anti-venom can be administered and these work well if given early enough. However, in other cases a pain killer is all that can be given but recovery should be rapid.

CHELICERATA
ARACHNIDA
PSEUDOSCORPIONES (PSEUDOSCORPIONS)

Pseudoscorpions are similar in structure to scorpions although they lack the post abdomen and sting. They are distinguished by their minute size and only measure between 1 and 7mm long. Their bodies are flattened in appearance and some species lack eyes. Their palpal chelae or claws are large, like those of scorpions, with a swollen "hand" and a moveable finger or digit. They use their chelae to climb up hairs of other animals. Although they normally walk forwards, they are equally good at going backwards. Sometimes they are gregarious and found in large groups.

Pseudoscorpions are predators and possess a poison gland at the base of their pincers which they use to anaesthetise prey. They feed on other tiny arthropods such as spring-tails (Collembola), book-lice (Psocidae), mites (Acari) and silverfish (Thysanurana). Food is digested externally by a fluid poured over the prey and the liquefied remains are ingested by the chelicerae. Pseudoscorpions regularly clean their palps to remove remains of food so that they can easily suck up their next meal through special grooves.

Some pseudoscorpions are phoretic which means that they use other animals for transport and dispersal over larger distances. They do so by attaching themselves to the legs of insects (such as flies) using their pincers. Others live under the elytra of large beetles where they prey upon parasitic or phoretic mites also living on the beetles. They have even been seen beckoning to beetles which then let them mount their bodies!

Despite their minute size pseudoscorpions demonstrate a tremendous variety and complexity of lifestyle. They have silk glands and construct nests of silk for moulting, brooding and hibernation. Their courtship dances may be very complicated. Females carry their eggs in a brood sac attached to their genitalia and actually provide nourishment in the form of a nutritive fluid which passes to the embryos in the brood sac. Some species exhibit parental care with the young riding on the back of females, but they generally disperse very quickly. The young are identical to adults in all but size and undergo three moults before they are fully grown. For further information on these minute but fascinating animals see Weygoldt (1969) and Legg & Jones (1988).

PSEUDOSCORPIONS IN UAE

Although pseudoscorpions are generally associated with moist habitats such as leaf litter and crevices, the families Olipiidae and Cheliceridae prefer dry habitats and may well occur in UAE. Manhert (1980) identified seven species of pseudoscorpions from the Arabian peninsula, four of them new to science and Manhert (1991) found 12 species from Oman alone. So far only two unidentified specimens have been found in UAE. They were both inside a light trap and had probably been using a fly or large beetle for transport.

CHELICERATA
ARACHNIDA
SOLIFUGIDA (SOLIFUGIDS OR CAMEL SPIDERS)

Solifugids have four pairs of long, hairy legs and enormous, well-developed jaws. They appear to have a large "head" which can be as long as the rest of the prosoma and houses the powerful muscles needed to operate the chelicerae. The teeth on the chelicerae consist of solid chitin (an extremely strong protein) and a solifugid bite can be severe. The chelicerae are covered with numerous spines and setae which help to remove solid prey so that they can ingest their liquid diet. Males are usually smaller than females and in some species, their teeth are reduced to a ridge preventing efficient feeding and they do not live long.

Camel spiders are one of the fastest running arthropods. Although they have four pairs of legs, they run using only three pairs. The first pair of legs or pedipalpi are held up in front of them and used in a similar manner to the antennae of insects. They have very long, silky setae and are constantly moving in order to locate and pick-up prey. On the underside of the last pair of legs are five malleoli or racquet organs which are thought to be sensory in nature and function like the pectines of scorpions. They use their second pair of limbs as rakes to push loose soil when constructing burrows and move the soil in rapid movements, looking like little bulldozers!

Despite their fearsome appearance and their strong bite, solifugids are unlikely to harm humans. In the past they were considered venomous and extremely dangerous but it is now thought that the only risk of injury resulting from them is caused by shock or infection following a bite. There is no evidence of venom in any part of their body.

Camel spiders are nocturnal predators of other arthropods including scorpions and are voracious feeders. Some species kill and feed on lizards and it is speculated that others kill mice and birds. They rely solely on their speed and stealth to catch their prey. In desert areas they are often attracted to lights

Camel spiders are called solifugids, because they avoid being out in the sun. If one accidentally uncovers a camel spider, it will frantically look for shade, usually found at one's feet. This characteristic has given it an undeserved reputation of aggression.

Camel spider,
Solifugid galeodes.

CHELICERATES
ARACHNIDA
SCHIZOPELTIDA, THELYPHONIDA AND AMBLYPYGI
(WHIP SCORPIONS AND TAIL-LESS WHIP SCORPIONS)

These obscure arachnids are very poorly-known and superficially resemble scorpions but lack a sting. However, the whip scorpions, Schizopeltida and Thelyphonida, have slender, whip-like appendages or tails and exhibit a defensive reaction, by discharging a caustic, dust-like cloud from an anal gland, which smells strongly of acetic acid or chlorine gas. Schizopeltida are similar in habits to scorpions but are only 5-7mm long. They are nocturnal and hide under stones or in burrows during the day. Thelyphonida are relatively large, nocturnal predators feeding on a wide variety of arthropods. They are quite ferocious in appearance and although their chelicerae are not claw-like their pedipalps are very powerful. The Amblypygi can be relatively large (8-45 mm in length) and are flattened in appearance. They lack a tail and are sometimes called tail-less whip scorpions. They are also nocturnal predators and have raptorial pedipalps armed with strong spines and a moveable hook with which they grab their prey.

There are no known records of these arachnids in UAE but Schizopeltida are common in other arid regions and may have been over-looked. Thelyphonida and Amblypygi are generally found in the tropics and could occur in moister environments such as wadis.

CHELICERATA
ARACHNIDA
OPILIONES (HARVESTMEN)

Opiliones or harvestmen are cosmopolitan predators inhabiting a wide range of habitats. They superficially resemble spiders but their legs are very long and spindly and the prosoma is not divided from the opithosoma. They feed on dead or recently dead tissues and probably require a humid environment. They have not been recorded from UAE, but probably occur in the more humid areas.

at night in search of food and their appearance can cause alarm if they enter tents. It is rare to see them during the winter months in UAE and they are thought to hide or hibernate during cold periods.

Females dig a burrow in which they lay over 200 eggs. They guard their young for two to three weeks until the first moult. Although they are quite large, solifugids are thought to live for less than one year.

CAMEL SPIDERS IN UAE

Despite their conspicuous appearance and size, little is known about these creatures and we are not even sure of their exact identity. There are probably three families of solifugids in UAE. These are the long-legged and sandy-coloured Galeodidae and Solpugidae, and the black-coloured Rhagodidae which has shorter legs and is better adapted for digging. The Galeodidae are commonly seen in sandy areas and the largest species is probably *Galeodes arabs* which is particularly hairy and bulky with limbs spanning up to 150mm. Other species probably occur in the mountains and Rhagodidae are thought to occur around Al Ain.

CHELICERATA
ARACHNIDA
ARANAEA

Aranaea are the true spiders and arid-zone species tend to be cryptically coloured, often with brushes of hair on their undersides to help them move through sand. Spider chelicerae are hook-like with moveable digits that carry poison glands, but most are harmless because their chelicerae are too weak to pierce human skin. They are predators and are further classified into separate families according to their anatomy and biology which reflect the way in which they capture their prey. For example, some spin webs and sit and wait for their prey while others are active hunters. Spiders are found world-wide and occur is all types of habitats.

SPIDERS IN UAE

At present little is known about spiders in the Emirates but current investigations by the American Museum of Natural History will soon tell us more. However, the spider fauna of the Sahara region is known, and includes a wide range of spider families such as ground hunting spiders (*Gnathosidae*), crab spiders (*Thomisidae*), giant crab spiders (*Sparassidae*), bark spiders (*Hersiliidae*), jumping spiders (*Salticidae*), wolf spiders (*Lycosidae*), sheet-web spiders (*Agelenidae*), comb-footed spiders (*Theridiidae*) and orb-weavers (*Tetragnathidae* and *Argiopidae*). All these families probably also occur in the Emirates.

Spiders of the Arabian peninsula as a whole are not well studied. Twenty-nine species of Salticidae have been found, many of which were undescribed but resembled African or Asian spiders (PrÛszynski,1993). Eight species from six genera of crab spiders or Thomisidae also occur (Dippenaar-Schoeman,1989). One of these, *Thomisus citrinellus*, has a wide distribution and probably inhabits UAE. In Saudi Arabia, two species of Linyphiidae have been recorded although they are not normally considered arid-zone species (JocquÈ,1981).

The crab spider, camouflaged by its colour, waits at the heart of a flower, to catch its prey.

BLACK WIDOWS (THERIDIIDAE; LACTRODECTUS SPP)

Two species of black widow are common in the Middle East, *Lactrodectus pallidus*, occurring from Libya to Azerbaidjan, and *Lactrodectus hysterix*, known from Aden and Yemen. In the Emirates, black widows occur along the coastal strip and hide in rubbish or objects left outside overnight. Care should therefore be taken when picking up debris etc. Their bite is rarely felt but is noticed later when the wound starts to swell and two tiny spots become visible where the fangs have penetrated the skin. The bite is very painful and the whole body can ache especially the legs. Other symptoms include shock, fever, nausea, headache, raised blood pressure, difficulty in breathing and heavy sweating. However most bite victims recover completely within two days. If bitten seek medical attention and always reassure the victim. Treatment includes intravenous salts and pain killers which alleviate symptoms.

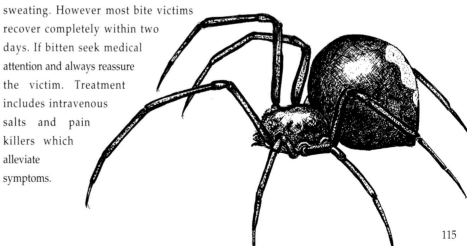

The velvet mite only appears above ground after rains.

CHELICERATA
ARACHNIDA
ACARINA OR ACARI (MITES AND TICKS)

The Acari are the smallest chelicerates but are also the most numerous world-wide in terms of the number of species. They are commonly known as mites and ticks. Adults have four pairs of legs while the young have three pairs. They include both parasites and predators which generally live on other animals or inside plants, although some inhabit the soil. Seven orders of Acari are recognised: Notostigmata, Tetrastigmata, Mesostigmata, Metastigmata, Cryptostigmata, Astigmata and Prostigmata.

The Notostigmata and Tetrastigmata are predatory mites frequenting warmer regions of the world, and probably live in the Emirates. The other orders are cosmopolitan and probably occur, but are relatively unknown because of their small size. However, the Metastigmata or ticks are better known because they are ectoparasites of terrestrial vertebrates and some are important pests of livestock and vectors of disease. Cryptostigmata are very small and dark in colour and live in soil and leaf litter where they feed on dead and decaying plant material. Astigmata are small and generally feed on fungus or detritus, but they also include some parasites of vertebrates known as fur and feather mites. Prostigmata are more heterogeneous and include free-living predators, phytophagous mites, parasites and aquatic mites.

Ticks are divided into two types: the hard ticks or Ixodidae and the soft ticks or Argasidae. Ixodids have a hardened dorsal scutelum which is absent in argasids. Argasids are most abundant in dry regions. The family Argasidae contains two genera: *Argas* which are associated with birds, bats or their nesting/resting places, and *Ornithodorus* which frequent burrows, corrals or houses. The larger Ixodidae family comprises six genera: *Hyalomma*, *Amblyomma*, *Rhicicephalus*, *Boophilus*, *Aponomma* and *Haemaphysalis*.

Tick bites can be painful and irritating, and severe cases of multiple tick infestation in a single animal, can result in anaemia, toxic reaction and paralysis. However, it is the tick's potential as a vector of pathogenic diseases that is more serious. Although man is only an incidental host and their natural

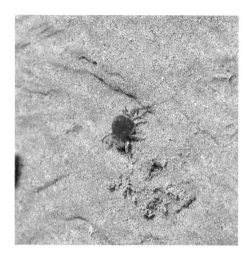

hosts are wild animals, some of the tick species present in Arabia can transmit human diseases. Many potentially infected ticks are accidentally imported along with foreign livestock but are equally able to feed on local livestock and could establish permanent populations. If they are infected with agents pathogenic to humans or domestic animals these may also be spread by local ticks. Although cases of tick-borne human disease are rare there is an element of risk.

TICKS FROM UAE

There are no published records of ticks for the Emirates but the following species are native to Arabia (Hoogstraal et al, 1984) and therefore likely to be part of the local tick fauna. *Hyalomma hyalomma anatolicum anatolicum* is very common and its hosts include domestic stock, lizards, rodents, hedgehogs, hares and humans. It is the major vector of Crimean-Congo Haemorrhagic Fever (CCHF) in the Southern Soviet republics, Pakistan and Nigeria. Other common Hyalomma ticks include *H.h.dromedarii* which is both a vector for CCHF and a natural reservoir of Q-fever; and *H.h.impeltatum* and *H.h.marginatum turcanicum* which have also been implicated as vectors for CCHF. The kennel or brown dog tick, *Rhipicephalus rhipicephalus sanguineus*, generally feeds on dogs as its name suggests, but can carry CCHF as can the closely related *R.r.turanicus*. Another vector of CCHF is *Boophilus annulatus* although its preferred hosts are goats. Human cases of CCHF are very rare in the Emirates, but it has been reported from Dubai.

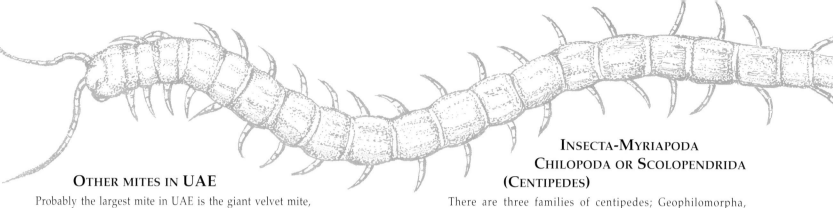

OTHER MITES IN UAE

Probably the largest mite in UAE is the giant velvet mite, *Dinonthrombium* sp. Adult mites measure up to 12mm and are covered in a thick and dense scarlet fur which warns predators that they are distasteful. Adults only emerge after heavy rain when they wander around sandy areas in search of termites. I have found them on several occasions near Sweihan and Al Samha. Their larvae are parasitic on grasshoppers.

Oribatid mites are one of the richest soil arthropod groups both in terms of numbers and species diversity. Bayoumi & Al-Khalifa (1985) report 48 species from Saudi Arabia but thought that the number of species was limited by soil humidity.

INSECTA-MYRIAPODA

The Insecta-myriapoda are the most numerically important group of animals in the UAE. As well as the insects this group includes millipedes (Diplopoda), centipedes (Chilopoda or Scolopendrida), and the lesser known Pauropoda and Symphyla. The name Myriapoda reflects the fact that these animals have many legs and, as will be seen, they are a diverse group.

INSECTA-MYRIAPODA DIPLOPODA

The diplopoda are commonly known as millipedes. Their body is made up of a large number of double-sided segments each bearing two pairs of legs. They are slow moving detritivores and are usually found in leaf litter and rotting vegetation. Millipedes are most abundant in the tropics and have not been recorded from UAE but probably occur in relatively humid areas such as wadis, parks and gardens.

INSECTA-MYRIAPODA CHILOPODA OR SCOLOPENDRIDA (CENTIPEDES)

There are three families of centipedes; Geophilomorpha, Scutigeromorpha and Scolopendromorpha. However, only the latter occur in the Emirates. Scolopendrid centipedes have an elongated, dorso-ventrally flattened body with a distinct head. The head bears a single pair of antennae and three pairs of feeding appendages (a mandible and two pairs of maxillae). The trunk can have from 15 to over 100 segments each bearing a single pair of legs which results in their characteristic locomotion, and centipedes can measure up to 120mm in length The first pair of trunk appendages is known as the maxillipedes or toxognatha and has powerful terminal claws at the tips, which have ducts leading to poison glands. Centipedes cannot usually pierce human skin and are unlikely to be poisonous but it is best to treat them with respect.

They are generally nocturnal predators and feed on other smaller arthropods. During the day they hide under rocks, stones and debris. Female Scolopendrids care for their young by making a protective basket between the body and legs, formed by curling their legs around the young.

CENTIPEDES IN UAE

Lewis & Gallagher (1993) mention various records of scolopendrids for UAE although they probably occur in most areas. *Scolopendrida mirabilis* has been found in Masah, Sharjah and Jebel Faiyah while *Scolopendrida valida* was collected near Sharjah. Both species are thought to be very resistant to desiccation.

CENTIPEDE BITES

The medical importance of centipedes was probably overestimated in the past since only very old records mention human fatalities (Lewis, 1986). However, the bite of *S.mirabilis* is though to be like that of a similar genus

Many interesting spiders remain as yet unidentified.

Trachycormocephalus which causes pain, swelling and subcutaneous bleeding. The area around the bite is particularly tender but most symptoms disappear within 24 hours. First aid treatment for a centipede bite is similar to that for scorpion stings although it is less likely to be life threatening

INSECTA-MYRIAPODA
PAUROPODA AND SYMPHYLA

These two groups of myriapods are less common than the others. They are both multiple-limbed, small and soft-bodied. They live in soil and leaf litter where they are thought to feed on fungi and detritus, although the Symphyla also feed on living plant material. Little is known of their biology and distribution and they have not been reported from UAE, but they could occur in the soil fauna of moderately moist environments.

INSECTA-MYRIAPODA
SUB-PHYLUM OR CLASS TARDIGRADA

I could not finish this chapter without mentioning the tardigrades. These minute animals only measure 50-500µm in size and cannot be seen without the aid of magnification. They have six legs ending in claws and are commonly known as water bears because of their rotund appearance. They live in the surface film of water covering mosses and in fresh and salt water. Since they can withstand prolonged periods of desiccation they could easily occur in temporal rain pools or beaches in UAE. To my knowledge, there is no published research work on the desert tardigrades but they would be an interesting subject for study.

Arthropods are very successful and many are able to flourish in the dry climate of the UAE either through adaptation to their environment or by behavioural avoidance of extreme conditions. They include a few detritivores and herbivores, but are predominantly predators. However they are all potential prey for vertebrates such as birds, mammals and reptiles. The larger species, such as scorpions and camel spiders, are particularly good sources of food for those able to catch them. However, there still remains much that we do not know about them, including which species actually occur in the Emirates. There are probably numerous new records and species waiting to be discovered all over Arabia. Next time you come across an arthropod be content to watch and admire it for its powers of survival.

ACKNOWLEDGEMENTS

I thank Dr John Balfour for information on public health pests, Dr Vojin Sjlivic for discussions about scorpions stings and Dr Patrick Osborne for commenting on an earlier draft of the text.

REFERENCES

Hoogstraal, H., Wassef, H. Y. & Buttiker, W. (1984). 'Ticks (Acarina) of Saudi Arabia. Family Argasidae, Ixodidae'. *Fauna of Saudi Arabia*, 3, 25-110.

Barnes, R.D. (1987). *Invertebrate Zoology*. Fifth edition. Saunders College,/Holt, Rhinehart and Wilson, USA.

Bayoumi, B. M. & Al-Khalifa, M. S. (1985).' Oribatid mites (Acari) of Saudi Arabia'. *Fauna of Saudi Arabia*, 7, 66-92.

Cloudsley Thompson, J. L. (1958). *Spiders, scorpions, centipedes and mites*. Pergamon Press, London.

Dippenaar-Schoeman, A. S. (1989). 'An annotated check list of Crab Spiders (Araneae:Thomisidae) of Saudi Arabia'. *Fauna of Saudi Arabia*,10 , 20-30.

Ferrara, F. & Taiti, S. (1985). 'The terrestrial isopods (Oniscoidea) of the Arabian Peninsula'. *Fauna of Saudi Arabia*, 7, 93-121.

Polis, G. A. (ed.) (1990). *The biology of scorpions*. Stanford University Press, USA.

JocquÈ, R. (1981) 'Araneae:Fam. Linyphiidae'. *Fauna of Saudi Arabia*, 3,111-113.

Legg, G. & Jones, R. E. (1988). 'Pseudoscorpions'. *Synopsis of the British Fauna* (New Series) Kemack, D. M. & Barnes, R. S. K. (eds.) No. 40. W. Backhuys, Leiden.

Lewis, J. G. E.(1986). 'Chilopoda of Saudi Arabia: centipedes of Saudi Arabia'. *Fauna of Saudi Arabia*, 8, 20-30.

Lewis, J. G. E. & Gallagher, M. D. (1993). 'Scolopendromrph and Geophilomorph centipedes from Oman and UAE'. *Fauna of Saudi Arabia*, 13, 55-62.

Manhert, V. (1980). 'Arachnids of Saudi Arabia: Pseudoscorpiones'. *Fauna of Saudi Arabia*, 1, 32-48.

Manhert, V. (1991). 'Arachnids of Saudi Arabia: Pseudoscorpions (Arachnida) from the Arabian Peninsula'. *Fauna of Saudi Arabia*, 12, 171-199.

Manton, S. M. (1977). *The Arthropoda - habits, functional morphology and evolution*. Clarenden Press, Oxford.

Meglitsch, P. A. (1967). *Invertebrate zoology*. Oxford University Press, Oxford.

PrÛszynski,J. (1993). 'Arachnids of Saudi Arabia: Salticidae (Araneae) of Saudi Arabia II'. *Fauna of Saudi Arabia*, 13 , 27-54.

Savory, T. H. (1964). *Arachnida*. Academic press, London.

Savory, T. H. (1977). *Spiders and other arachnids*. The English Universities Press Ltd, London.

Sheals, J. G. (1973). 'Arachnida'. In: Smith, K. G. V. (Ed*) Insects and other arthropods of medical importance*, pp 417-472. Trustees of the British Museum (Natural History), London.

Sheals, J. G. (1973). 'Other Arthropods' In: Smith, K. G. V. (Ed) *Insects and other arthropods of medical importance*, 473-482. Trustees of the British Museum (Natural History), London.

Taiti, S. & Ferrara, F. (1989). 'Terrestrial isopods of Saudi Arabia (Part 2)'. *Fauna of Saudi Arabia*, 10, 78-86.

Taiti, S. & Ferrara, F. (1991). 'New species and records of terrestrial isopods (Crustacea) from the Arabian Peninsula'. *Fauna of Saudi Arabia*, 12, 209-224.

Vachon, M. (1989). 'Arachnids of Saudi Arabia. Scorpions'. *Fauna of Saudi Arabia*, 1, 30-65.

Weygoldt, P. (1969). *The biology of pseudoscorpions*. Harvard University Press, Harvard.

119

TERRESTRIAL ARTHROPODS IN UAE

Major Taxa

Species

Sub-phylum Crustacea

Sub-class or class Isopoda

Super-family Oniscoidea

Littrorophiloscia stronhali

Somalodillo paeninsulae

*Porcellionides pruninosus

*Protracheonisus inexpectatus

*Porcellio assimilis

*Porcellio evansi

*Koweitoniscus tamei,.

Sub-phylum Chelicerata

CLASS ARACHNIDA

Sub-class Scorpiones

Family Buthidae

Androctonus crassicauda

Apithobuthus pterygocercus

Buthacus yotvatensis nigroaculeatus

Compsobuthis arabicus

Parabuthus liosoma;

Vachoniolus minipectibinus

and/or *Vachoniolus globimanus.*

*Orthochirus innesi

Sub-class Pseudoscorpiones

Family Olipiidae

Family Cheliferidae

Sub-class Solifugida

Family Galeodidae

Galeodes sp.

*Galeodes arabs

Family Solipugidae

Family Rhagodidae

Sub-class Schizopeltida

Sub-class Thelyphonida

Sub-class Amblypygi

Sub-class Opiliones

Sub-class Aranaea

Family Gnaphosidae

Family Sparassidae

Family Thomisidae

*Thomisus citrinellus

Family Hersiliidae

Family Salticidae

Family Lycosidae

Family Agelenidae

Family Theriidae

Lactrodectus sp.

Family Tetragnathidae

Family Argiopidae

Sub-class Acarines

Order Notostigmata

Order Tetrastigmata

Order Mesostigmata

Order Metastigmata

Sub-order Argassidae

Sub-order Ixodidae

Hyalomma sp

*Hyalomma hyalomma anatolicum anatolicum

*Hyalomma hyalomma dromedarii

*Hyalomma hyalomma impeltatum

*Hyalomma hyalomma marginatum turcanicum

*Rhipicephalus rhipicephalus sanguineus

*Rhipicephalus rhipicephalus turanicus.

*Boophilus annulatus

Order Cryptostigmata

Order Astigmata

Order Prostigmata

Dinothrombium sp.

Sub-phylum Insecta-Myriapoda

Class Diplopoda

Class Scolopendrida

Family Scolopendromorpha

Scolopendrida mirabilis

Scolopendria valida

CLASS PAUROPODA

CLASS SYMPHYLA

Phylum Tardigrada

* indicates probable species.

Terrestrial Reptiles and Amphibians

Christian Gross

Saw-scaled viper changing its skin.

Opposite Page: Two saw-scaled vipers, one with milky eyes.

Most reptiles are characterised by having a scaly skin which prevents them from drying out in arid environments and generally helps to protect their bodies. They have adapted to most habitats around the world, their only serious limitation being their inability to control internal body temperature without recourse to external heating or cooling sources. A level of around 25 - 30 degrees Celsius is necessary for them to function properly, depending on the species. In the UAE they are rarely unable to reach the required body temperature, but on the contrary, they have to take care for most of the year that they do not overheat, which could cause death. Therefore many species emerge from their hiding places only in the early morning and late afternoon, or they are active only at night.

Spiny-tailed lizards, or dhabs, have developed special adaptations. In the morning they are dark grey to black when they are still cold from the chilly desert night. The dark colour absorbs the solar heat which warms them up very quickly. Once the optimal body temperature is reached, the spiny-tailed lizard changes its colour to a very light sandy beige, that reflects the sunlight and therefore prevents the animal from overheating. Many reptiles are able to change their colour slightly, but for the majority it is only a camouflaging adaptation to the environment in which they live and not part of a cooling mechanism as is the case with the spiny-tailed lizard. Such colour variation can make the identification of the different species extremely difficult and very often proper identification can only be achieved by counting scales on the body and the head.

A spiny-tailed lizard is warming up at the entrance to its burrow.

House Gecko moulting its skin in large flakes.

Unlike the scales of fish, which are attached to the skin, reptile scales are an integral part of it, formed from localised thickened areas. Snakes usually have a single row of wide scales on the ventral surface of the body, each corresponding to a vertebra and a pair of ribs. The reptiles' scales serve to take the wear and tear associated with friction during movement and in some cases to help in locomotion. To accommodate growth and to renew the scales that are subjected to considerable wear, the reptiles periodically moult the outer layer of their skin. This process is known as sloughing. As they continue to grow, the skins are shed at regular intervals throughout their lives. Young animals grow rapidly and therefore moult more frequently than older ones. The moulting is

preceded by the secretion of fluid between the old layer of the epidermis and the new one beneath it. This causes the reptile's colour to become dull, while its eyes appear to swell and take on a milky appearance. Two to three days later the eyes clear, and then, after a further four or five days, the skin is sloughed. Snakes usually shed their skin in one piece by sliding out of it, after tearing around the edges of the mouth. Lizards tend to loose their skin in large flakes that tear off.

Horned Viper (without horns) showing the tip of its tongue.

None of the reptiles in the UAE have eyelids and whilst moulting, they also shed the outer layer of their cornea. This is necessary, since without an eyelid the cornea is neither protected nor lubricated. Hence the eyes becoming milky and swelling prior to moulting. There are no external ears and in some species the eardrum or tympanum is clearly visible on the outside.

Most reptiles are carnivorous, but in the United Arab Emirates the adult spiny-tailed lizard is a true vegetarian. The food of the other reptile species includes virtually everything from insects to amphibians, fish, small mammals, birds and other reptiles.

One of the best known anatomical features that is found in many reptiles, and certainly in all snakes, is the forked tongue which is extended at regular intervals through a notch in the upper jaw. The purpose of flicking the tongue for several seconds before it is withdrawn is to pick up minute particles of scent from the air. These are then deposited in openings in the roof of the mouth, which lead to the Jacobson's organ. In this organ, the information is then transmitted through sensitive cells to the brain. This helps to explain how a viper can follow and find a mouse it has bitten and injected with poison even at night, or in places where there is no light.

Certainly the most infamous and feared feature of many reptiles is its bite. While there are only two species of venomous lizards, the gila monster and the Mexican beaded lizard both from the Americas, there are numerous poisonous snakes, in various forms on all the continents, except Antarctica. However, the majority of snakes encountered are non-venomous, some are mildly toxic and only a few can be considered to be dangerous to man.

The harmless snakes have numerous short teeth, solidly embedded in their jaws and slightly curved to the rear of their mouth. There are no toxic glands producing venom and the sole purpose of the teeth is to keep a solid grip on a prey animal. Mildly toxic but still harmless snakes have teeth as described above, but in between they have one or several pairs of slightly longer fangs with a groove, through which slightly toxic venom trickles into the wound of the prey that is being bitten. These snakes are also called "rear-fanged" since the teeth described above are located very much to the rear of the mouth and usually only come into action when the reptile has started to swallow its prey. There are a few rear-fanged snakes that are highly toxic, but they do not occur on the Arabian Peninsula.

Two groups of snakes are dangerous: those with long erectile fangs and those with short, curved fangs in the front of the upper jaw. Both types have tubular fangs that are connected to poison-producing glands and the toxin is injected by muscular compression of those glands. In the Emirates it is the vipers that have erectile fangs, their teeth being so long that they need to be hinged in order to enable the animal to fold them back so it does not injure itself with its own weapons. Long teeth enable the snake to inject a large quantity of venom deeply into the victim.

The only snakes that occur in the UAE with fixed short tubular fangs are the sea snakes which are discussed in a separate chapter, along with other marine reptiles.

Saw-scaled Viper.

SNAKES IN THE UAE

The most common snake in our region with long erectile fangs is the saw-scaled viper (*Echis carinatus*). It is found along the coast, in the open desert and in the mountains. Its name derives from the fact that along the sides of its body it has several rows of diagonal scales with minute projections. If aroused, it starts rubbing these scales against each other by making undulating movements with its body, producing a rasping sound, similar to the rattle of the rattle snake. The smallest of the locally occurring vipers, it reaches a maximum length of approximately 60 cms, at which size it will have fangs over 5 mms long! The saw-scaled viper is often referred to as a "sidewinder" due to its unusual manner of travelling over soft sand. It has adapted superbly to moving on the unstable substrate found in the sand desert, by travelling at an angle of about 45 degrees to the approximate line of its body. The head is raised and thrown forward in the direction of travel, and as it makes contact with the ground a loop of the body follows it. By the time half of the body has been moved, the head is raised for the next step and so the process continues.

Only two points of the body are in contact with the ground at one time. This leaves the characteristic, shallow "S"-shaped parallel markings on the sand. All side-winders, however, will revert to moving in normal sinuous movements when reaching firm ground.

A very close relative of the rather common saw-scaled viper is the rarely seen carpet viper (*Echis coloratus*) which only occurs in the mountains. With a maximum length of 70 cms, it is slightly stockier and a little more colourful than the widespread saw-scaled viper, from which it can only be distinguished by counting the rows of facial shields under its eyes. Three rows or more are specific for the carpet viper whilst the saw-scaled viper has only one row. Both animals are principally nocturnal and becoming active after dusk. They probably eat lizards and geckos, but in captivity they show a definite preference for small rodents. The carpet viper also has diagonal scales, which produce a hissing noise when it rasps the sides of its body together, and can also move in side-winding undulations if it encounters soft sand.

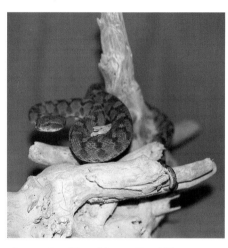

Carpet Viper.

Another rare viper that lives in the mountains of the UAE is the false horned viper (*Pseudocerastes persicus*). It does not occur at altitudes lower than 400 m above sea-level and it does not venture out into the open desert. With a typical bulky viper-like body, it has a very broad head with short horns above the eyes. It is hinge-fanged like the other vipers and lacks a very distinct colour pattern on its body, being rather uniform dark grey or brown, blending well with the rocky habitat it favours. At 90 cms total length it is the largest of the vipers occurring in the United Arab Emirates.

Similar in appearance to the false horned viper, is the horned viper (*Cerastes cerastes gasperetii*) often also referred to as the sand viper. Confusion arises in the identification of this animal, because some have horns, whereas others completely lack any trace of horns. It reaches a length of about 85 cms, with the typical stocky viper body and a very broad head. They have long hinged teeth and also move in a side-winding manner in soft sand, which is their favoured habitat. Adapted to the open desert it is creamy-beige in colour, with darker blotches on its back. In the Emirates it is found in all the sandy deserts from the coast up to the mountain plains where there is virtually no shade available. The horned viper is almost entirely nocturnal, spending the day under anything that provides a little shelter from the sun. If no shade is available it buries itself in the sand by moving its ribs forward, and at the same time upward, causing the sand to be pushed to the side and allowing the otherwise motionless animal to sink below the surface in a manner reminiscent of a submerging submarine. Within a very short time nothing is visible but the eyes, which are set very high on top of the vipers head.

There are no other dangerously poisonous, terrestrial snakes known to inhabit the deserts and the mountains of the United Arab Emirates and although the Arabian cobra, the black desert cobra, the puff adder and the burrowing asp occur on the peninsula, they have never been confirmed in this region.

The most widespread of the "rear -fanged", or mildly toxic, snakes in this area is the sand snake (*Psammophis schokari*) and at 155 cms maximum length it is also the longest snake in the Emirates. It can move at incredible speed and is probably one of the most elegant of snakes. Even in soft sand it moves in a normal sinuous way, since the distribution of its body weight over a long thin surface prevents it from sinking in and permits it to find a grip even on the most unstable of substrates. Active during daytime, it is found near cultivations, gardens and scrubland in the mountains as well as on the open plains and around fertile areas bordering onto the sandy deserts, where it searches for lizards, small mammals and even climbs trees in pursuit of freshly hatched birds. When in search of rodents it investigates any holes in the ground and if it has found a nest of mice it usually consumes the whole litter. Since it is not dangerous to man its contribution to pest control should be highly valued. It is brown to grey in colour, with black and white streaks, which, on young animals, extend along the side of the body, but on older specimens only reach from the snout to the back of the neck.

Also mildly toxic and harmless to man is the false cobra (*Malpolon moilensis*). Thicker bodied than the sand snake it favours similar habitats and the same food species, but is able to handle and overcome slightly larger prey than the latter. If cornered or irritated it will spread the skin of its neck in a cobra-like

fashion and produce a hissing noise. However, as its name suggests, it is not related to the cobra. It is pale brown in colour with dark spots along its back and sides, and with conspicuous red eyes bearing round black pupils. It grows to a length of approximately 150 cms and appears to occur in lower numbers than the sand snake, but it is also very widespread and has regularly been found sharing the burrows of spiny-tailed lizards. As with the sand snake, its contribution to mouse and rat control should not be underestimated.

The last of the "rear-fanged" snakes found here is the cat snake (*Telescopus dhara*). Growing to 95 cms it is the smallest of the three mildly toxic snakes represented in the region. Its most outstanding feature is the very large head

with the distinct neck and the slit pupils that give it a viper-like appearance. It occurs in a range of colour variations, from reddish, to grey, to brown, with some animals being uniformly coloured whilst others are spotted. A nocturnal snake, it lives in the mountains and is absent from the open desert. An agile climber, it investigates trees for birds' nests with fledgelings, rock crevices for lizards and rodents and it is said to regularly prey on bats. Due to its night time activity, and since it is confined to the mountains and hills, it is seldom encountered. It is most probably the rarest of the three "rear-fanged" snakes in the area. This brings us to the completely harmless snakes that have neither fangs nor toxin producing glands.

The wadi racer (*Coluber rhodorachis*) is similar to the sand snake in appearance, but grows only to 130 cms. It has a long and slender body with a very long tail and it can move at incredible speed. It displays considerable colour variations depending on the habitat which it occupies. Although it is confined to the rocky areas of the United Arab Emirates, it can occur in regions bordering on to sandy habitats, where its colour pattern will adapt accordingly, ranging from uniformly sand-coloured to dark grey with heavy black speckling that can give it an almost banded appearance. In all colour phases of the wadi racer, the dark markings become indistinct towards the tail, which is usually olive-green to brown in hue. It completely lacks the black and white streaked face mask of the sand snake which makes separation from this species relatively easy. Its favoured habitat is a wadi with running water, where it is active by day or at dusk, feeding, like most of the other snakes, on other reptiles, small mammals and birds, but also preying on wadi fish and toads, the latter being pursued in the water.

Certainly one of the prettiest serpents is the diadem snake (*Spalerosophis diadema*). It is boldly marked with large dark spots on a creamy-beige

The amphisbaenid is neither a lizard nor a snake.

background. Feeding mainly on rodents it is often found near, or around, cultivations but is absent from the open desert. Growing to about 130 cms it has a body shape similar to the cat snake, but with a distinctly oval head. This snake should also be regarded as beneficial to cultivations since it helps to keep small rodents under control.

Hardly ever seen, but present in all the sand deserts of the United Arab Emirates, is the sand boa (*Eryx jayakari*). A nocturnal member of the Boidae family, it lives almost permanently under the sand. With its very smooth scales it is able to glide through the soft substrate without surfacing. Its eyes and nostrils are located on the uppermost parts of its head, allowing it to lie buried under the surface, with only these organs protruding. Thus it lies in wait for an unsuspecting prey animal to walk past. Once it has caught a small mammal or reptile, it constricts it in typical boid fashion before swallowing the prey whole. The smooth scales give the body a very glossy appearance. It's basic colour is yellow, with an irregular pattern of brown bars and blotches. It has a thick, strong body with no defined neck and grows to approximately 40 cms in length.

The thread snake (*Leptotyphlos macrorhynchus*) is one of the smallest snakes in the world. It grows only to about 15 cms and remains very thin. With its uniformly pink body, it is often mistaken for an earthworm. It dislikes light and burrows if the texture of the soil allows it to, or hides under dry leaves and grass. It feeds on small insects such as termites and is usually found in and around cultivations and gardens. Widespread in the United Arab Emirates it is rarely found in the dry open desert.

One reptile-like animal that is neither snake nor lizard, is the amphisbaenid (*Diplometopon zarudni*). Its short stocky body grows to approximately 20 cms in length. Much stronger than the thread snake and equipped with a spade-like snout, it is able to burrow in fairly compacted soil but is very rarely seen, since it is nocturnal and spends most of its time underground. Completely harmless, it feeds on insects which it hunts mainly underground, leaving a clearly visible raised trail on the surface. It is pinkish to purple in colour, dotted with small black spots and squares.

LIZARDS IN THE UAE

Besides snakes and the amphisbaenid, there is a multitude of lizards and geckos endemic to the Arabian Peninsula and most probably there are still many species waiting to be discovered. As mentioned earlier, only the spiny-tailed lizard in the Emirates is a vegetarian, whilst all the others are insect-eaters, with the exception of the monitor lizard that takes larger prey. Like all reptiles, lizards and geckos require external heat sources to regulate their body temperature. In order not to overheat, the majority of species have become nocturnal and are not very often seen.

The spiny-tailed lizard (*Uromastix microlepis*) can grow to a length of 65 cms and usually lives in loose colonies. There is rarely one burrow on its own but usually several, at some 20 to 50 m distance from its neighbour. Colonies can extend over large areas, depending on the availability of food. Feeding on shrubs, the spiny-tailed lizard never drinks water and has special glands that help its body to dispose of uric acid. The spiny-tailed lizard, called "dhab" locally, often allows other creatures, such as snakes, scorpions and hedgehogs to share its burrow. Despite its dragon-like appearance it is a very placid animal that prefers to flee rather than enter into conflict. If cornered, however,

Toad-head Agama.

Monitor Lizard.

it can give painful blows with its spiny tail. With its strong jaws that have no teeth, but possess sharp bone plates, it can give a nasty bite. The dhab used to be a welcome source of protein for the bedouin and the strong leather of its skin was widely used.

One of the most aggressive reptiles in the UAE is the monitor lizard (*Varanus griseus*). Growing to about 120 cms, its body only makes up for about one third of its total length, whilst the rest consists of tail. As with the spiny-tailed lizard it uses its tail for self-defence and lashes out with it in a whip-like fashion. It does not have any teeth, but sharp bone-plates and will bite any attacker readily. It will eat anything it can catch and overpower, from rodents to reptiles, insects, birds and it has a liking for carrion, which, with its deeply forked tongue it can detect from considerable distances. Sandy in colour with darker speckling, it blends in superbly in the desert environment. It lives in

Sand skink

burrows which it excavates itself and where it spends the hottest hours of the day, being mainly active at dawn and dusk.

The last of the larger lizards that is regularly encountered in the open desert is the toad-head agama (*Phrenocephalus arabicus*). Growing to some 25 cms it often sits conspicuously on top of a rock or sand-dune. During the mating season the throats of the males become bright orange in colour, which they display from their vantage point, in the hope of attracting a mate.

A small, but common lizard of the sandy plains, dunes and sabkhas is the fringe-toed sand lizard (*Acanthodactylus schmidti*). It is easily recognised by a row of white oval spots on its flanks. Although it can move at lightning speed, it can be approached quite closely if one moves very slowly and avoids casting a shadow over it. The fringes on its toes help it to move across the sand more rapidly.

Various species of nocturnal geckos occur in the loose sands of the dunes and sandy plains. *Stenodactylus arabicus*, *S. doriae* and *S. leptocosymbotis* are all very similar and need an expert eye to be identified correctly. The most colourful nocturnal gecko is the pretty *Teratoscincus scincus*.

Adapted like the sand boa to live in the soft sand is the sand skink (*Scincus mitranus*) popularly known as the *sand fish*. In the early morning it can be observed basking on the sunny flank of a sand-dune but will "dive" into the soft sand and glide away under the surface at the slightest disturbance. It has a wedge-like snout and smooth scales enabling it to move rapidly in the soft substrate. Very glossy reddish-pink to brown in colour it feeds on insects and grows to about 15 cms .

The common garden skink (*Chalcides ocellatus*) is only found in and around cultivations as well as in gardens in the cities and seems to be absent from the open desert or the dry mountains. Reaching a length of approximately 20 cms it lacks the spade-like snout of the *sand fish* but has the same smooth scales and glossy hue. Dark brown in colour it favours dry leaves as a hiding place and is very often found living in compost heaps, where it hunts for insects.

The largest lizard known in the wadis of this region is the Oman lizard (*Lacerta jayakari*). Blue-grey and brown in colour, it can reach a length of 60 cms, two-thirds consisting of the long thin tail. It is active in the middle of the day in the hot months of the year, although it stays in the shade and close to water. It is possible that it hibernates in the winter months, as it is rarely seen during that time.

Smaller in size than the Oman lizard is the blue headed agama (*Pseudotrapelus sinaitus*). Frequently found in the wadis of the UAE, it is, in typical agama fashion, less shy than most other reptiles and allows relatively close approach. Only about 18 cms in length it preys mainly on small insects. The male is very noticeable, as its head and upper body turn a bright blue, when it is sexually aroused or angry.

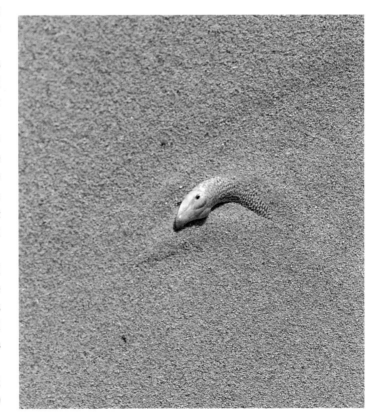

The streamlined wedge-like snout of a sand skink and its smooth scales enable it to move underneath the surface of the sand like a fish swims through water.

132

In rock crevices and caves the fan-toed gecko (*Ptyodactylus hasselquisti*) is regularly encountered. As with other geckos it has a very delicate and fragile appearance and grows to no more than about 18 cms. It is nocturnal, and emerges after dusk to hunt for small flying insects. Some fan-toed geckos that live in larger caves may never leave them at all and are probably active for longer periods. Their enlarged toe-pads are covered with tiny lamellae, which in turn are coated with thousands of microscopic "hook-like" structures. With each step, the gecko first lifts its toes, thus "unhooking" its foot, then brings it forward and only pushes the toes downwards again once its footpad has touched the surface it is walking on. These movements are executed so quickly that they are not visible to the human eye.

Of the many species of dwarf rock geckos, *Pristurus rupestris* must be mentioned as it is most often encountered in the day time. It likes to sit on rock walls of plantations, signalling to fellow-lizards by curling and uncurling its tail.

The yellow-bellied house gecko (*Hemidactylus flaviviridus*) is known to every household in the UAE. Active from dusk to dawn it is found in and around houses and apartments all over the region. Their faint bark-like calls can be

This small gecko (Stenodactylus doriae) *lives in the sandy desert.*

133

AMPHIBIANS

In the United Arab Emirates the amphibians are only represented by two toads the Arabian toad (*Bufo arabica*) and the Dhofar toad (*Bufo dhofarensis*), the latter having been confirmed in our region only recently, during a survey undertaken in the mountains. The Arabian toad is slightly larger, with a rounder head and golden speckling, whilst the smaller Dhofar toad has a flatter head with green markings on its body. They occur together in the wadis that have water and can be encountered in large numbers. If wadis dry out, they probably escape desiccation by entering deep and permanently damp crevices, where they possibly burrow. They feed mainly on insects, but cannibalism is widespread. In summer, when small pools dry out, they also feast on the helpless wadi fish whose escape into deeper water is cut-off.

The toads of the UAE can be distinguished by the size and position of their eardrum. Bufo arabicus (above) has a large drum close to the eye, Bufo dhofarensis (right) has a small drum at a small-distance away from the eye.

heard only by those with sensitive ears. Hunting mainly for flying insects it is often seen lying in wait near a garden lamp, in the hope of catching an insect that is attracted by the light. Beige to brown in colour, they grow to about 15 cms. If not disturbed they will happily spend the day in a dark ceiling corner inside a room of a house and will defend their territory fiercely against others of their kind who approach too closely.

TERRAPINS

There is the caspian terrapin (*Mauremys caspica*) in the Arabian Peninsula, and in the UAE it is only in Wadi Ishi that these animals have been seen in the artificial lake created by the dam. As the lake is large, no specimen has been caught for proper identification as yet but they have been seen on numerous occasions. Terrapins eat vegetable matter as well as fish, insects and tadpoles.

THE GENERALLY HIGH SEA WATER TEMPERATURES of the UAE suit the needs of the reptilian form and help to explain the relative abundance of the two represented marine groups; sea turtles and sea snakes.

SEA TURTLES

Of the seven recognised species of marine turtles in the world, four occur in the waters of the UAE; the green turtle (*Chelonia mydas*), the hawksbill turtle (*Eretmochelys imbricata*), the loggerhead turtle (*Caretta caretta*) and the huge leatherback turtle (*Dermochelys coriacea*). A fifth species, the olive ridley turtle (*Lepidochelys olivacea*) is known from neighbouring Oman and from Pakistan and India and is certainly a visitor to UAE waters from time to time. All five are listed as species endangered with extinction throughout their worldwide range. Two of the five, the green and hawksbill turtles nest on beaches in the UAE as well as feeding in UAE waters, and while little is known about the other three, the huge leatherback turtle, which may grow to an astonishing ten feet in length and weigh almost one thousand kilograms, has been seen on just a handful of occasions feeding on the vast seasonal abundance of jelly fish (the sole component of its diet) in Arabian Gulf waters. The loggerhead turtle has recently been confirmed to occur in the Arabian Gulf waters of UAE, but next to nothing is known about its status or distribution in this country. The olive ridley turtle has only twice been recorded in the UAE, but it nests in neighbouring Oman and also in India, where mass nesting in synchronised waves or 'Arribadas' sometimes includes tens of thousands of nesting turtles in a single season. Even if this species is unlikely to nest in the UAE, it is worth looking closely at the turtles you see as you may discover the occasional stray.

Both green and hawksbill turtles are sometimes seen by divers and snorkellers in the UAE, either feeding, mating or simply resting on or near coral reefs and seagrass beds. Hawksbill turtles feed on soft corals, sponges and other reef animals, clipping them from the bedrock with their hawked beaks. On occasion both hawksbill and green can be found sleeping amongst the coral, motionless and unaware of any other presence. This offers excellent opportunity for underwater photographs and a good close look at these remarkable reptiles. In some parts of the world, and possibly the UAE, turtles are thought to sleep underwater for weeks, or even months, in a state of semi-hibernation. As they possess lungs just like you and I, it is hard to imagine how this can be possible, but it is thought to be achieved by slowing the heartbeat to a bare minimum and through the use of minute capillaries in the soft skin of the neck and cloaca, which facilitate gaseous exchange directly with the sea water.

The most commonly seen turtle in the UAE is the green, thousands of which come to feed on the vast, rich seagrass and algal communities particularly in the shallow offshore waters of western Abu Dhabi. Many a boater will have heard the sharp exhalation of a turtle that has surfaced nearby, and turned in time to see a rounded head poking up from beneath the surface. On still, windless days when the water is calm, it is surprising just how frequently turtles can be seen surfacing to breathe in between feeding on the seabed. It is likely in fact, that the UAE shallow water environments constitute part of an Arabian Gulf ecosystem of global importance to the feeding requirements of green turtles. The exact number of feeding green turtles that visit the UAE is undetermined. However, the density of turtle congregations seen from helicopters and research boats suggests that the area is critical to the regional population of this species and it is probable that turtles migrate hundreds, if not thousands of kilometres from all over the north-western Indian Ocean to feed here. It is certainly worth keeping an eye open for turtles that may bear a silver-coloured titanium tag at the base of the left fore flipper. Tens of thousands of green turtles have been tagged in Oman where the nesting population is thought to exceed 20,000. Some of these have turned up over 2,000 kilometres from where they were tagged. A few have been found around the corner in UAE waters, and it seems logical that many swim here after having nested in Oman and spend much of the rest of their time in UAE waters.

Seagrass meadows, often interspersed with algal growth, are the most productive of shallow, sedimentary environments in the sea. Green turtles take full advantage of this and graze the meadows day and night. They are the only

Hawksbill turtle tracks in the sand.

herbivorous turtle and possess bacteria in their stomachs which aids the digestion of cellulose. In the UAE four species of seagrass have been identified all of which can be expected in the green turtle's diet. Probably the most common of these is the elongate, double-stranded seagrass (*Halodule uninervis*), the shoots of which superficially resemble blades of grass in a municipal garden. Also common are the broad and narrow leafed seagrasses (*Halophila ovalis* and *H. stipulacea*) both of which have leaf-shaped shoots, the first rounded and delicate, the second narrower, fleshier and ribbed. The only other kind of seagrass (*Syringodium isoetifolium*) is locally sparsely distributed and quite distinctive, closely resembling the shoot of an onion or chive and is hollow in cross-section.

Knowledge of the diet of green turtles in the UAE can provide clues both to their behaviour and distribution and also helps in identifying habitats in need of conservation for the sake of the turtles. Do the green turtles, for example, prefer seagrasses to algae? Do they preferentially feed on one species of seagrass over another? Will other food, such as algae or even sponges, substitute for seagrasses if these are not available?

The seagrasses, *Halodule uninervis* and *Halophila ovalis,* appear in the diet of most green turtles sampled in the UAE. However, examined specimens indicated a mixed diet that included three species of seagrasses, numerous species of algae, sponges and ascidians. Others showed a preference for just one species of seagrass (not necessarily the same one in each individual case), whilst others ate a mixture of any two or three seagrass species in equal or unequal proportions, but appeared to avoid algae. Interpreting this information is difficult. Food preferences may not necessarily apply to the species as a whole, but may, for example, differ between sub-populations. Green turtles are probably opportunist to an extent, possibly preferring one food item over another, especially if it is of greater nutritional value, but only selecting that if it is abundant. Otherwise, they will eat whatever is there for the taking. Age is also a determining factor influencing the diet and green turtles seem to begin life as carnivores, turning vegetarian when they are about one year old. Continued research on feeding green turtles in the UAE will

provide a better understanding of their natural history, helping conservationists to delineate areas and seasons of particular importance to the survival of this endangered reptile.

Unlike the males which spend their entire life at sea, female turtles must visit the land for a single part of their life cycle - egg laying. In addition to the UAE's function as an important feeding area, hundreds, if not thousands, of female turtles use the country's beaches as nesting sites. To date only green and hawksbill turtles have been confirmed as nesting in the UAE, although there is a possibility of both loggerhead and olive ridley turtles also doing so. Precise data, in terms of both numbers and nesting locations is not yet clearly defined, though some important beaches have been identified on the shores of Ras al-Khaimah and on offshore islands west of Abu Dhabi. In addition, scattered nesting sites have been found along much of the mainland coast, including developed areas on the east coast near Fujairah. Both green and hawksbill turtles tend to nest in late spring and summer, hawksbills mostly completing their nesting season before the greens. They often use the same beaches for their egg laying, although greens tend to be more selective, favouring beaches that are relatively steep with fine, deep sand.

Watching turtles during their nesting activity provides a rare insight into these fascinating animals. It requires patience and the following of a few simple rules. Always move slowly and keep low, preventing the chance of a turtle noticing your silhouette against the night sky and keep behind the turtle where possible. Never approach or touch turtles moving along the beach. Handling hatchlings can disrupt their olfactory imprinting mechanism and may cause females to be unable to locate the beach again when they return to nest decades later. Use lights sparingly behind the beach and never on the beach where they will disturb turtles and disorient hatchlings. Use flash photography only when a turtle is laying its eggs, never if there are other turtles nearby and never angle the flash so that it points towards the sea where other turtles may be contemplating coming ashore. Avoid photographing turtles head-on and try to wait for the natural light of early morning to take your photographs. Finally, don't impede nesting or disturb nests by driving on the beach, leave pets at home and take all your litter with you.

A turtle emerging from the sea in the cool moonlight and hauling herself up the beach to a point above the high tide line bears little resemblance to the graceful movement of the turtle underwater, but it is a sight for privileged eyes. Turtles reach maturity anywhere between the age of 25 to 50 years and are believed to return to nest on the same beach on which they themselves hatched decades earlier. Little is known about how they navigate with such

precision, but it is thought to involve celestial as well as magnetic cues. The sense of smell has also recently been identified as a means by which adults 'remember' the beach of their birth.

Hawksbill turtle digging her nest.

Male turtles, distinguished by their long, thick tails and a stout, curved claw on each fore flipper, establish mating territories around nesting beaches and each female may lay two, three or more times in a season at intervals of about two weeks. Once she leaves the relative security of the sea, the turtle, and particularly her eggs, are at risk from predators and she may spend several hours in the surf lifting her head and checking for danger before emerging. Pushed in to shore by a breaking wave, the turtle cautiously looks around and begins the arduous task of dragging her huge bulk over the sand. Resting for a moment, the deep breaths of a mature adult green turtle, weighing perhaps two hundred kilograms, are clearly audible. Soft sand flung by the fore flippers surprises unwary turtle watchers, as she begins to dig her nest. If the conditions are judged to be good and there is no sign of danger the body pit, sometimes almost a metre deep, is completed and work begins on the egg chamber. The rear end of the shell lifts to the left, then to the right as the hind flippers carefully fashion the neat chamber in the bottom of the nest,

139

scooping out sand to a depth of about 40 centimetres. Don't be tempted to use flash photography and keep quite still while the turtle performs these tasks, which may take an hour or more, as any disturbance may cause her to return to the sea.

Green turtles lay approximately 110 eggs per clutch. The eggs are spherical and soft-shelled, about the size of a golf ball. Three or four glistening white eggs slip out at a time as the turtle gently raises her body to allow them to fall. A small hand held torch angled beneath the heaving turtle will allow you to see the entire egg laying process without any real risk of disturbing her, as now she is concentrated in her task and apparently ignores the world around her. You may notice a few deformed eggs, half the size of the others or a misshapen ovoid. These will often be laid last and indicate the end of the egg-laying process. Turtle watchers should retreat while she carefully covers the chamber with sand, moves forward a few feet, throws soft sand behind her with her fore flippers to disguise the nest from would-be predators, such as foxes, and makes her way back to the sea. Her duties as a mother have been fulfilled and though she may return every two to four years to lay on the same beach until she is well over 70 years old, she will never see her offspring.

The eggs remain buried in the sand for approximately 55 days before hatching. The warmth of the sand alone incubates the clutch and it is the precise temperature at which the eggs are incubated, rather than any genetic mechanism, that determines the sex of the hatchling turtles. Warmer temperatures produce females, cooler temperatures produce males and intermediate temperatures a mixture of both. However, it is impossible to distinguish the sex of a hatchling using external features and only histological examination can reveal the answer. The threshold temperature above which all hatchlings will be female has not been measured in the UAE, but it is probably about 29-30 degrees Celsius.

The temperature-dependent mechanism for sex determination in turtles is crucial in determining a successful and popular nesting beach. Regardless of all the other factors that may be important to nesting, such as the composition and depth of the sand, grain size, moisture content, stability of the beach,

or more before returning to the nearshore to feed on seagrasses and algae. However, even before reaching the pounding waves of a vast and threatening ocean full of predatory fish, land predators such as cats and dogs, foxes, seagulls and crabs, see to the demise of most of the hatchlings. Before long most will have died and under natural conditions, as little as two or three in every ten thousand have been estimated to survive to adulthood. Add to natural threats the recent and far greater man-made threats that sea turtles face and it is easy to see why all surviving species are in danger of extinction.

The precarious survival of turtles, so delicately balanced around natural events, is even further exacerbated by a whole gamut of threats generated by our own kind. Excessive egg-collecting, direct hunting of turtles for their meat, shell, bone, oil and leather, disturbance of nesting turtles by tourists and beach development have all been implicated in different countries as direct factors leading to the disappearance of feeding, breeding and, in particular, nesting

Hatchling green turtles.
Opposite Page:
The sex of future hatchlings is determined by the temperature at which eggs incubate. Outer ones generally become males.
Turtle hatchlings are prone to predation, especially in the early morning.

likelihood of flooding, level of predation and harvest, ocean current patterns and human disturbance, if the incubation temperature favours males the beach will never develop into a major nesting site.

When the heat of day gives way to night, an eruption of sand is followed by the appearance of energetic hatchling turtles, small enough to rest easily in the palm of a hand and exact replicas of the huge adults. An egg tooth, or caruncle, at the end of the beak allows the hatchlings to cut open the soft shell. The first to emerge from the nest are those who tunnel their way through the sand to the surface. Layers of hatchlings below successively push the excavated sand beneath them, causing the whole group to rise together, as if on an escalator, towards the surface. Then begins an impulsive race for the sea and a life-long struggle for survival. They are apparently attracted to the lightest horizon, which is usually the sea. In recent years, however, development has led to the electrification of coastal areas and lights often cause hatchlings to head inland, in the opposite direction to the sea. The stars also play a role and the journey from nest to sea may be the start of a strategy of imprinting on stellar constellations as a future navigational aid.

The hatchlings are thought to swim out to sea continuously for many days and to subsequently drift on ocean currents, feeding on zooplankton for a year

Green turtle skull and carapace.

populations. Ships and boats often strike and kill turtles at sea and pollution of the sea affects turtles on an unknown, but possibly drastic scale. Perhaps worst of all are fishing nets that catch and drown thousands, if not tens of thousands of turtles every year. As with turtles throughout the world, those in the UAE

Fishing nets can ensnare turtles.

This green turtle was killed by the propeller of a boat.

are affected by all these pressures and it remains uncertain as to how long they will survive here.

A large proportion of turtles nesting on mainland beaches are unsuccessful in their attempts to add new recruits to the population, either being disturbed before or during nesting or losing eggs or hatchlings to one causal threat or another. Slaughter of turtles for their meat, which is considered to have medicinal qualities, is widespread, the turtles either having been harpooned or accidentally caught in fishing nets, particularly those set for sharks, rays and other large fishes. The death toll of turtles on one recently investigated offshore island reached into the hundreds in just three fishing villages. Increasing use of nylon nets and modern, large fishing boats with powerful engines and extensive ranges is placing increased pressure on the UAE turtle population. Disturbance and destruction of vital habitats, such as seagrass beds and coral reefs, is a further indirect threat that provides cause for serious concern.

Conservation management of turtles is by no means a simple task, particularly as the turtles may cross several international boundaries whilst migrating between feeding and nesting grounds. International cooperation is needed to ensure protection during all phases of the life cycle. In the UAE a national research effort has focused on local turtle populations, generating information that can be used for management of this precious natural resource. Links with international organisations and researchers are now well-established and government interest in ensuring the continued survival of UAE's turtles may aid and contribute to a regional effort to safeguard these ancient marine reptiles for the benefit of future generations.

DESCRIPTIONS OF SEA TURTLES IN THE UAE

GREEN TURTLE

(*Chelonia mydas*)

Family Cheloniidae

Description: A green turtle carapace (upper shell) can measure up to 1.2m in length and an adult of this size may weigh in excess of 200 kgs. The smooth, rounded carapace has four pairs of large plates (costal scutes) on either side and is generally dark brown in colour with lighter patches, although the colour can vary considerably. The head is relatively small, the beak blunt and rounded. A single pair of plates stretch from the nostrils to the forehead between the eyes. Green turtle nests are distinctly circular and may be over a metre deep. The tracks left by a nesting green turtle are easily recognisable as the fore flippers are swept backwards together pulling the turtle along the beach, the right flipper leaving a distinct linear groove in the sand exactly opposite the left flipper, creating a series of parallel, horizontal tracks either side of the body.

Habitat: Feeding grounds are in shallow water over seagrass and algal beds. Nesting beaches tend to consist of fine deep sand in the UAE and include offshore islands and mainland sites.

Range: Green turtles are known to migrate great distances (several thousands of kilometres in some cases) and may be seen almost anywhere in UAE waters. However, largest numbers occur on feeding grounds to the west of Abu Dhabi.

Comments: Green turtles, locally known as 'Hamas' or 'Shiree', nest during summer months and feed at all times of year in the UAE. Many die each year in fishing nets and their bones and shells frequently wash ashore.

HAWKSBILL TURTLE

(*Eretmochelys imbricata*)
Family Cheloniidae

Description: Hawksbill turtles are smaller than green turtles, adults measuring about 80cm in length and weighing a maximum of about 50 kgs. They are named after their pointed, slightly hooked beak, which is accentuated by a narrow head. They can however be mistaken for young green turtles. Both are similar in colour and have four costal scutes on each side of the carapace. The thick costal scutes of the hawksbill tend to overlap in all but the oldest individuals and the trailing edge of the carapace often appears jagged. There are two pairs of plates between the eyes, compared to just one in the green turtle.

Hawksbill turtle nests are roughly circular and shallow, usually less than half a metre deep. Unlike the technique used by green turtles, hawksbills move along the beach by alternately sweeping the fore flippers backwards, much like a freestyle swimming stroke. The tracks left by each flipper either side of the body are therefore parallel, but not directly opposite each other as they are in the green turtle.

Habitat: Feeding grounds are in shallow water over coral or rocky reefs where they feed on soft corals, sponges, ascidians and other animals. Nesting beaches may consist of anything from fine sand to rocky, coarse sand beaches in the UAE and include offshore islands and mainland sites.

Range: Hawksbill turtles probably occur wherever there are coral reefs, which suggests a range including much of the Gulf of Oman and Arabian Gulf coasts of the country. Most have been seen near the shallow, offshore coral reefs to the west of Abu Dhabi.

Comments: The nesting season of hawksbill turtles is during spring months when they emerge on scattered beaches covering a wide area. The carapace of hawksbill turtles is known as 'tortoise shell', a popular collector's item among tourists in many parts of the world. The trade in 'tortoise shell' is now banned by international treaty.

LOGGERHEAD TURTLE

(*Caretta caretta*)

Family Cheloniidae

Description: Adult loggerhead turtles are slightly smaller than green turtles, the carapace usually measuring a little less than 100cm in length, and weighing up to 160 kgs. There are five pairs of costal scutes, as opposed to four in both green and hawksbill turtles. The carapace is relatively flat and is often a light brown colour. The leathery skin has an orange tinge. The broad head is on a thick neck and is very large relative to body size. The beak is sharply pointed but thick and solid.

Habitat: Loggerheads feed on crabs, molluscs and other reef animals relatively deep down on the reef. Nesting beaches in neighbouring Oman are composed of coarse sand.

Range: Knowledge concerning the presence of loggerhead turtles in the UAE comes only from discoveries of a few skulls and carapaces of dead animals on offshore islands to the west of Abu Dhabi. No confirmed live sightings have been recorded.

Comments: Loggerhead turtles are not well known by fishermen of the UAE, but one identified a skull as belonging to 'Murah'. Numbers in the UAE have never been assessed, but Oman hosts the world's largest nesting population, numbering 30,000.

LEATHERBACK TURTLE

(*Dermochelys coriacea*)

Family Dermochelyidae

Description: Leatherback turtles are the giants among turtles. The largest on record is reputed to have weighed nearly 1,000 kilograms and to have measured an astonishing 3 metres in length. Most are substantially smaller than this, weighing perhaps 400 kilograms. They are unusual turtles, placed in their own family. They do not have plates like other turtles, but a soft skin covering the shell with seven prominent ridges running the length of the carapace. They are mostly black with scattered white markings. The large smooth head on a thick, short neck has a rounded beak with two cusps at the end of the upper jaw. Their huge nests and deep tracks have not been recorded in the UAE.

Habitat: Leatherbacks are truly pelagic, avoiding coral reefs and coastal areas much of the time. They feed almost exclusively on jelly fish and planktonic organisms such as sea squirts, in the open ocean. Nesting sites elsewhere in the world are on steep beaches with deep sand, often in areas of heavy surf with deep water close to shore.

Range: Leatherbacks are known only from a few sightings in the UAE, which were made near Dubai in the Arabian Gulf. It is likely that they may also occur off the east coast, in the Gulf of Oman.

Comments: Fishermen of the UAE claim to see leatherback turtles from time to time in the Arabian Gulf. Worldwide they are known to travel great distances, and have even been found within the Arctic circle. One individual was found in open ocean a remarkable 6,800kms from the nesting site at which it had previously been tagged.

SEA SNAKES

Sea snakes occur throughout the UAE sea area. There are at least seven species, all of which belong to one family, the Hydrophiidae. They are excellent swimmers and the laterally flattened tail makes them easily recognisable and distinguishes them from eels, such as the harmless yellow and black banded snake eels that often feed in sandy seabeds in UAE waters, but are rarely seen on the surface alive. Sea snakes are most abundant in the warm shallow seas of the Arabian Gulf, where they are frequently seen resting motionless on the sea's surface. The striking bright yellow and black bands of the Arabian Gulf sea snake (*Hydrophis lapemoides*) catch the eye against a sea of turquoise blue and draw a cautious curiosity among on-looking boaters. Often the snakes too show their natural curiosity, raising their small heads up to two feet above the water to eye the surface surroundings and directly approaching a stationary craft. The seemingly unmistakable pattern of the Arabian Gulf sea snake is in fact shared by a

Opposite page:

Arabian Gulf sea snake on a seagrass bed.

number of other species which can easily be confused. The annulated sea snake (*H. cyanocynctus)* is very similar and both the yellow sea snake (*H. spiralis)* and Shaw's sea snake (*Lapemis curtus)* could be mistaken for either. The first two are generally fairly large and bulky, reaching lengths of over a metre, but not as large as the yellow sea snake which can easily exceed 2 metres. Confusingly, the colour varies among them from yellow to green to grey and the black banding too is variable in extent and shade. In Shaw's sea snake the bands often take on a rough diamond shape, thicker over the spine and converging to points at the flanks. The yellow-bellied sea snake (*Pelamis platurus)* is one of few that is easily recognisable being uniform brown above and yellowish on the undersides with the black tail baring a bold yellow pattern.

Like all snakes, sea snakes have scales, but unlike their land-dwelling relatives they lack belly plates, or gastrosteges, which makes them helpless on shore. It is not uncommon to find a live sea snake washed ashore, or left stranded on the beach by a rapidly falling tide. Unable to move, they must wait for the high tide in order to return to their watery world. A sea snake lying motionless on a beach may appear dead, but it is wise to resist any temptation to handle such specimens, for they could well be alive. Although not aggressive, unwanted handling may provoke an attack.

Sea snakes are the most venomous of the world's snakes. One drop of sea snake venom is reputed to have the potency to kill five men. This high toxicity enables them to disable their cold-blooded prey, such as fish, crabs and squid on which they feed. The venom also has a secondary role in actively aiding digestion. The fixed fangs which are just a few millimetres in length hang from the upper jaw at the front of the mouth. Injection is effected by compression of the poison glands, delivering a lethal combination of neurotoxins and myotoxins, although the exact make-up of the venom varies between species and even individuals. Neurotoxins, as their name suggests, act on the nervous system and can completely paralyse the muscles. Myotoxins work by destroying muscle fibres and debilitating prey. Even young sea snakes, that are born live at sea, have a venom as potent as any adult.

People are rarely bitten by sea snakes. Their apparently docile nature largely precludes the chance of a deliberate sea snake attack and they are anyway generally recognised as dangerous and avoided. The small mouth restricts their ability to bite any but the smallest appendage, such as a finger, although the gape can be greatly extended. Fishermen in the UAE are sometimes struck, having unintentionally angered a sea snake by hauling one into a boat in a fishing net. One of the first signs of the venom acting on a victim is a difficulty in breathing and swallowing, aching muscles and drooping eyelids. Although undoubtedly very dangerous, sea snakes, like all snakes, do not necessarily inject venom at each bite and symptoms of shock are often misidentified as serious snake bite cases.

Slow-moving, docile, yet inquisitive is the general impression that sea snakes often leave with observers. It is surprisingly easy to approach them, and you may soon find yourself closer than you would expect or desire. Underwater, they generally move with calm deliberation and can be seen hunting amongst coral heads and rocks and may frequently investigate holes in the sand, made by blennies and other burrowers, in the hope of a meal. Their docile demeanor however, should not prevent you from treating sea snakes with the caution and respect that they deserve.

There is at least one occasion of an outright attack by a sea snake on a pleasure boat. Having passed many sea snakes on a typically calm day in the Gulf the skipper stopped his boat in order to observe and photograph a mating pair of sea snakes, their bodies entwined and writhing, forming constantly changing slipknots. Suddenly noticing a third sea snake, partially wrapped around the shaft of the outboard motor engine, with the rest of its body trailing, apparently lifelessly, behind the boat, the boatman was naturally concerned that he had accidentally killed the snake. As he reached down to pull it clear of the engine, the snake slipped free and reared its head, violently striking the side of the boat. The frightened helmsman immediately jerked the boat into gear and sped forward, only to be chased for nearly half a kilometre by the enraged snake.

Common species of sea snakes in the UAE

Arabian Gulf sea snake

(*Hydrophis lapemoides*)

Family Hydrophiidae

Description: 100cm or more in length. Bulky, but with a relatively small head. Yellow, sometimes pale dull green or grey, with dark bands along the length of the body. Top of the head usually dark with a narrow yellow band forward of the small eyes. Undersides pale. Laterally flattened tail, diagnostic of all sea snakes. Very similar in appearance to the annulated sea snake (*H. cyanocynctus*).

Habitat: Warm, shallow waters over reefs, seagrass or sand.

Range: Throughout the UAE. Common in the Arabian Gulf. In the Gulf of Oman, only in nearshore shallow water.

Comments: Named after the Arabian Gulf, this species is nevertheless apparently found throughout the Arabian region. Like all sea snakes, it is dangerous and a bite can be fatal. However, it is generally docile.

Yellow sea snake

(*Hydrophis spiralis*)

Family Hydrophiidae

Description: 220cm or more in length. Relatively less bulky than the Arabian Gulf sea snake, though much larger overall. Colour pattern very conspicuous yellow with black bands along the length of the body. Top of the upper jaw often fringed with reddish brown scales. Undersides pale. Laterally flattened tail, diagnostic of all sea snakes.

Habitat: Warm, shallow waters over reefs, seagrass or sand.

Range: Throughout the UAE, including the Gulf of Oman and the Arabian Gulf, but restricted to shallow water.

Comments: The yellow sea snake is perhaps an exception to the generally docile nature of sea snakes and is reputably aggressive. It is large and dangerous, the bite potentially fatal.

Yellow-bellied sea snake thrown upon the beach. Even though it looks dead, it may not be and therefore it can be very dangerous if handled.

SHAW'S SEA SNAKE

(*Lapemis curtus*)

Family Hydrophiidae

Description: Less than 100cm in length. Yellow with dark bands, which often take on a rough diamond shape, thicker over the spine and converging to points at the flanks. May have dark patches above each eye. Undersides pale. Laterally flattened tail, diagnostic of all sea snakes. Juveniles more strikingly coloured, bright yellow against black.

Habitat: Warm, shallow waters over reefs, seagrass or sand.

Range: Throughout the UAE, including the Gulf of Oman and the Arabian Gulf, but restricted to shallow water.

Comments: This species is less often seen than the Arabian Gulf and yellow sea snake. Dangerous, with a potentially fatal bite.

YELLOW-BELLIED SEA SNAKE

(*Pelamis platurus*)

Family Hydrophiidae

Description: Generally less than 90cm in length. The upper surface along the back is uniform brown (often very dark), sides and undersides pale yellow and the tail black with a bold yellow diamond shaped pattern. The head is small and narrow and bares the pattern of the rest of the body, dark above, pale below. The eye is relatively large compared with other species. Laterally flattened tail, diagnostic of all sea snakes.

Habitat: Unlike all other species of sea snake in the UAE, this species prefers deeper water.

Range: Throughout the UAE in deeper, offshore water, particularly in the Gulf of Oman.

Comments: This species' colour pattern is unique and not easily mistaken for any other species. Like all of the other sea snakes it is dangerous and the bite is potentially lethal. Look out for it along distinct surface current lines over deep water where it has often been observed.

Birds & Birdwatching

Colin Richardson

Houbara bustard,
Chlamydotis
undulata

Opposite page:
Socotra cormorant,
Phalacrocorax
nigrogularis.

Little green bee-eater,
Merops orientalis.

Nearly 400 species have been found in the United Arab Emirates since records began, with about 310 recorded annually. Of these about 90 breed regularly, the balance being passage migrants, winter visitors and accidentals. The reason for such a wealth of birdlife in such a relatively small country is its geographical location and the diversity of habitats found there. The UAE is situated on a migratory cross-roads where a north-south flyway conveys species between the main Palaearctic landmass and Africa, while a less-used east-west route takes birds between the Near East and the Indian subcontinent. Add to this an influx of Indian Ocean seabirds in summer and a scattering of Siberian vagrants in autumn and you have a recipe for exciting birdwatching throughout the year.

For the keen European birdwatcher the UAE offers considerable interest, with Socotra cormorant *Phalacrocorax nigrogularis*, sooty gull *Larus hemprichii*, white-cheeked tern *Sterna repressa*, chestnut-bellied sandgrouse *Pterocles exustus*, black-crowned finch lark *Eremopterix nigriceps*, Hume's wheatear *Oenanthe alboniger*, plain leaf warbler *Phylloscopus neglectus* and yellow-throated sparrow *Petronia xanthocollis* plus dozens of other Asian specialities, within relatively easy reach. A visit of eight to 12 days should allow enough time to see all the resident specialities and most of the interesting migrants for which the region is famous. The number of species likely to be found varies from month to month, with a maximum of about 230 recorded in October and March and about 190 in mid winter. In summer the numbers dip to about 105 species.

Ornithological importance

At any one time during migration periods (July - November and April - May) probably in excess of 250,000 waders are present on intertidal areas of the country's Gulf coast. Taking into account the likely turnover of shorebirds on this Eurasian/West Asian - Arabian Gulf - African flyway, the mudflats of the southern Gulf probably support several million individuals over the course of a year.

The current UAE population of Socotra cormorants is around 200,000, which is about 15-33% of the estimated total world population. Persecution is a problem as it is the only species which may be hunted under UAE law, and a number of island populations have been lost since 1980. Only seven known colonies remain. This is due to a perceived threat to fish stocks, whereas, to the contrary, the species may be a vital component in nutrient cycling within Gulf waters, actually maintaining fish stocks rather than reducing them.

Individual sites are regionally important for wader species, namely Abu al Abyadh for its crab plover *Dromas ardeola* colony and migratory populations of lesser sand plover *Charadrius mongolus*, Kentish plover *Charadrius alexandrinus*

and grey plover *Pluvialis squatarola*, Khor Dubai for its high densities of Kentish plover, greater sand plover *Charadrius leschenaultii*, lesser sand plover and broad-billed sandpiper *Limicola falcinellus* and Khor al Beidah for its large wintering population of crab plover and parties of up to 90 wintering great knot *Calidris tenuirostris*. The summer population of crab plover is estimated at over 1,200 shared between Abu al Abyadh and another colony on the island of Umm Amim, while the largest wintering population of over 500 birds is at Khor al Beidah.

Several islands hold important seabird populations and all are (or were) important in some way. Siniyah, Yasat and Ghagha Islands hold large Socotra cormorant populations; Qarnayn Island alone has breeding red-billed tropicbird *Phaethon aethereus*, sooty gull and several tern species and other islands in the south-west hold exceptional numbers of white-cheeked, lesser crested *Sterna bengalensis* and bridled tern *Sterna anaethetus*. The UAE holds the Gulf's largest breeding population of sooty falcon *Falco concolor*, a strongly migratory species the bulk of which winters in Madagascar. The species is considered to be threatened since most of its known nest sites are on strategic offshore islands which are quickly being developed. Osprey *Pandion haliaetus* has practically disappeared from its former mainland nest sites, now confined almost exclusively to islands, where its numbers appear healthy.

Of passerines, populations of many Middle Eastern restricted range species appear healthy. In the Hajar mountains Hume's wheatear and yellow-vented bulbul *Pycnonotus xanthopygos* are common residents, with eastern pied wheatear *Oenanthe picata*, red-tailed wheatear *Oenanthe xanthoprymna* and plain leaf warbler widely distributed in winter. The mangrove-lined creek at Khor Kalba holds the country's only population of white-collared kingfisher *Halcyon chloris*, of the endemic subspecies *kalbaensis*. This subspecies is endangered, with a population of only 44 pairs remaining at the site. Also here is the country's only breeding site of booted warbler *Hippolais caligata*, and regular wintering site of Indian pond heron *Ardeola grayii*.

Opposite page:
Red-billed tropicbird, Phaethon aethereus.

Yellow-spotted rock sparrow,
Petronia xanthostema.

Sooty Gull, Larus
hemprichii, *adult.*

Opposite page:
Chestnut-bellied
sandgrouse,
Pterocles exustus.

Sooty Gull, chick.

Certain local problems need to be addressed, including the increasing use of 4-wheel drive vehicles, on beaches, damaging tern and turtle nest sites, and inland, destroying fragile desert eco-systems in the process. The rapid increase in human population (2.3 million in 1995) continues to put pressure on remaining coastal areas, while former vast expanses of inland deserts and plains are being developed for agriculture or other purposes, inevitably affecting wildlife. In addition, over-grazing is a major problem, herds of goats and camels inhibit new growth or regeneration of *Prosopis*, *Acacia* and other perennials. Branches of trees are regularly cropped and in some cases trees are pulled over to allow the tops to be grazed clean. This has already had an effect on Arabian babbler *Turdoides squamiceps,* which, through lack of low cover has become scarce in many formerly well-populated areas. Other species which rely on these trees include lappet-faced vulture *Torgus tracheliotus*, striated scops owl *Otus brucei*, red-tailed wheatear, eastern pied wheatear, Upcher's warbler *Hippolais languida*, desert lesser whitethroat *Sylvia minula*, Hume's lesser whitethroat *Sylvia althaea*, plain leaf warbler and yellow-throated sparrow.

DESERTS AND DUNES

The south and west of the country close to Arabia's great Empty Quarter, consists of high, wind-blown sand dunes interspersed with flat areas of stony plain or sabkha (salt flats). Where there is natural ground water, obtained by pumping from prehistoric wells, cultivations and settlements occur. In some cases the government has embarked on afforestation projects. Hundreds of hectares of *Prosopis* and other evergreen desert trees have been planted in former desert areas. Drip irrigation and sprinklers are transforming desert areas to fodder fields, large areas of woodland, cultivations and palm plantations, so changing the natural desert ecology. Larger towns are also being established in some areas and acres of sand desert are usually bulldozed in advance of development.

The natural desert region lies almost entirely to the west of the mountains. It ranges in width from 20 kms in the north to over 150 kms in the south and west. Inland Abu Dhabi emirate consists almost entirely of sand dunes and gravel plains. In the northern emirates the sand desert is punctuated by groves of trees, *Prosopis cinerea*, (which are usually heavily grazed by camels and goats), which nevertheless host desert lesser whitethroat in winter, Upcher's warbler in spring and nesting yellow-throated sparrow from April to August. Open desert is the best place to find hoopoe lark *Alaemon alaudipes*, desert warbler *Sylvia nana* and desert wheatear *Oenanthe deserti*, while the flat gravel areas between the dunes is favoured by flocks of Black-crowned finch lark. Brown-necked ravens *Corvus ruficollis* are usually encountered in the sand desert areas, particularly inland from Umm al Quwain.

Nearer the mountains, east of a line from Al Ain to Ras al-Khaimah, the sand dunes give way to a broad gravel plain scattered with *Acacia tortilis*. This savannah plain is relatively rich ornithologically, particularly as you approach the base of the mountains. Red-tailed wheatear (mid October to March) and Arabian babbler are most likely here, while eastern pied wheatear (a scarce winter visitor late September to February) is likely to be found perched low in a tree at the base of the foothills. Qarn Nazwa, an interesting rocky outcrop between Dubai and Hatta has been a regular winter site for the species in recent years. Twelve species of wheatear occur in the Emirates and are best separated using a good field guide (see Further Reading).

Desert wheatear,
Oenanthe deserti.

Variable wheatear,
Oenanthe picata.

Hooded wheatear,
Oenanthe monaca.

Opposite page:
Desert lark,
Ammomanes
deserti.

157

MOUNTAINS AND WADIS

The mountains are reasonably untouched by development, by virtue of their inaccessibility, and hold many varied and interesting species of birds, animals and plants. They form an easterly backbone to the Emirates and contain a web of wadis (river beds), some wet throughout the year, and a scattering of villages and small towns. The area around the mountain village of Masafi has a number of sites worth visiting, particularly on the road to Dibba, where one passes through a range of pale foothills and on to Tayibah plain. The area is quite unspoilt away from the towns and there are lots of wadis to explore. Probably the most interesting bird for visitors is the Hume's wheatear, a mountain resident and easily identified by its contrasting black-and-white plumage. Most of the mountains are best visited by four-wheel drive vehicle as walking can be quite hard going.

Short-toed eagle,
Circaetus gallicus.

These dark 'ophiolitic' mountains (see chapter on geology) support resident sand partridge *Ammoperdix heyii*, desert lark *Ammomanes deserti* and pale crag martin *Hirundo obsoleta*, while Indian roller *Coracias benghalensis* and little green bee-eater *Merops orientalis* are found in the shaded, more cultivated wadis. The key birds for birdwatching visitors occur in winter and include species such as eastern pied & red-tailed wheatear, desert lesser whitethroat and plain leaf warbler.

The highest mountain is Jebel Hafit, near Al Ain which, at 1,500 metres, towers above the surrounding plain. A drive up the superbly-engineered highway to the top of Jebel Hafit should provide a few good views of Hume's wheatear and possibly a glimpse of the more elusive hooded wheatear *Oenanthe monacha*.

Most of the indigenous species inhabiting the mountains rarely stray far from this habitat so it is worth spending a day or two searching some of the Acacia plains and the more promising looking wadis. Yellow-vented bulbul and pale crag martin are easy to find, but scrub warbler *Scotocerca inquieta* and house bunting *Emberiza striolata* (subspecies *striolata*) need more determined work. Arabian babbler favours more cover, sometimes in short supply in this overgrazed land. Lichtenstein's sandgrouse *Pterocles lichtensteinii* can be

encountered anywhere in the mountains but is more reliably seen (or at least heard) shortly after dusk at a favoured water hole.

Of the migrants, red-tailed wheatear and desert lesser whitethroat are the most common. Less common, plain leaf warbler can usually be located by its insistent, though quiet "tch, tch, tch...." call.

Birds of prey are rather scarce in the Emirates. A few pairs of Bonelli's eagles *Hieraaetus fasciatus* and barbary falcons *Falco pelegrinoides* nest on the higher crags, while the mountains are also favoured by migrant short-toed eagles *Circaetus gallicus* and long-legged buzzards *Buteo rufinus*. The most interesting raptor in the area is the lappet-faced vulture. This *negevensis* dark-race can be a real prize if encountered, usually soaring high like a giant flying carpet, north and east of Al Ain.

*Indian roller wing
feathers and adult*
Coracia
benghalensis.

Greater flamingo,
Phoenicopterus
ruber.

COASTS AND MUDFLATS

Wader watchers are in their element in the Northern Emirates, where a visit to one of the major wetlands should produce an exciting abundance of Palaearctic shorebirds. The Arabian Gulf and its shallow saline lagoons and extensive mudflats serve as important winter feeding grounds for millions of Arctic and central Asian migrant shorebirds. One hundred and twenty six thousand wetland birds were counted in January during the 1995 Asian Waterfowl Census, including 41,000 wildfowl, 42,000 waders, 38,000 gulls and 4,200 terns, so it is worthwhile spending some time watching the coasts and lagoons.

The sheltered tidal lagoon at Khor Dubai can hold about 12,000 birds at any one time during the winter season, including hundreds of the much sought-after species broad-billed sandpiper and lesser sand plover. This site has been declared a Wildlife Sanctuary by Dubai's Crown Prince, General Sheikh Mohammed bin Rashid Al Maktoum, whose interest in the high numbers of greater flamingos *Phoenicopterus ruber* occurring throughout the year encouraged him to build a breeding island in the centre of the lagoon. Other species of interest here are spotted eagle *Aquila clanga* (late October to March only), greater sand plover and Pacific golden plover *Pluvialis fulva* (September to April). Khor al Beidah, at Umm al Quwain is the most accessible site to see crab plover in winter, when over 300 birds are present at their high tide roost. Great knot is regular here too. One of the world's largest colonies of Socotra cormorants nests nearby in late autumn and there are often flocks of several thousand flying offshore, visible from the coastline. About 100 kms north-east of Dubai is Al Jazeerah Khor, another network of lagoons. It is a good place to see terek sandpiper *Xenus cinereus*, while flocks of slender-billed gull *Larus genei* and Saunders' little tern *Sterna saundersi* in winter, best viewed from the high dunes which guard the bay. These scrub-covered dunes usually host several species of *Sylvia* warbler in winter and spring, including desert, orphean *S.orpheus* and Ménétries' warbler *S.mystacea* and 'Siberian' lesser whitethroat *Sylvia curruca (blythi)*.

The UAE's eastern coastline situated at the northern extremity of the Indian Ocean holds a marvellous diversity of bird and marine species. Khor Kalba,

Crab plover, Dromas ardeola.

about 12 kms south of Fujairah town, facing the Gulf of Oman, is by far the most interesting site on the country's east coast. It is unique in many ways, not least for the fact that it holds Arabia's oldest stand of black mangrove *Avicennia marina*, which thrive in the slack tide inland from the fishing harbour. This is the home of the white-collared kingfisher, generally rare and localised in Arabia and here belonging to the distinctive race *kalbaensis*, named after the site which shelters it.

The sea here is rich in marine life (including several species of turtles, sharks, rays and dolphins) and seabirds are usually abundant. Socotra cormorant, sooty gull, bridled tern, swift tern *Sterna bergii*, lesser crested tern, white-cheeked tern, pomarine skua *Stercorarius pomarinus* and Arctic skua *Stercorarius parasiticus* are seasonally common. Less common, Audubon's (Persian) shearwater *Puffinus lherminieri (persicus)* and Wilson's storm-petrel *Oceanites oceanites* are sometimes visible from the shoreline.

161

GARDENS AND AGRICULTURAL AREAS

A bird-watching visit to the Emirates is not complete without touring the numerous golf courses, city parks and agricultural areas. In Abu Dhabi, a visit is recommended to Bateen Gardens and the adjacent Mushref Palace Gardens and the Khalidiyah Spit at the western end of the Corniche. In and around Dubai are Safa Park, the Creek Park, the Emirates golf course (where special permission is required to birdwatch) and the cultivations around Al Awir and Al Habab. The grass fields around Digdaga and Hamraniyah (Ras al-Khaimah), the central grassed areas of Al Wathba (Abu Dhabi) and the Al Ain camel race tracks are usually full of migrants and associated birds of prey. In addition there are a number of other sites, less known for their beauty, though teeming with birdlife. These include sewage lagoons and water treatment plants, which sometimes hold the country's greatest variety of wetland species.

Without the irrigated man-made habitats many Arabian migrants would probably not otherwise survive the rigours of the desert. The UAE government has planted tens of thousands of trees in the desert. There are vast grass fields in the oases and golf courses and parks in all the large cities. These sites attract thousands of migrant birds and are "must visit" sites for bird-watchers. All are irrigated by desalinated water or from natural aquifers beneath the desert.

The well-established agricultural area around Digdaga and Hamraniyah, south of Ras al-Khaimah has produced more than its fair share of excitement in the last few years. Besides its resident population of hundreds of Indian rollers and little green bee-eaters the area is well-known for its ability to draw in migrant birds of prey. Six species of eagle have been recorded, including imperial eagle *Aquila heliaca* and booted eagle *Hieraaetus fasciatus* and both pallid and Montagu's harrier *Circus macrourus* and *C. pygargus* are regular from September to March. The most interesting phenomenon was the number of lesser kestrels *Falco naumanni* attracted by the grass fields in spring 1993 and 1994. Numbers peaked at 109 in early April 1994, with most birds departing by 19th April. They were found to be feeding on larvae of the large convolvulus hawk-moth *Agrius convolvuli*, which were in abundance during those years. Unfortunately the quality of water pumped from the wells dropped in late 1994 and many fields were abandoned and lesser kestrel numbers subsequently dropped in 1995. The varying ecology of these large fields seems to appeal to a number of opportunist colonists. The site hosts the country's only breeding spanish sparrows *Passer hispaniolensis* (largest flock of over 300 recorded in March 1995) and European rollers *Coracias garrulus*, while bank mynahs *Acridotheres ginginianus* take their chances nesting in old wells between some of the fields. Flocks of over 500 pale rock sparrows *Petronia brachydactyla* are recorded here from mid March to early April.

Also regular at cultivations are a number of interesting central Asian sub-species which occur from September to April. These include masked wagtail *Motacilla alba personata*, Siberian stonechat *Saxicola torquata maura*, Caucasian bluethroat *Luscinia svecica magna*, eastern black redstart *Phoenicuroides ochruros phoenicurus* and steppe great grey shrike *Lanius excubitor pallidirostris*. The latter species is a regular migrant and it is interesting to compare it with the very black-masked local *aucheri* subspecies.

The camel race tracks at Al Ain and Al Wathba are grassed and irrigated inside the race track perimeter. These large areas act as magnets for larks, pipits, wheatears and other tired and hungry migrants. The rare specialities found here from October to February include bimaculated lark *Melanocorypha*

Montague's harrier, Circus pygargus.

Opposite page: *White-collared kingfisher,* Halcyon chloris kalbaensis.

bimaculata, oriental skylark *Alauda gulgula* and Blyth's pipit *Anthus godlewski*. Between 08.00h and 09.30h throughout the year flocks of up to 200 chestnut-bellied sandgrouse arrive and by mid morning from September to March half-a-dozen pallid and Montagu's harriers are often seen foraging over the fields. Immatures and females are most common but with care most can be identified by those unfamiliar with both species, simply by studying their face and wing patterns. Small groups of cream-coloured coursers *Cursorius cursor* are attracted to the Al Ain camel track in autumn and winter while Caspian plover *Charadrius asiaticus* and long-toed stint *Calidris subminuta* can occur between August and October. Since 1993 the nearby plantations at Al Wathba have regularly attracted small groups of hypocolius *Hypocolius ampelinus* in November and March. As the fruit trees mature it is expected that this may become a regular stopover site for this enigmatic species.

A regular site to see striated (Bruce's) scops owl in a spectacular fashion is only 15 minutes drive from the centre of Dubai. Several pairs nest in Mushrif National Park and individuals can sometimes be seen in the evening feeding under spotlights near one of the leisure centres. At least one pair of 'desert' eagle owls *Bubo bubo (ascalaphus)* nests on the rocky outcrop at Qarn Nazwa. A trip there at sunset can be rewarded by a pair calling from the summit, just visible in silhouette in the glow from a nearby oilfield flare.

Late autumn is the traditional time for Siberian vagrants and the parks and gardens of Dubai and Abu Dhabi are the best places to find them. Such interesting species as oriental pratincole *Glareola maldivarum*, pintail snipe *Gallinago stenura*, lesser noddy *Anous tenuirostris*, White-throated Bee-eater *Merops albicollis*, Forest Wagtail *Dendronanthus indicus*, dusky & radde's warbler *Phylloscopus fuscatus* and *P.schwarzi* and white-capped bunting *Emberiza stewarti* are just some of the vagrants recorded between October and November.

REFERENCES

Aspinall, S. 1996. Status and Conservation of the Breeding Birds of the United Arab Emirates. Hobby, Liverpool & Dubai.

Aspinall, S. & Richardson, C. 1994 Asian Waterfowl Census 1994. *Emirates Bird Report* 18:117-123.

Clement, P. & Harris, A. 1987. Field Identification of West Palearctic Wheatears. *British Birds* 80:137-157, 187-238. April & May 1987.

Richardson, C. (compiler) 1987-93. *Emirates Bird Reports:* 1-18. Emirates Bird Records Committee, P.O. Box 50394, Dubai, UAE.

Richardson, C. 1990a. *The Birds of the United Arab Emirates*. Hobby, Warrington & Dubai.

Richardson, C. & Aspinall, S. 1996. *A Checklist of the Birds of the United Arab Emirates*. Emirates Bird Records Committee, P.O. Box 50394, Dubai.

Uttley, J.D., Thomas, C.J., Green, M.G., Suddaby, D. & Platt, J.B. 1988. The autumn migration of waders and other water birds through the northern United Arab Emirates. *Sandgrouse* 10:58-70.

FURTHER READING

Gallagher, M. & Woodcock, M. (1980) *The Birds of Oman*. Quartet Books, London (hardback only).

Gensbol, B. (1984) *Birds of Prey of Britain and Europe*. HarperCollins, London.

Hayman, P., Marchant, J. & Prater, T. (1986) *Shorebirds*. Croom Helm, London.

Heinzel, H., Fitter & Parslow. (1995) The Birds of Britain and Europe with North Africa and the Middle East. Collins, London.

Hollom, P.A.D., Porter, R.F. *et al* (1988) *The Birds of the Middle East and North Africa*. Poyser, Calton.

Jonsson, L. (1992) *The Birds of Europe*. Helm, London.

Lewington, I., Alstrom, P. & Colston, P. (1991) *A Field Guide to the Rare birds of Britain and Europe*. HarperCollins.

Local bird guides and information:

Aspinall, S. (1996) *Conservation and Status of the Breeding Birds of the United Arab Emirates*. Hobby, Dubai & Liverpool. Price £14.99 (plus £6 p&p) from C.Richardson.

Hardwick, M. (1994) *United Arab Emirates March/April 1994. A Detailed Guide to Species and Sites*. Published privately £5.50 per copy from Mark Hardwick, The Garden Flat, 13 Southcote Road, London N19 5BJ. Tel 0171 700-2645.

Richardson, C. (1990) *The Birds of the United Arab Emirates*. Hobby, Warrington. ISBN 1-872839-00-2. Price £17.00. (also available from the author, plus £6 p&p).

Richardson, C. & Aspinall, S. (1996). *A Checklist of the Birds of the United Arab Emirates*. Published by the EBRC, P.O. Box 50394, Dubai. Price £6 (plus £2 p&p) from C.Richardson.

Richardson, C. (Compiler) 1987-94. *Emirates Bird Reports 1-18*. Editions 16 & 18 price £7.00 each (post free) (EBR15 & 17 are out of print) from C.Richardson.

MARINE FISH

Mike Shepley

THE FOLLOWING TREATMENT is by no means exhaustive. It is based on personal observation, unpublished studies and available literature, and focuses on the species a diver or fisherman is most likely to meet. The order of the families is alphabetical rather than by evolutionary hierarchy. Unless otherwise stated, fish mentioned occur in both the Arabian Gulf and eastern waters of the UAE.

side-swiping movement of their tail. Sohal favour the wave-turbulence zone adjacent to shallow rocky outcrops interspersed with coral, and are often observed grazing in large schools. Most surgeon fishes graze on bottom-dwelling algae and some also feed on zooplankton. *Acanthurus sohal; Zebrasoma xanthurus.*

Surgeon fish or sohal *Acanthurus sohal*
Distinctive and colourful with high forehead and lunate caudal fin with blue margins. Dark blue dorsally with dark horizontal stripes over silvery sides, yellow sub-laterally. Pectorals yellow with dark edges. Matching long dorsal and ventral fins also have electric blue edges. Bright orange spine on caudal peduncle. Arabian Gulf and east coast coral reefs, inshore rocks and islands. One of the commonest coral reef fishes, and easily observed inshore in the inter-tidal surf zone on shallow reefs, where they work the marginal rocks, scraping algae with their sharp teeth. They can be inquisitive and aggressively defend their home range. Often caught in nets and traps and discarded by fishermen as unmarketable. 30-75 cm

Yellowtail surgeonfish *Zebrasoma xanthurum*
Deep-bodied, high forehead; dark blue-black body with caudal fin bright canary yellow. Dark horizontal stripes which break into spots on shoulder and head. Another colourful resident of the inshore reefs which can often be seen while snorkelling. 22 cm

The surgeonfish Acanthurus sohal is common in shallow, turbulent water, usually with corals.

ACANTHURIDAE
SURGEON FISHES

Elongate and deep compressed body shape; thick-skinned with small roughish scales. Small mouth with incisor-like teeth for grinding, used to remove tiny invertebrates and algae from rocks. Colourful residents of the inshore reefs, surgeon fishes are so-called because of their ability to slash at other fish aggressively with their sharp, scalpel-like spines forward of the caudal fin, by a

ALBULIDAE
BONEFISH

Represented by a single species. The bonefish is elongate, streamlined cigar-shaped with a conspicuous protruding snout. Large-scaled, they are known to game anglers as 'silver ghosts'. They possess a second fleshy dorsal adipose fin. Not surprisingly, this fish takes its name from the many small bones which also make it a poor contender for the fish souks. Occasional specimens do turn up, generally taken in inshore gill nets. They are grazers using their

ARIIDAE
CATFISHES

Blunt, flattened head, with strong bony shield, scales absent. Paired maxillary and mandibulary barbels on chin. Deeply forked caudal fin, adipose fin present. Venomous spine present on soft-rayed dorsal fin. Silvery with bronze sheen, elongate. Feeds on small fish and crustaceans over shallow sand bars near the coast and offshore over sandy bottoms around structures. Powerful fish regularly caught by shore anglers and their venomous dorsal spine can inflict a nasty wound. *Arius thalassinus*, 100-150 cm.

ARIOMMIDAE
DRIFTFISHES

Fish are among the few truly wild animals that still form part of our staple diet. In the UAE a wide variety of fish are harvested. These are Lutjanus coeruleo-lineatus, the blueline snapper, which lives in shallow water.

underslung mouth to feed on crustaceans and invertebrates as well as predating on small fish. In shallow water, they can be observed with their tails above the surface as they grub along the bottom for crabs and shrimps. Local concentrations are found in shallows with good tidal flow and often associated with sea grasses.

Bonefish *Albula vulpes* Arabic name, *Bonouk*
Silvery, ghost-like, conspicuous protruding snout, streamlined, large-scaled. They possess a second fleshy dorsal adipose fin. Shallow inshore grassbeds, tidal sandy inlets and creeks. Local distribution uncertain and not significant as food fish. Feeds on shrimps, molluscs, small fish and invertebrates. 120 cm.

Driftfishes are small, slender fishes with rounded to compressed bodies and small mouths. Two distinct but closely positioned dorsal fins; caudal peduncle square cross-section with two low fleshy lateral keels present either side of caudal base. Associated with inshore reefs.

ATHERINIDAE
SILVERSIDES

Diminutive, semi-transparent fishes found in huge shoals in shallow water, mainly over sand. Dorsally light opaque sandy colour, their name derives from the broad lateral silvery stripes present along either side of the body. Often taken in fine-mesh gill nets along the shoreline, then dried and used for fertliser.

BALISTIDAE
TRIGGERFISHES

Triggerfishes are related to the puffer fish and trunk fishes. They are curiously shaped with high foreheads, with the eyes also very highly placed above a longish pointed snout. Small to medium-sized fishes with deep, compressed body shape covered with minute rough scales. Gill opening reduced to small slit. First dorsal spinous and restricted to no more than three spines. Pelvic fins either absent or fused. They move by propelling themselves with their second dorsal and ventral fins in an undulating motion, and only use their tails in an emergency when under threat. They vary from the colourful and aptly-named Picasso triggerfish to darker and much larger specimens. Triggerfishes have three dorsal spines compared to filefishes or leatherjackets which have either one or two dorsal spines. *Abalistes stellaris, Rhinecanthus assasi, Sufflamen chrysopterus , Sufflamen albicaudatus, Sufflamen capsitratus.* See also Monacanthidae.

Starry triggerfish *Abalistes stellaris* Arabic name: *Homarah*
Grey-green dorsally, vividly marked with small, light blue spots, blotches and 'brain' lines anteriorly. High set small eyes, small powerful jaws. First dorsal fin with three spinous rays, caudal peduncle small. Pectoral fins small and rounded, pelvic fleshy, merging with underbelly. Indo-Pacific, Arabian Gulf and east coast coral reefs, rocks and structures. These attractive trigger fishes are normally caught in fish traps and nets set for other species. 60 cm.

Picasso triggerfish *Rhinecanthus assasi*
Pointed snout, caudal fin pale and slightly rounded. Caudal spines with three horizontal black bands. Vertical dark brown stripe with blue edges from eye to gill rakers, preceded by yellow bar lined with pale blue stripe. Ventrally black surrounded by bright orange. A colourful and distinctive triggerfish. Coral reefs and inshore rocks. Feeds on zooplankton, crabs, and molluscs. 25 cm

BELONIDAE
NEEDLEFISH, GARFISH

Elongate, silvery body, dorsally bluish-green, either compressed or cylindrical. Large eyes, extended beak-like mouth, needle-sharp teeth. Gill rakers absent. Larger specimens offshore around structures in strong tidal flows. Caught by gillnets commercially. Bones and parts of the meat are green. *Ablennes hians* garfish or needlefish, *Tylosurus crocodilus* garfish. Arabic name: *Kharam* or *Hagool.*

A garfish (Belonidae) caught in an intertidal set net.

BOTHIDAE
SOLES AND FLOUNDERS

Flatfish with eyes on left side of body, generally dark or pale sandy-brown dorsally with extended marginal dorsal and ventral fins, and separate caudal fin. Flatfish range over sandy bottoms, from very shallow water to offshore. They conceal themselves by burying in the soft sand or sediment until only the eyes are visible. They are subject to parasites, and are not popular food fish. *Bothus pantherinus*, leopard sole; *Pseudorhombus arsius* , Moses sole.

Leopard sole *Bothus pantherinus*

Eyes on left of head, body flattened dorsally, mottled brown on back, with profuse spots and blotches. Partially curved lateral line with large dark blotch midway along straight section. Pale white translucent underneath. Male has elongate pectoral fin. Found on shallow inshore sandy bottoms. Feeds on bottom dwelling invertebrates and fish fry.
25 cm.

Moses sole *Pseudorhombus arsius*

Eyes on left of head, closer set than *B. pantherinus*. Pale sandy-brown dorsally with numerous ocellated spots. Semi-translucent to white underside. Feeds on bottom dwelling invertebrates and fish fry.
30 cm.

CARANGIDAE
JACKS, TREVALLY, QUEENFISH, AND SCAD

Body deep and moderately to highly compressed. Two dorsal fins, ventral fin preceded by two separate spines, caudal fin deeply forked. Scutes sometimes present along lateral line. Jacks or trevally are powerful, strong-swimming fish which feed on other fishes, cuttlefish and crustaceans. Many of the species are large, free-roaming fish that gather around offshore structures and wrecks, and also in open water. Inshore reefs and creeks are home to smaller species such as the orange-spotted jack, *Carangoides bajad* . Most species in this large family are overall silvery-grey in colour, with distinctive individual markings, including dark blotches, indistinct patches and black or orange spots. Carangidae swim in schools of a hundred or more fish, although larger species tend to be more solitary or hunt in smaller numbers. *Alectis indicus, Alepes mate, Carangoides bajad , Carangoides chrysophrys, Carangoides malabaricus, Carangoides sexfasciatus, Gnathanodon speciosus, Megalaspis cordyla, Scomberoides commersonianus, Scomberomorus lysan, Seriola dumerili, Seriolina nigrofasciata, Trachinotus blochi, Ulua mentalis.*

African pompano or threadfinned trevally *Alectis indicus*
Dark blue dorsally, black opercular spot, blunt high forehead. Dorsal and ventral fin rays elongated in young specimens. On offshore reefs, around structures, and in open water. 100 cm.

Indian threadfinned trevally *Alectis ciliaris*
Silver-blue dorsally, silver below with black opercular spot. The young of this species have a striking appearance, with long filamentous rays extending from both the high dorsal fin and the leading edge of the ventral fin. 90 cm.

Rainbow Runner *Elagatis bipinnulatus*
Bluish-green dorsally, silvery white with two blue stripes on either side of wide golden yellow mid-lateral band; terminal two-rayed finlets to both dorsal and ventral fins. Streamlined, powerful fish. Offshore pelagic in open water. Predatory on shoal fishes including mackerel, sardines, and occasionally cuttlefish. These torpedo-shaped fish have the appearance of giant fusiliers and are highly prized by sports fishermen. Seldom seen in the fish market, but increasing inshore in recent years. 90 cm.

A grey reef shark swims towards the camera. Although such species are present in UAE waters, they are generally not considered dangerous to well-trained divers.

Trevally *Caranx sem* Arabic name: *Jash Farrow*
Bluish-green dorsally, silvery with numerous small orange spots. Offshore: deep-water reefs, wrecks, offshore structures. Predatory on fishes and cuttlefish; and on cigale during their vertical migration in November and December for spawning. 90 cm.

Yellowfin jack *Caranx ignobilis* Arabic name: *Jash Yep*
Bluish-green dorsally, silvery with caudal fin dusky, except for pale leading edge. Highly curved lateral line. Extended leading edge to second dorsal and ventral fins. Offshore: deep-water reefs, wrecks and other structures. Predatory on fishes, cuttlefish and crustaceans. 115 cm

Bigeye scad or horse mackerel *Selar crumenophthalmus*

Bluish-green dorsally, silver, translucent sides; pale yellow band laterally. Large eyes set high on forehead. Slim caudal wrist and deeply forked tail. Arabian Gulf and east coast. Pelagic in large shoals, feeding on small fish and crustaceans. Shoals of these free-ranging, silvery fishes move close inshore and are often taken in nets by local fishermen. 30 cm.

Talang Queenfish *Scomberoides commersonianus*

Dark greeny-blue dorsally, bright yellowy-gold dorsally fading to silver and white underbelly. Five to eight large dark spots above lateral line. Scales oval shaped. Blunt head, large powerful jaws. 7 to 12 lower gill-rakers. Gulf and east coast, inshore reefs and creeks, also wrecks and offshore structures. Predator on fish, cuttlefish and crustaceans. While the kingfish is slim and elongate, queenfish are deep-bodied with powerful, crushing jaws and large eyes. 100 cm.

Queenfish *Scomberoides lysan*

Dark greeny-blue dorsally, with five to six parallel rows of dark spots on either side of the lateral line. Slim, streamlined shape, head mackerel-shaped. 15 to 20 lower gill-rakers. On inshore reefs and creeks, also wrecks and offshore structures. Predatory on fish, cuttlefish and crustaceans. 100 cm.

CARCHARHINIDAE
REEF SHARKS AND REQUIEM SHARKS

Elongate, streamlined body, head compressed. First dorsal prominent and in front of pelvic fins. Lower caudal lobe extended. All sharks have a number of rows of distinctive, serrated teeth. These are an important means of species identification. Tropical to temperate seas throughout the world and the largest family of sharks represented in the Arabian Gulf and UAE waters. Large powerful predators, some of which are considered potentially dangerous. There are at least ten different species of sharks in the Arabian Gulf. Tiger sharks, which are considered dangerous, rarely come close enough inshore to

come into contact with swimmers. Isolated shark attacks have been recorded in the days of the pearl divers, but they considered barracuda to be more dangerous. *Carcharhinus melanopterus*, blacktip reef shark; *Carcharhinus plumbeus*, whaler shark; *Carcharhinus brevipinna*, spinner shark; *Carcharhinus limbatus*, blacktip shark; *Galeocerdo cuvier*, tiger shark; *Hypogaleus hyugaensis*, blacktip houndshark. Also reported: *Carcharhinus sorrah*, spottail shark; *Negaprion acutidens* sicklefin lemon shark; *Isurus oxyrinchus*, shortfin mako which is not recorded from the Arabian Gulf, but one confirmed hook-up off Fujairah on the east coast.

Blacktip reef shark *Carcharhinus melanopterus*

Black tip to second dorsal and lower caudal lobe; colour of ventral and pectoral fins varies. Young less than 70 cm have unmarked fins. Inshore reefs, offshore structures. Opportunist predator, scavenger. Small, blacktip reef shark are found on coral reefs and around rocky headlands and islands. 200 cm.

Whitecheek shark *Carcharhinus dussumieri*

Small, sleek streamlined shark, pointed snout. Distinctive black blotch on second dorsal fin, first unmarked. Abundant in coastal waters and regularly in shrimp trawls. Originally reported from the Arabian Gulf as *Carcharias menisorrah*. 125 cm.

Sandbar shark or whaler shark *Carcharhinus plumbeus*

High dorsal fin, deep body, blunt snout, dark colouration. Potentially dangerous. Around wrecks and other structures, also oceanic. Opportunistic predator on fish and cuttlefish. 220 cm.

Spinner shark *Carcharhinus brevipinna*

Black tip to second dorsal and lower caudal lobe; ventral and pectoral fin colour varies. Young less than 70 cm have unmarked fins. Inshore reefs and around offshore structures. Opportunistic predator and scavenger. 280 cm.

The tiger shark, Galeocerdo cuvieri, is a rare visitor to UAE waters, most likely to occur off the east coast.

Blacktip shark *Carcharhinus limbatus*
Black tip to dorsal, caudal lobes colour varies. Status unconfirmed. Inshore reefs, offshore structures. Opportunist predator, scavenger. 150 cm.

Black-tipped shark *Carcharhinus sealei*
Black tip to dorsal, caudal lobes colour varies. Inshore reefs and around offshore structures. Opportunist predator and scavenger. 95 cm.

Tiger shark *Galeocerdo cuvieri*
Juveniles strongly marked dark vertical bars which fade in adults; very blunt snout, mid-lateral keel on caudal peduncle. Potentially dangerous. Offshore, occasionally inshore, around structures. Uncommon. Opportunistic predator, will feed on other smaller sharks, sea turtles and reputedly also dolphins. Immature specimen 80 cm recorded off Jebel Ali caught on rod and line. Female specimen caught in non-UAE Gulf waters was 4m in length. 550 cm.

Grey reef shark *Hypogalius balfouri*
Overall greyish, darker dorsally; small spiracle behind eye. Found on offshore reefs and also wrecks and other structures; less frequently inshore reefs. Opportunistic predator and scavenger, mainly feeding on fish, crustaceans, cuttlefish. 200 cm.

CHAETODONTIDAE
BUTTERFLYFISH, CORALFISH

Members of the butterflyfish family have deep compressed bodies and moderate ctenoid (rough) scales. Dorsal and ventral fins are well developed and extended. Small protractile mouth with bristle-like teeth. Snout can be extended. With the exception of a few species, such as *C. obscurus.*, butterflyfish are brightly coloured. *Chaetodon obscurus* dark butterflyfish; *Chaetodon melapterus* orange butterflyfish; *Heniochus acuminatus*, pennant coral fish; *Chaetodon lineolatus* , lined butterflyfish (only off east coast).

Dark butterflyfish *Chaetodon obscurus* Arabic name: *Anfooz, Qunfuth*
Main body oval shaped, dark brown overall with darker spots on scales

forming streaks. Snout paler and pointed. Most common butterfly fish on the east coast where it is found on coral reefs and rocky outcrops. Omnivorous. These pretty little fish are easily observed in shallow water, and are sometimes swimming in large groups, although two or three is the more usual number. Smaller and less colourful than the orange butterflyfish which is the other common species on UAE reefs. 12 cm.

Orange butterflyfish *Chaetodon melapterus*
Main body oval shaped, bright orange-yellow with head dark purple to black with two orange bands vertically. Pectoral fins hyaline, others including caudal are dark brown-black, banded exteriorally orange. Found on coral reefs and rocky outcrops. Omnivorous. These colourful butterflyfish are often seen on reefs in pairs, and can be observed by snorkellers, but tend to rush for cover if swimmers approach too closely. Sadly they are often trapped in inshore gargours set among coral reefs, and are discarded by fishermen as being unmarketable. 20 cm.

Pennant coral fish *Heniochus acuminatus*
Main body oval shaped, with prominent dorsal membrane prolonged in

pennant shape. Yellowish colour to second dorsal and caudal fin, with strong vertical dark bars from eye, shoulder and sub-dorsally along the second dorsal fin. Found on coral reefs and rocky outcrops. Omnivorous. Graceful and beautiful fishes, these butterflyfish prefer deeper water, and can often be seen in large groups along the seaward drop-off to coral reefs. 18 cm.

The Arabian butterfly fish, Chaetodon melapterus.

175

CHIROCENTRIDAE
WOLF-HERRINGS

Elongate, highly compressed body; scutes absent from belly. Single dorsal fin set close to deeply-forked caudal fin. Scales large, soft and bright silver. Large, needle sharp canine teeth to both jaws. Two species present in the Arabian Gulf and east coast, i.e.*Chirocentrus dorab* and *C. nudus* .

Dorab wolf herring *Chirocentrus dorab*
Dark-green dorsally, silvery. Large scaled, flattened, elongate body. Large needle-sharp teeth, underslung mouth. Dorsal fin black. Oceanic and pelagic. Predator of small fishes and crustaceans. This species looks very much like a giant elongated herring, with large silvery scales which easily come off when handled.
100 cm.

Whitefin wolf herring *Chirocentrus nudus*
Dark-green dorsally, silvery. Large scaled, flattened, elongate body. Large needle-sharp teeth, underslung mouth. Dorsal fin pale, contrasting with the black dorsal fin of *C. dorab*. Oceanic and pelagic. Predator on small fishes and crustaceans.
100 cm.

CLUPEIDAE
HERRINGS AND SARDINES

Elongate, compressed body, underside keeled with scutes along ventral edge. Equal-jawed largish mouth. Scales shed easily and are thin and smooth to touch; lateral line absent. Silver overall, olive to bluish dorsally. Predated on by numerous other fishes including sharks. Taken in inshore gill nets in huge quantities.

CORYPHAENIDAE
DOLPHINFISHES OR DORADO

Represented by a single species, the fish is more common on the east coast, but generally widely distributed. As their name implies, they are a bright golden colour in life, but this fades rapidly on death. Highly regarded as sportsfish by anglers, dorado leap spectacularly when hooked. Their other name dolphino or dolphinfish often leads to confusion with the various species of dolphin which are of course marine mammals. In Hawaii they are known as mahi-mahi.

Dorado or Dolphinfish *Coryphaena hippurus*
Female elongate and compressed; male develops prominent bony crest on head. Spectacular gold colouration with large blue spots on sides and long dorsal fin. Oceanic, pelagic, offshore often in shade around anchored oil tankers. Predator mainly on fish and cuttlefish. The brilliant colouration which gives this fish its 'golden' name, fades rapidly with death, to an overall silver-grey.
200 cm.

CYPRINODONTIDAE
KILLIFISH

Elongate, ovoid, slightly compressed body with head flattened dorsally. Small mouth, teeth villiform. Single rounded dorsal fin set back. Soft rays to all fins.

DASYATIDAE
STING RAYS

Body flattened and disc shaped with elongate, whip-like tail with venomous spine. Spiracles large, adjacent and behind the eyes. Dorsal and ventral fins absent. Upper surface of disc either smooth or with tubercles, colour varies from brown to dark bluish-grey, often with mottled blotches or spots. Sting rays are bottom-dwelling fish, with a preference for soft mud, sand or shale ground. Most rays are ovo-viviparous, i.e. they produce eggs that hatch within the body of the parent female. Most species of ray present in the Arabian Gulf have sharp spines on their elongated tail, and can inflict a nasty wound if inadvertently stood on by bathers. *Dasyatis kuhlii, Himantura gerrardi, Himantura uarnak, Taeniura melanospila* .

Spotted stingray *Dasyatis kuhlii*
Dark brown with lighter mottled spots; spine on tail. Inshore lagoons, shallow water bays, creeks and sharms. 160 cm.

Long-tailed stingray *Himantura uarnak* Arabic name: *Ruget*
Light sandy to dark brown with proliferation of darker spots. Venomous spine on tail. 155 cm.

Stingray *Taeniura melanospila*
Rounded disc; brown with darker mottling; two spines on tail. Found on mud, shale and sand near reefs. Feeds on small fish, crustaceans and molluscs. 130 cm.

ECHENEIDAE
REMORAS, SUCKER FISH

Elongate body, head flattened with modified oval sucking disc on dorsum, used to attach to host fish, generally sharks or rays. Attaches to a wide variety of hosts but aalso free ranging.

Caesio sp. photographed at night.

Remora or sucker fish *Echeneis naucrates*
Indistinct broad black band through eye and mid-laterally, widening dorsally on body; oval-shaped sunction disc on top of flattened head. 120 cm.

EXOCOETIDAE
FLYING FISH

Elongate, fusiform shape with enlarged pectoral fins which allow the fish to glide above the surface of the water to escape predators. The lower lobe of the caudal fin is extended and acts as a keel.

Flying fish *Cypselurus oligolepis* Arabic name: *Yaradah*

FISTULARIDAE Flutemouths
Tubular snout with small terminal mouth. Elongate body with tiny scales. Mid caudal ray filamentous.

Flutemouth *Fistularia petimba*
Reddish-brown dorsally to silver sub-laterally; tubular body shape. Long caudal filament. 120 cm.

177

Silver pomfret, Pampus argenteus, appear at certain times of year in schools around the UAE's offshore oil rigs.

FORMIONIDAE
POMFRET OR JACK-POMFRET

Deep oval or rhomboid, highly compressed body. Lateral line arched anteriorly, scales small. Dorsal and ventral fins elevated anteriorly, caudal fin forked. Two species present in the Arabian Gulf, one silvery-white, the other larger and dark brown. Offshore in deeper water, generally forming demersal shoals, but occasionally found sub-surface. Pomfret are highly prized as food fish, with firm white flesh. Some authors place fish from this family in the Stromateidae.

Silver pomfret *Pampus argenteus,* Arabic name: *Zobaidy*
Smooth-scaled, deep-bodied, compressed, deeply forked caudal fin. Small mouth and eye placed close to front. Near offshore reefs. 30 cm.

Dark pomfret *Formio niger*
Smooth scaled, deep bodied, compressed; overall brown to dark brown dorsally. Deeply forked caudal fin. Young have three to four distinct pale vertical bars on the body, and several darker blotches on both lobes of caudal fin, both bars and blotches fading in adults. 152 cm.

HAEMULIDAE
GRUNTS AND SWEETLIPS

Sweetlips or grunts, sometimes grouped under the family name Pomadasyidae, Gaterinidae or Plectorhynchidae, are superficially similar to snappers, but they have a smaller mouth in which the upper jaw generally projects to form a somewhat pronouced lip. Moderately sized fish, oblong compressed bodies, small to moderate mouths, thick lips and wide gill openings. Characteristic grunting noise created by grinding their teeth together. Colouration highly variable. Common in shallow waters around coral reefs and rocky headlands.

Spotted grunt *Plectorhynchus fangi* Arabic name:*Hellaly*
Silvery grey with dark round blotches from below front of leading dorsal. Dorsal fins and caudal fin heavily spotted. 60-75 cm.

Blackspotted grunt or sweetlips *Plectorhynchus gaterinus*
Silvery white with prolific black spots to body, dorsal and caudal fins. Bright yellow to fins and dusky back. Prominent forehead, large eyes, and small underslung mouth. On coral reefs where it grazes on algae and minute crustaceans. 50 cm.

HEMIRAMPHIDAE
HALFBEAKS OR BALAO

Halfbeaks are grouped with the needlefishes and flyingfishes in the order Beloniformes. Most halfbeaks have a long extended lower jaw, generally tipped with red, and short upper jaw, triangular shaped when viewed from above. Offshore and on inshore reefs, seagrass beds, harbours and khors. Main prey of the sailfish, *Istiophorus platypterus* . At least two species in UAE waters.

Spotted halfbeak *Hemiramphus far*
Greenish-brown dorsally, shading to silvery with pinkish sheen. Longitudal row of four or more black blotches above lateral line; anterior dorsal fin pronounced fork and suffused with yellow. Extended lower lobe to caudal fin, and upper lobe suffused with yellow. Lower jaw tipped with red. 45 cm.

Hyporhamphus sp.
Smaller and more elongate than *H. far*. Bluish-green dorsally, shading to silver. Weak black dots sometimes present. Lower jaw tipped with red. Similar to *H. gambarur* , Red Sea halfbeak, which is regarded as endemic to the Red Sea and Gulf of Aden. 20 cm.

ISTIOPHORIDAE
BILLFISHES

The sailfish, *Istiophorus platypterus,* is the main billfish present in UAE waters, and is seasonally common in both the gulf and on the east coast, peaking in late August through November, and again in March and April. Oceanic and pelagic, capable of extended migration. Feeds predominantly on halfbeaks and other small shoal fish. Sailfish often work together forcing the baitfish into a tight ball before attacking with slashing movements of the bill, then feeding at leisure on any damaged or dead fish. Popular sports fish with big-game anglers; generally tagged and released in UAE waters. Marlin have not been recorded from the Gulf. A single striped marlin,*Tetrapturus audax,* caught on rod and line off Khorfakkan, and other sightings confirm presence of marlin in offshore east coast waters, possibly including black marlin, *Makaira indica* , and blue marlin, *Makaira mazara* , both of which occur in the Gulf of Oman.

Indo-Pacific Sailfish *Istiophorus platypterus* Arabic name: *Kheil al-bahr*
Upper jaw extended to form prominent pointed bill. Distinctive sail-like dorsal fin, irridescent blue with segmented lines of three to ten large black spots on anterior rays. Dark bluish-black dorsally to purple or bluish bronze on sides, often showing broad darker barring. Larger average size on east coast. Tends to school by size, the young forming denser schools than adults. 150 to 300 cm.

coast. *Cheilinus lunulatus, Labroides dimidiatus, Hemipteronotus hypospilus, Thalassoma lunare, Halichoeres sp.*, and possibly present, *Stethojulis interrupta*.

Broomtail wrasse *Cheilinus lunulatus*
Distinctive filamentous caudal fin, blunt head, sharp incisor teeth. Dark green dorsally with dark double vertical bars on body. Small scattered orange dots on head, bright orange-yellow blotch and smaller spots on gill cover. Bright orange on pectoral fins. As with many of the wrasses, there are marked colour differences between males and females. The above description refers to the more prominent male, whilst females are smaller and drabber. On inshore coral reefs. Feeds on crustaceans, worms and other invertebrates. 50 cm.

LEIOGNATHIDAE
SLIPMOUTHS

Small, sedentary fish, shoals in shallow coastal water. Feeds on invertebrates. Elongate oval compressed body with naked, bony ridges to dorsum of head. Conspicuous concave lower jaw profile produces pointed snout. Terminal mouth protractile and maxilla absent from external edge of mouth. Eyes relatively large. High lateral line closely concurrent to dorsum profile. Extended spinous front dorsal almost continuous to soft-rayed portion. At least six species present in the Arabian Gulf.

The moon wrasse,
Thalassoma lunare,
is a common fish in
UAE waters.

LABRIDAE
WRASSES

Wrasses come in a multitude of shapes, colours and sizes, from the small cleaner wrasse and lunar-tailed wrasse, to the large broomtail wrasse, which, as its name implies, has a large brush-like tail with ragged, split ends. They can often be seen on inshore coral reefs, especially around Khorfakkan on the east

LETHRINIDAE
EMPERORS

Familiar to many residents of the UAE as one of the prime food-fishes, emperors, related to the snappers, are among the most important fish caught in local waters and are greatly prized. There are at least three species represented in UAE waters.

Spangled or blue-spotted emperor *Lethrinus nebulosus* Arabic name: *sheiry*
Brownish-grey with distinctive blue spots on scales and blue starry effect around head. Spinous rays to front of dorsal and ventral fins. Dorsal fin and caudal fin barred spots. On coral reefs, rocky outcrops and around inshore structures. Carnivorous, feeds on small fish, crustaceans and molluscs. 60 cm.

Longfaced emperor *Lethrinus miniatus* Arabic name: *sheiry*
Slimmer, more elongate and larger than *L. nebulosus*. Snout long and pointed, compared to other snappers present in region. Arabian Gulf and east coast, on coral reefs, rocky outcrops and around inshore structures. Feeds on small fish, crustaceans and molluscs. 90 cm.

Redspot Emperor *Lethrinus lentjan* Arabic name: *sheiry*
Characteristic gill cover edge bright red. Smaller and less common than *L. nebulosus*. On coral reefs, rocky outcrops and inshore structures. Feeds on small fish, crustaceans, and molluscs. 40 cm.

LUTJANIDAE
SNAPPERS

A large family of commercially important fish, the snappers are common on UAE coral-reefs and around other structures, where they hunt for small fish and crustaceans. Many of them are brightly coloured.

Malabar red snapper *Lutjanus malabaricus*
Orange-red to deeper red dorsally. High, curved lateral line, scale rows above,

Previous page:
*Yellowtailed snapper,
schools in UAE
waters, attracted by
the shade of
an oil-rig.*

directed obliquely towards dorsal fin. Young are red with pale-rimmed black spot on caudal peduncle and dark bar on head and darker horizontal lines which fade in adults. On coral reefs and offshore wrecks and structures. Feeds on small fish, crustaceans and cuttlefish. Commonly seen in the fish souq. Young can be seen on coral reefs when snorkelling, but don't show their true colours, and can be mistaken for the black-spotted snapper which is far more common. 100 cm.

Pinjalo snapper *Pinjalo pinjalo*
Dusky-red to deeper pink laterally. Dorsal fin with dark margin; caudal lobes pointed and more concave than *L. malabaricus*. Head uniform with no underslung lower jaw. Eye placed centrally. On coral reefs and offshore wrecks and structures. Carnivorous on small fish, crustaceans and cuttlefish. Less common than *L. malabaricus* . 85 cm.

Pinjalo snapper *Pinjalo pinjalo*
Dusky-red to deeper pink laterally. Dorsal fin with dark margin; caudal lobes pointed and more concave than *L. malabaricus*. Head uniform with no underslung lower jaw. Eye placed centrally. On coral reefs, offshore wrecks and structures. Carnivorous on small fish, crustaceans and cuttlefish. Less common than *L. malabaricus*. 85 cm.

Mangrove snapper or **river snapper** *Lutjanus argentimaculatus*
Robust, dusky bronze to rusty-red. Opaque pale blue line sometimes present on snout. Capable of living in freshwater. Feeds on crustaceans and small fish. Recorded from Khor Khalba on east coast. 40 cm. but can attain 80 cm.

Blackspot snapper *Lutjanus ehrenbergi*
Small robust, dark olive dorsally to olive yellow sides with strong longitudinal golden-yellow stripes. Eyes relatively large and set close to forehead. Curved lateral line with black blotch anteriorly below junction of spinous and soft rays

of dorsal fin. On inshore reefs and rocky headlands. Feeds on invertebrates and smaller fish and fry. 30 cm.

Dory snapper *Lutjanus fulviflamma*
Single black spot, margins indistinct, above lateral line behind gill plate. 13 dorsal fin rays compared to 14/15 in *L. russelli*. Around coral reefs and rock outcrops. 30 cms.

John's snapper *Lutjanus johni* Arabic name: *Hobara, Naisarah*
Moderately deep, silvery green body with longitudinal rows of scales above and parallel to curved lateral line, and horizontal rows below. Scales tipped with black giving distinct linear pattern. Dark blotch may be present at lateral line below junction of spinous and soft dorsal rays. Offshore and coastal waters. Feeds on invertebrates and small fishes. 50 cm.

Bluestripe snapper *Lutjanus kasmira* Arabic name: *Hobara, Naisarah*
Moderately deep bodied, orangey-brown dorsally with orange to yellow sides. Five longitudinal blue lines bordered brown from cheek, top two oblique and others horizontal. Pale blotch above lateral line, below junction of spinous and soft dorsal rays. Offshore on rough ground or reefs. 25 cm.

Bigeye snapper *Lutjanus lineolatus*
Robust body, orangey-brown dorsally to silvery sides. Large eyes. Several longitudinal yellow lines below thicker dark yellow band from snout through eye to caudal fin. Scales above high curved lateral line, with darker brown margins produce oblique pattern. On shallow coral reefs. feeds on invertebrates and smaller fish. Not very common. 25 cm.

Russel's snapper *Lutjanus russelli*
Pale reddish-brown to silvery flanks with darker golden-brown stripes. 14/15 dorsal fin rays compared to 13 in *L. fulviflamma*. Prominent black spot posteriorly. 40 cm.

MOBULIDAE
MANTA RAYS

The largest of the rays present in UAE waters, manta rays are oceanic plankton feeders which can grow to considerable size, with a wing span of around 3 m., although most sightings in UAE waters are of generally of much smaller fish. Dark brown, whitish ventrally, with fleshy projections or horns either side of the head, used to funnel plankton to the mouth; short whip-like tail. Often accompanied by remora and schools of smaller fish. When senn from a distance, manta rays may sometimes be confused with eagle rays, which also leap out of the water.

MOLIDAE
SUNFISH

The sunfish family contains three species of ocean travelling, distinctively-shaped laterally compressed fish, which appear on first sight to be all head and no body! Mouth small with

teeth to both jaws fused to form sharp beak; large, paired dorsal and ventral fins. Sunfishes grow to a considerable size, up to 3 m. long and weighing in excess of 1000 kg. Offshore surface and sub-surface, they feed on plankton. *Mola mola, Mola ramsayi.*

Sunfish *Mola ramsayi*
Confirmed from a single specimen recorded from east coast. Dark, large pointed dorsal and ventral fins. The specimen was estimated at around 500 kg. 121.5 cm.

MONACANTHIDAE
FILEFISHES AND LEATHERJACKETS

The filefishes or leatherjackets are closely related to the triggerfishes (Balistidae). They differ from triggerfishes with more compressed body shape with generally more pointed snout, prominent longer first spine, with small or absent second spine and no third spine. unlike triggerfishes, they can adapt their colouration to their surroundings. Tend to be secretive; found on reefs and seagrass beds. *Paramonacanthus choirocephalus, Paramonocanthus oblongus, Pseudotriacanthus strigilifer, Stephanolepsis diaspros, Triacanthus biaculeatus.*

183

MONODACTYLIDAE
MONOS

A small family consisting of two genera. Common around harbours and khors in UAE waters, and capable of living elsewhere in freshwater.

Mono *Monodactylus argenteus.*
Body highly compressed and silvery with high curved lateral line; head angular with small oblique mouth with protruding lower jaw. Vestigial pelvic fins, matching dorsal and ventral fins very elevated lobes tinged with black; caudal fin emarginate.
23 cm.

MUGILIDAE
MULLETS

Generally seen in large or small schools, mullets are moderate-sized, large scaled, silvery fishes; the back is bluish-back. Head depressed and blunt, with short and rounded snout. Body nearly cylindrical anteriorly and compressed towards the tail. Leading spinous dorsal and second soft-rayed dorsal well separated. Mullets are restricted to shallow inshore waters, particularly in creeks, khors, around harbour walls and inshore coral reefs and rocky outcrops.

Flathead mullet *Mugil cephalus* Arabic name: *Biah*
Wide ranging species, with characteristic blunt, flattened head. One of the largest mullets in UAE waters and most common mullet in the fish souk.
60 cm.

Largescale mullet *Liza macrolepis* Arabic name:*Biah Sfaiti , Beyah*
Greenish head and back, silvery sides, dorsal and ventral contour equally convex. Thin lips with fine teeth to upper. Dorsal and caudal fins dusky, pectoral fins hyaline with indistinct spot at axil.
35 cm.

Blue-spot mullet *Valamugil seheli* Arabic name:*Biah arabi Araby, Beyah*
Bluish-silver above, silvery on sides and underbelly, indistinct longitudinal lines on upper body. Pectoral fins yellow with darkish blue spot at axil. Attracted to good tidal flow, it inhabits coastal waters, sharms and lagoons, forming large schools. Feeds on small organisms and algae. Potentially viable species for marine farming.
25 cm - 45 cm.

MULLIDAE
GOATFISHES

Small to moderate fishes, easily recognised by the paired chin barbels equipped with chemosensory organs used for probing the sand for minute invertebrates. Found in shallow coastal waters, over sandy and seagrass beds, generally in small groups or shoals. Although small, they are important food fish. *Parupeneus cyclostomus, Hedi ; Parupeneus macronema, Parupeneus pleurotaenia, Upeneus asymetricus, Upeneus sulphureus, Upeneus tragula, Mulloidichtys auriflamma, Mulloides flavolineatus.*

Black-striped goatfish *Upeneus tragula* Arabic name: *Hamer*
Light brown to reddish body with darker brown lateral band and numerous dark spots dorsally, with fewer brownish spots below. Barbels yellowish-brown. Dorsal fins may be tipped dusky red. Pectoral fins reddish. Caudal fin pale with distinct oblique darker bands to each lobe.
25 cm.

Golden-striped goatfish *Mulloidichtys auriflamma* Arabic name: *Hamer*
Olive-brown head and body, paler sub laterally to silvery white. Golden-yellow band on sides of body above lateral line. Fins hyaline with darker blotches to dorsal fins. Caudal fin light brown darker marginally.
40 cm.

The moray eel,
Gymnothorax
javanicus *lays at the entrance of a hole in the reef for most of the day, emerging in the evening and at night to feed. Here it is being attended to by a cleaner wrasse.*

MURAENIDAE
MORAY EELS

Moray eels are easy to recognise by their distinctive eel shape. They are usually observed poking their head out from a crevice, mouth agape, sometimes with a pair of cleaner shrimp picking at their teeth or cleaning their scales. There are a number of moray eels present in UAE waters.

Snowflake moray *Echidna nebulosa*
Origin of dorsal fin just anterior to gill slit. Light grey to whitish with irregular black blotches giving mottled or dappled effect; smaller yellow spots and irregular, broken black bars, most distinct sub-laterally. Frequents shallow inshore coral reefs and rocky headlands. 75 cm.

Moray eel *Gymnothorax favagineus*
Elongate with oval body section. Light grey, with irregular darker blotches. On coral reefs, offshore wrecks and other structures. Predator and scavenger, feeding on small fish and crustaceans.
200 cm.

185

MYLIOBATIDAE
EAGLE RAYS

Moderate to large sized, often found close inshore in shallow water. Often leap clear of the water, which sometimes causes them to be confused with larger manta ray. Feed on small fish, crustaceans and molluscs which they crush with their powerful jaws and grinding teeth. Long whip-like tail carries a barbed spine which can inflict a painful wound if stood on or handled. Fishermen working the shores on the east coast normally discard these handsome fish. Body disc-shaped with raised head and eyes set to the sides rather than on top, giving the appearance of a 'dolphin-like marine mammal' rather than a fish. Pectorals fused along sides of head and pectoral flap united below snout forming rostral lobe. Five small gill openings to underside of disc. White underside and dark brownish-grey dorsally, one with large profuse pale spots. *Aetomyleus nichofii, Aetobatus narinari, Rhinoptera javanica* .

Eagle ray *Aetomyleus nichofii*
Brown or mottled, long whip tail, prominent head and pointed wings. Occurs in open water over sandy substrate where it feeds on molluscs, small fish and crustaceans. Disc 150 cm.

Spotted Eagle ray *Aetobatus narinari*
Large spots, long whip tail, prominent head and pointed wings. Occurs in open water over sandy substrate. A bottom and mid-water fish feeding on molluscs, small fish and crustaceans. Disc 175 cm.

Java cownose ray *Rhinoptera javanica*
Brown or mottled, long whip tail, prominent head and pointed wings. Open water over sandy substrate, feeds on crustaceans and squid. Disc 150 cm.

NEMIPTERIDAE
THREADFIN BREAMS AND SPINECHEEKS

The threadfin breams are generally fairly small, slightly compressed fish with a small mouths at the tip of the snout. They include several species that are found in quite deep water, beyond diving range.

Japanese Threadfin Bream *Nemipterus japonicus*
Pinkish to red; one to three yellow lines above lateral line, bright yellow on ventral surface; elongate filament to upper caudal lobe. Can be confused with *N. metopias*, which occurs in the Gulf of Oman and has similar caudal filament and a bright orange band from upper jaw to eye but lacks the pattern of lateral yellow lines on the main body. Shallow coastal waters, often near reefs. 32 cm.

Delgoa Threadfin Bream *Nemipterus delagoae*
Pinkish to red with silvery sheen: scale rows ascend obliquely on sides. Inshore shallow water near reefs. 30 cm.

Arabian Threadfin Bream *Scolopsis ghanam*
Pretty, distinctively marked fish, with olive to brown back and silvery sides; 2-3 dark horizontal variegated lines along the back with a pattern of small black spots on the lower flanks, up as far as the curved lateral line. Dorsal fin long with ten spinous filaments to front. Eyes large and set forward. On inshore reefs and creeks. Feeds on crustaceans and small fish. This is one of the prettiest and commonest fishes found on inshore reefs, and easily seen whilst snorkelling. It lives amongst the coral and rocks, often in groups of several fish. 25 cm.

Threadfin bream *Nemipterus tolu*
Reddish pink with indistinct darker random blotches dorsally. Upper lobe of caudal fin extended. 30 cm.

Threadfin bream *Scolopsis ruppelli*
Dark olive to creamy flanks, with prominent dark patch below base of dorsal fin. 35 cm.

PLATACIDAE
BATFISH

The batfish's body is highly compressed and deep. Young batfish have long dorsal and ventral fins which shorten as the batfish grows into an adult.

Round Batfish *Platax orbicularis*
Grey to black dorsally, rounded and laterally compressed. Darker greyish-black vertical bands through head and pectorals, with third band more diffuse. Large extended soft dorsal and ventral fins especially in young forms. On coral reefs and offshore structures. Grazes on sea weed. Inquisitive and friendly towards scuba divers, often in large groups. Occasionally seen on shallower reefs accessible to snorkellers. 50 cm.

Long-finned Batfish *Platax teira*
Deep-bodied, compressed, silvery with three broad vertical bars through eye, pectoral fins and across dorsal and ventral fins. Often seen in shoals adjacent to reefs and offshore structures. 30 cm.

The bat fish, Platax orbicularis is often found swimming near ship-wrecks or shallow rocks.

PLOTOSIDAE
EEL CATFISHES

One of 30 families of catfishes (Siluriformes), the Plotosidae is one of only two truly marine species. Both Ariidae and Plotosidae are each represented in UAE waters by one species. Plotosid catfishes are known as eel catfishes because of their highly elongate, tapered shape, with extended second dorsal and ventral fins joining with the caudal fin to form the pointed tip of the tail. Superficially can be confused with goatfish due to their habit of probing the sandy bottom, on seagrass beds and over reefs.

187

A juvenile yellowbar angelfish,
Pomacanthus
maculosis

Striped eel catfish *Plotosus lineatus*
Chocolate-brown with two prominent whitish stripes above and below the eye, from snout to tail. Sides brown, with silvery white underbelly. Juveniles are darker with yellowish stripes. The separate first dorsal and pectoral spines are serrated and venomous, and should be regarded as potentially dangerous. Not very common. *P. anguilaris* and *P. arab* are synonyms. 30 cm.

POMACANTHIDAE
ANGELFISHES

Angelfishes are among the most attractive of the shallow-water reef fishes in the UAE. They are laterally compressed and somewhat triangular in profile. Their young have markedly different colour

patterns to the adult forms and are often mistaken as different species. Angelfishes generally eat sponges and are frequently found around underwater structures or wrecks to which these invertebrates have attached.

Emperor Angelfish *Pomacanthus imperator*
Beautifully marked fish, with bright yellow longitudinal stripes over a blue-brown background, marginally blue. Eyes masked. Mouth small with comb-like teeth. Juveniles dark blue with whitish whorl marking. Found around sponge encrusted rocks and corals. 40 cms.

Yellowbar Angelfish *Pomacanthus maculosis*
Dark blue, with electric blue edges to fins; vertical yellowish bar on flanks, tail fin bright yellow with orangey-brown spots. Shoulder mottled with dark blue-

black streaks. Strong spine to lower edge of cheek below gill cover. Long dorsal and ventral fins. Found on coral reefs, inshore structures, wrecks and outcrops. Grazes on sponges, algae and crustaceans. This colourful inhabitant of the coral reefs is the most common and largest of the angelfish in UAE waters. 45 cm.

POMACENTRIDAE
DAMSELFISHES

The Pomacentridae is a large family of small, often colourful fishes associated mainly with coral reefs, wrecks and rocky headlands. Deep compressed body shape, small mouths either conical or incisiform teeth, lacking teeth on the roof of the mouth. Scales moderately large and ctenoid. Territorial and aggressive as demonstrated in UAE waters particularly by the clownfishes. Damselfishes lay elliptical demersal eggs which are guarded by the parental male. The young of many species are brightly coloured in shades of blue, yellow and orange.

Sergeant major *Abudefduf saxatilis*
Yellowish-green to bluish dorsally, shading to silvery-white, with five broad black bars, the first from front of the dorsal to upper base of pectoral fin, and the last on the caudal peduncle. Shallow-water species usually forming colonies on reefs, rocky headlands and harbours. One of the commonest and most prolific of the damselfishes on UAE coral reefs. 10 - 18 cm.

Scissortail sergeant *Abudefduf sexfasciatus*
Bluish dusky-green dorsally shading to greyish white ventrally, with five black bars which broaden dorsally. Last bar at caudal fin base joins a sub-marginal black oblique bar in upper lobe of caudal fin. Similar and opposite marginal bar on lower lobe disconnected. 19.5 cm.

Domino *Dascyllus trimaculatus*
Dusky black with centre of scales brownish. Whitish spot or blotch above lateral line below and between VIII and IX dorsal rays. Juveniles have more pronounced larger white spot and another on forehead. Young associated with anemones and branching corals. 14 cm.

Violet damselfish *Pomacentrus sindensis*
Head and body dark violet, paling to underside. Scales on back and sides with lighter blue central spot, giving appearance of

longitudinal lines laterally. Operculum with obscure light blue lines and dots. Dorsal and caudal fins posteriorly marginate canary-yellow. Caudal fin deeply emarginate, upper lobe pronounced. Very common in Arabian Gulf. *Pristotis jerdoni* is a synonym. 13 cm.

Clark's clownfish *Amphiprion clarkii*
Colourful dark brownish-black fishes with two broad white vertical bars. Head and mouth bright orange, with orangey-yellow fins. Juveniles yellow not brown, and could be misidentified as *A. bicinctus* which occurs in the Red Sea and Gulf of Aden. Clownfishes have a symbiotic relationship with the giant sea anemones *Stoichactis* and *Radianthus* found on coral reefs. They are territorial and fiercely protective of their homes and in spite of their diminutive size will attempt to chase off any snorkellers or divers who get too close. 12 cm.

The two-bar anemonefish or clownfish, Amphiprion bicinctus, *is not stung by the anemone's tentacles.*

A white-spotted shovelnose ray, Rhynchobatus djiddensis.

PSETTODIDAE
TOOTHED FLOUNDERS

A member of the order Pleuronectiformes, or flatfishes, this family contains a single species, the Queensland halibut, also known as the oriental halibut. Unlike most flatfishes, the asymmetry is less pronounced and individuals may be left or right handed. Spines in dorsal and pelvic fins.

Oriental halibut *Psettodes erumei*

Dark brown eyes normally ranged right on top of head but can be to left or right side; white to viscous underbelly; large mouth with sharp teeth and powerful jaws. Offshore in deeper water, over mixed bottom and on sand near reefs. Predatory on small fish and crustaceans. 60 cm.

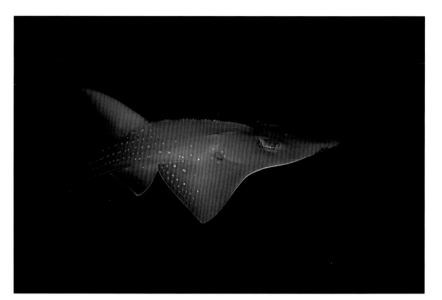

RACHYCENTRIDAE
COBIA OR LEMON FISH

Represented by a single species. Cobias are powerful fish, highly regarded by anglers. Excellent eating and fetch a high price at market. Normally caught commercially on lines.

Cobia or lemon fish *Rachycentron canadus*

Streamlined body, with distinctive bands of black and creamy-grey. Head broad and flat, powerful underslung jaw. Series of short spines precede dorsal fin. Superficially similar to the remora excluding sucker disc on head. Inhabits wrecks and reefs. A predator on fish, even larger specimens. A specimen of 22 kgs taken trolling between Chicago Beach and Jebel Ali had consumed an 45 cm black-tip reef shark. Also feeds on crustaceans and cuttlefish. 180 cm.

RHINOBATIDAE
SAND SHARKS, SHOVELNOSE RAY OR GUITARFISH

Sand sharks or guitarfish have a body shape between that of sharks and rays; male possesses claspers as in rays. Mouth on underside, powerful jaws, translucent nose. Dorsum varies from few spots to heavily spotted with fairly large tubercles. Larger specimens offshore. Also off beaches and shoreline, on sandy bottom near reefs. Feed on fish, cuttlefish and crustaceans. They are powerful and voracious bottom-dwelling predators which are not however considered dangerous. *Rhinobatis annulatus, Rhynchobatus djiddensis, Rhinobatus granulatus.*

Guitarfish *Rhinobatis annulatus*

Depressed body, sandy-brown, frequently with blueish grey spots; pointed, flattened, semi-translucent snout. High, distinctive first dorsal well behind pelvic fins. 150 cm.

White-spotted shovelnose ray *Rhynchobatus djiddensis*

Depressed body, dark greyish-brown with scattered white ocelli forming regular lines laterally. Translucent snout, narrow and produced. Disc elongate and powerful; first dorsal opposite pelvic fins. More common than *R. annulatus*. Predator on fish, cuttlefish and crustaceans. 300 cm.

Granulated guitarfish
Rhinobatos granulatus
Arabic name: *Sous*
Depressed body, sandy-brown; pointed, flattened, semi-translucent snout. High, distinctive first dorsal well behind pelvic fins. 200 cm.

SCARIDAE
PARROTFISHES
Parrotfish have remarkable beak-like mouths with horny fused teeth, which they use to scrape algae from rocks and coral. Graceful swimmers, they can often be observed on inshore shallow reefs and around breakwaters.

Parrotfish *Scarus scaber*
Brightly coloured, large scales; blunt head with characteristic parrot-like beak. Small eyes set high on forehead. Colouration variegated blues, greens and pinks. Mature males with orange wash and blue markings, often with striking blue borders to fins. On coral reefs, rocky outcrops and harbours, where it grazes on algae, crustaceans and molluscs. 100 cm.

SCOMBRIDAE
TUNAS AND MACKEREL
Most species in this family of medium to large size fish form large schools and feed in mid-water where they hunt fish or feed on planktonic forms. They are important commercial fish, generally caught in nets.

cf. Scarus psittacus
photographed at the
Umm Shaif oil field

191

Bearded scorpionfish, Scorpaenopsis gibbosa.

Frigate mackerel or frigate tuna *Auxis thazard* Arabic name: *Tabban*

Dorsum black-blue to metallic green with darker oblique bands. Silvery-grey to white below lateral. Spinous first dorsal deeply concave with 12 spines. Pelagic but also comes close inshore where it hunts in shoals for small fish, shrimp, and cuttlefish. 100 cm.

Eastern Little Tuna, Bonito or kawkawa *Euthynnus affinis* Arabic name: *Sadah*

Dorsum black-blue to metallic green with darker oblique bands. Silvery-grey to white below lateral; several large dark spots can be present between pelvic and pectoral fins. Spinous first dorsal deeply concave with 12 spines and more extended than *A. thazard*. Common off both coastlines, pelagic but also comes close inshore where it hunts in shoals for small fish and shrimp. 100 cm.

Narrow-barred Spanish mackerel or kingfish *Scomberomorus commerson* Arabic name: *Chana'd, Khabbat.*

Dorsum black-blue to metallic green with numerous vertical variegated bands. Silvery-grey to white below lateral. Spinous first dorsal; second dorsal and ventral fins pointed. Pelagic but smaller specimens also close inshore, especially in strong tidal flows. Shoal predator, feeding on fish, shrimp and cuttlefish. 200 cm.

Yellowfin tuna *Thunnus albacares*

Dorsum black-blue to metallic green with golden-yellow laterally. Dorsal and ventral fins bright yellow. Larger specimens develop elongate second dorsal and ventral fins. Generally small fish in Arabian Gulf to 10 kgs, whilst up to 30 kgs off east coast. Oceanic pelagic shoal predator, feeding on fish, shrimp, and cuttlefish. 195 cm.

SCORPAENIDAE
SCORPION OR LIONFISH

Lionfish like shaded areas and caves, and divers often observe them upside down or moving gracefully in vertical loops. Their fin spines are venomous and should never be handled. They can give a nasty sting, although they are not as dangerous as the stone fish. Other smaller bottom-dwelling scorpion fish are duller in colour with remarkable pectoral fins which have the appearance of scallop shells, adding to their superb camouflage. *Pterois miles,* Indian lionfish; *Pterois russelli,* Russell's lionfish; and *Synanceia verrucosa,* common stonefish.

Russell's lionfish *Pterois russelli*

Striking, distinctive body shape and colouration. Spots absent from fins (present in *P. volitans,* closely related species which also occurs in UAE). First dorsal fin filamentous. Eyes high set, and head and body feature striking vertical bars of alternate reddish-brown, ochre and brown. On coral reefs,

The rabbitfish,
Siganus rivulatus
*feeds on benthic algae
and is often seen
resting like this,
particularly during
night dives.*

rocky reefs, in caves and around other structures. Feeds on small fish and crustaceans. 45 cm.

Stonefish *Synanceia verrucosa*
Large pectoral fins look like scallop shells. Head carbuncles and filamentous. Spinous first dorsal fin. Relatively uncommon but highly camouflaged, often resting on top of rocks, unseen by divers. Occurs inshore on coral reefs and rocky substrates where it feeds on small fish and crustaceans. Poisonous and considered dangerous, particularly if touched inadvertently by swimmers or

snorklers. Scorpion fish, which are similar but less venomous, are sometimes confused with the rarer stonefish, but should also be treated with respect and left well alone. 38 cm.

SERRANIDAE
GROUPERS OR SEA BASS
The groupers are resident hunters on many reefs and include among their numbers the giant groupers of man-eating proportions, up to 3 m long and weighing almost half a ton in weight! The largest recorded from the southern

193

gulf, taken off the Musandam in 1977, was 180 cm long and weighed 178 kg. The more familiar groupers in shallow waters around the UAE's coastlines are much smaller however, generally around 30 to 50 cms in length. Nearly all groupers begin life as females and change to males if there is space for them in the social hierarchy. This maximises reproductive efficiency since a single male will fertilise the eggs of many females.

Halfspotted grouper *Cephalopholis hemistiktos*
Brightly coloured grouper, ranging from orangey-brown to red with multitude of blue and whitish spots on body and fins. Pale yellowish blotch on upper caudal peduncle. Powerful jaws often used for scraping crustaceans and small molluscs from rocks as well as attacking fish. On coral reefs and rocky outcrops where it hunts for small fish, crustaceans and molluscs. Often easily viewed on inshore reefs on the east coast from Khorfakkan to Dibba, but appear olive-brown underwater, although the lighter blotch near the tail is distinctive. Normally disappear quickly under the nearest coral branches or rocks at the approach of swimmers. 25 cm.

Coral grouper *Cephalopholis miniata*
Background colour is bright orange-red to red-brown, covered by a fairly even distribution of blue spots on head and body. Young fish can be more yellow. On coral reefs and rocky outcrops. feeds on small fish, crustaceans and molluscs. 50 cm.

Tawina grouper or hamour *Epinephelus tauvina*
Heavily spotted mottled reddish-brown over olive-brown with bars and blotches of deeper ochre. Large powerful jaws. Long dorsal fin with 10 spinous rays. Ventral and caudal fins convex. Found around inshore reefs, wrecks and offshore structures where it feeds on fish, cuttlefish and crustaceans. This grouper, one of several species known as hamour in the fish souks, is the most common of the groupers found locally, and is highly prized as a food fish. 180 cm.

Brownspotted grouper or hamour *Epinephelus chlorostigma = Serranus angularis*
Olive brown to whitish, darker dorsally, with numerous close-set dark-brown spots on body and fins. Ventral fin angular, caudal fin straight and slightly emarginate. Can be confused with *E. areolatus* . 100 cm.

Areolate grouper *Epinephelus areolatus*
Pale reddish-brown dorsally to whitish with numerous brown to brownish-yellow spots, not so close-set as *E. chlorostigma* .

SIGANIDAE
RABBITFISH
An unusual feature in rabbitfish is that their pelvic fins are formed by two spines, one at each end, and three soft rays between these. They also have dorsal and ventral rays so are well protected, especially so since their rays are venomous. Despite these features, rabbitfish are regarded by local people as one of the finest fish in the sea.

Rabbitfish *Siganus canaliculatus* Arabic name: *sigan*
Light brown or greenish-blue, silvery belly. Dark blotch behind upper gill cover, and body heavily spotted with large pale, silvery-white spots. 15 cm.

Javan Rabbitfish *Siganus javus* Arabic name: *sigan*
Greenish-brown with silvery-grey belly. Heavily spotted with large pale, silvery-white spots and stripes and horizontally regulated blotches. 15 cm.

SPARIDAE
SEABREAMS
Seabreams are related to snapper and threadfin breams and have spiny fins and sharp incisor like teeth at the front of the jaw, whilst strong teeth at the sides of the jaws are adapted for crushing molluscs and other similar food items.

Opposite page:
The great white shark is an Indian ocean species that is a rare visitor to UAE waters, mainly on the east coast. It has not been recorded inshore.

Two-bar bream *Mylo bifasciatus*
Silvery-grey with two broad stripes on the head, interspersed with bright silver. Prominent dark spotted scales and strong lateral line. Dorsal, caudal and pectoral fins bright yellow. Inshore coral reefs, islands and structures. Feeds on molluscs, crustaceans and algae. Another relatively common reef fish which can be observed around harbour walls and rocks in the Arabian Gulf. Common on coral reefs between Khorfakkan and Dibba, particularly Sandy Beach Island and along Dibba Bay where some reefs accessible from the beaches offer safe inshore snorkelling. 30 cm.

SPHYRAENIDAE
BARRACUDAS
Barracudas have a partially-deserved reputation for being fearsome and attacking anything smaller than themselves. Slim, very elongated fishes, they have a powerful underslung jaw with rows of needle-sharp teeth, spinous first dorsal, and paired second dorsal and ventral fins. In the UAE, barracuda frequent the creeks and inshore reefs, as well as free-ranging offshore. Larger fish may swim as solitary individuals, but also hunt in groups. Some of the smaller species and juveniles swim in quite large schools.

Yellowtail barracuda *Sphyraena flavicauda*
Slim, streamlined. Green dorsally, silvery with two longitudinal stripes laterally. 2-3 gill rakers on first arch. Offshore and inshore reefs, structures and in creeks. Predator and scavenger on fish and crustaceans. 50 cm.

Blackfin barracuda *Sphyraena qenie*
Slim, streamlined. Green dorsally, silvery with darker vertical bar chevron-shaped bars. Lateral line pores. Offshore and inshore reefs, structures and creeks. Predator and scavenger, feeding on fish and cuttlefish. 125 cm

Great barracuda *Sphyraena barracuda*
Slim, streamlined. Blue-black dorsally, silvery with darker vertical bar chevron-shaped bars. Lateral line pores. Spinous first dorsal. Powerful underslung jaw with rows of needle-sharp teeth. Larger specimens solitary and considered potentially dangerous. Offshore reefs, and structures, open sea. Predator and scavenger on fish and cuttlefish. 200 cm.

SPHYRNIDAE
HAMMERHEAD SHARKS
One of the larger sharks in the Arabian Gulf and east coast. Two species present. Head characteristically flattened and expanded to form hammer-shape. Eyes positioned on the extremities of the head lobes. Both species considered potentially dangerous, but rarely found inshore. Occasional seasonal sightings of large numbers of hammerhead off Ras al-Khaima, and east of Abu Dhabi.

Great Hammerhead *Sphyrna mokarran*
Front margin of head median indentation. Trailing margins of pelvic fins concave. This is a migratory species that may visit UAE waters whilst on-passage. Feeds on other sharks, rays, fish, squid and crabs. Generally accompanied by a flotilla of pilot fish. 600 cm.

SYNGNATHIDAE
PIPEFISHES AND SEAHORSES
Pipefishes and seahorses are small fishes whose bodies are encased in bony rings. Distantly related to the cornetfishes, they also have tubular snouts and small mouths, very small gill openings and no spines in the fins. The caudal fin is absent from the seahorses and a number of the pipefishes; the seahorses using their tail as a prehensile organ. Well-developed spiny projections on the head and body, including two conspicuous ones on the top of the head. Colour variable. Found on seagrass beds and coral reefs. The vertical orientation of the seahorses' body and horizontal position of the head is unique. Eggs are reared by the male in a ventral brood area. They feed on tiny crustaceans drawn in through their mouth with a rapid intake of wate. Pipefishes and seahorses of

the Arabian Gulf in general are not well-known taxonomically, but the following may be present in UAE waters. *Hippocampus histrix*, Thorny seahorse; *Hippocampus kuda*, spotted seahorse; *Sygnathus analaricens*, pipefish.

SYNODONTIDAE
LIZARDFISHES

Elongated body, almost cylindrical. Adipose fin present. Mouth large and terminal, numerous small needle-like teeth. Feeds on small fish and intertebrates. Frequent shallow, sandy areas, particularly adjacent to structures, rocks and reefs. *Saurida undosquamis, Saurida tumbil.*

THERAPONIDAE
THERAPONS

Pretty, small bass-like fishes with oblong slightly compressed bodies. Mouth moderate. Single soft rayed dorsal separated by notch, spinous anteriorly. Generally found in shallow and brackish water. *Therapon theraps, Therapon puta.*

TETRAODONTIDAE
PUFFER FISH

Short, stout-bodied fishes. Fused teeth form powerful beak. Gill plate absent, only small slit. Matching soft-rayed dorsal and ventral fins. Skin below lateral line covered with small spines or naked. Pelvic fin absent, pectorals rounded. Caudal fin rounded and truncate. These curious little fish have powerful beak-like jaws for crushing molluscs and crustaceans. Often caught off piers and breakwaters, and should be handled carefully. When alarmed, they blow themselves up like small balloons and make a loud squeaking noise! Although some species are considered a delicacy in other parts of the world, most have highly poisonous livers, and should be left well alone!

Puffer fish *Lagocephalus lunaris*
Olive-green dorsally through yellow to white underbelly. Body sub-cylindrical, smooth, tough skin covered on belly by small spines. Dorsal and

The giant, or black-spotted puffer fish, Arothron stellatus.

ventral fins soft and opposite each other; used by the fish for directional control. Pectoral fins round, pelvic fins absent. Common inshore over soft ground and around reefs. Feeds on small fish, crustaceans and molluscs. 24 cm.

Spotted puffer *Arothron stellatus*
Pale yellowish-brown dorsally to creamy-white under, profuse darker brown spots cover body and fins. Paired dorsal and ventral fins, broad convex caudal fin. Slow moving, docile fish found on coral reefs, structures, wrecks and rocky outcrops. Feeds on crustaceans and molluscs. 50 cm.

197

TORPEDINIDAE
ELECTRIC RAY

Torpedo rays are bottom-dwelling species, with rounded flattened disc and fleshy tail. Paired electric organs behind the large spiracles can produce a severe electric shock when touched and are used both as protection and to numb or kill their prey. Normally found in shallow coastal water over soft sand or shingle substrate. Relatively uncommon in UAE waters.

Mottled electric ray *Torpedo panthera*
Circular disc, broader than long; caudal fin triangular, truncate. Spiracles almost as large as eyes. Mottled reddish-brown variegated lines and darker blotches. Separate paired fins also speckled. Can give powerful shock. Uncommon. Inshore sandy areas near reefs. Feeds on crustaceans and small fish. 60 cm.

MARINE MAMMALS

Robert Baldwin

THE STUDY OF WHALES AND DOLPHINS is a relatively new subject in the UAE and many recorded species come from single brief sightings or dead animals washed ashore. However, the richly diverse and productive seas of both the east and west coasts provide suitable habitat for many more cetaceans than had previously been expected to occur here. Perhaps a third of the 80 known species of whales and dolphins, or cetaceans as they are collectively called, may occur off the shores of the United Arab Emirates. Some are far more common than others and many, such as the shy beaked whales, have yet to be confirmed in UAE waters but are thought to occur here due to sightings in neighbouring Oman, or simply due to their known habitat preferences. The deep underwater canyons and cliffs on the edge of the continental shelf off UAE's east coast is where most species can be found, including deep water cetaceans like the mighty sperm whale (Physeter macrocephalus) and the Risso's dolphin (Grampus griseus). The warm, sandy shallows of the Arabian Gulf are in strong contrast to the east coast environment, and host some species adapted for shallow water life, such as the Indo-Pacific humpback dolphin (Sousa chinensis) and the rare finless porpoise (Neophocaena phocaenoides). Many other species are at home in either environment.

WATCHING WHALES AND DOLPHINS

Whale and dolphin watching requires considerable patience, as well as luck, and many cetaceans, if they choose, barely create a ripple upon surfacing to breathe. Dolphins are easier to find than the bigger whales, as they are more common, tend to be in larger groups and surface more frequently. Usually, whales will surface just a few times, then disappear underwater for 10 to 30 minutes, or possibly for as long as an hour, and are easily missed. The lack of thorough study of the UAE's cetaceans leaves us with many uncertainties about the occurrence and identification of some species, and the keen-eyed whale and dolphin watcher could be rewarded with the discovery of new records for the area.

It is possible to view whales and dolphins in the UAE's waters most of the year, although a choppy sea provides remarkably good cover for an arching back and dorsal fin of even the largest of whales. Conditions are ideal in the UAE from late March to July, when the sea-surface is calm although the humidity and temperatures in May and June can be uncomfortable. However, whale and dolphin watching can be rewarding at almost any time. Only the northerly winter winds, or 'Shamal', of December to February are likely to create viewing difficulties.

Early mornings and evenings are usually the best times to look for cetaceans, as the sea is often calmer and the light better. They can be found any zshore, whereas whales are more often found well offshore. It is possible to watch some cetaceans from the land, including both whales and dolphins. Most likely to be seen are the bottlenose and Indo-Pacific humpback dolphins. Far better, however, is to venture slowly out to sea by boat, sit back, wait, watch and listen.

It is possible to hear the blow of a whale from quite a distance, even before you have seen it. Listen too, for splashes. The thunderous sound of a breaching whale can carry over a couple of kilometres and whales in such a mood have been sighted from as far away as 8 to 10 kms. On days when the sea is calm, however, the general atmosphere created by the quiet, glassy water often pervades through schools of dolphins and whale pods, which loll peacefully on the surface, allowing boats to approach to within a few metres. On occasion whales 10 to 12m long have slowly swum under boatloads of onlookers, providing captivating and memorable close-up views as they surface nearby.

With experience, whales and dolphins become easier to locate by eye. At first, you may find yourself surprisingly close to a large school of dolphins before you notice them. Keep a sharp eye out for the dark hump of a dolphin's back and any dark, floating mass, that may be a resting whale. Regular splashes and areas of disturbed water may well be caused by whales or dolphins. A pair of binoculars will help to confirm that distant splashes are caused by them, and not fishes like sailfish or marlin. Tell-tale signs also include sunlight glinting off the wet, sheeny surface of an arching back and flocking seabirds, which may betray schools of feeding dolphins.

Spinner dolphins.

BALEEN WHALES

The mysticetes, commonly known as baleen whales, are a small group of just eleven species worldwide, most of which are large whales. Of three families, the largest is the Balaenopteridae, consisting of six species, at least four of which may be found in UAE waters. They range in size from the Bryde's whale *(Balaenoptera edeni)* with a maximum recorded length of 14m, to the enormous blue whale *(Balaenoptera musculus)* with a pre-whaling era maximum of 31m. A female blue whale of this size could weigh over 130 tonnes at the end of the feeding season, making it by far the largest animal ever to have lived on earth, dwarfing even the extinct dinosaurs. Two other species of baleen whale, the sei whale *(Balaenoptera borealis)* and the minke whale *(Balaenoptera acutorostrata)* are thought to occur in UAE waters but have yet to be confirmed.

201

DESCRIPTIONS OF THE BALEEN WHALES

Blue whale
(*Balaenoptera musculus*)
Family Balaenopteridae
This enormous whale, named after the silvery blue sheen of its mottled skin, frequently exceeds 25m in length and may weigh well over 100 tonnes. It is probable that it is represented by the pygmy race of the species, the pygmy blue whale - a misleading name as individuals may still exceed 21m in length. A single ridge runs along the top of the broad head from the snout to the blowholes. The dorsal fin looks disproportionately small and is situated very far back on the body towards the tail - features that help to distinguish it from other baleen whales. The tail is often lifted on diving. It is a pelagic species that often enters shallow water regions. The blue whale's range in the UAE, as evidenced by skeletons found along the coast and unconfirmed sightings, includes the Arabian Gulf and probably the Gulf of Oman.

The blue whale moves through the water with sleek grace, belying its gigantic mass, which equates to the mass of 30 bull elephants. With arteries large enough for a child to crawl along, even new-born calves can be seven metres long and may weigh more than 2.5 tonnes. On a diet of 600 litres of nutrient-rich milk a day, the blue whale calf grows rapidly, at a rate of over 500 kgs a week. After six or seven months the calf is weaned, but its habit of taking huge meals hardly dwindles. In the Southern Ocean, adult blue whales may swallow over four tonnes, (four million individuals) of their favourite food, the shrimp-like krill, every day. Today, the UAE's blues are among less than 5,000 whales of this species in the northern hemisphere.

Fin whale
(*Balaenoptera physalus*)
Family Balaenopteridae
Second in size only to the blue whale, the largest fin whale recorded in waters of the Emirates near Jebel Ali measured nearly 20m in length. It is slender looking compared to the blue whale and capable of travelling at great speeds, perhaps exceeding 30 km/h. Recognisable by the asymmetrical colour pattern peculiar to this species. A pattern of white pigment extends from the undersides of the whale over the right lower jaw and into the mouth, sometimes even spreading as far as the upper right jaw. The coloration pattern is also borne by the baleen: the first third of the plates on the right side are white. The rest of the body is dark grey. Like the blue, sei and minke whales, with which the fin can be mistaken, there is a single ridge running along the top of the head from snout to blowholes.

Known as an open-ocean dweller, this species also swims into coastal areas and often enters shallow regions to breed. Fin whales usually feed in polar regions, although those of the UAE may be an exception. Its range includes both the Gulf of Oman and the Arabian Gulf, where it may enter very shallow water leading to occasional strandings.

Bryde's whale
(*Balaenoptera edeni*)
Family Balaenopteridae
Those observed in the UAE have measured about 10m in length, but this species may reach 14m. Subtle grey mottling covers the broad back on the otherwise dark skin. It is almost identical to the sei whale in appearance, but can be distinguished by three prominent ridges that run in parallel along the top of the rostrum back to the blowholes. The central of the three ridges is the most pronounced, and the only one present in sei, minke, blue and fin whales. Circular dish-sized scars are the result of cookie-cutter sharks that attack the whales, taking bites out of the flesh on the back and tailstock. The dorsal fin is pointed and curves backward, set about two thirds of the way back along the body. The tail is rarely seen, as it is not lifted on diving as in other species such as the humpback, and the flippers are small and may go unnoticed. Like the minke, however, Bryde's whales in the UAE may approach a boat quite closely, and there may be the added attraction of a glimpse of a calf, as this species seems to breed here. Its normal habitat is warm, preferably deep,

water. In the UAE it probably feeds on small shoaling fish. Its range may include the Gulf of Oman, although it has only been seen in the Arabian Gulf.

Humpback whale

(*Megaptera novaeangliae*)

Family Balaenopteridae

So named for the way in which it arches its back on diving, can be 15 metres long and has a robust body but a relatively slim head. It is recognisable especially due to the long, slender flippers that are usually white on the undersides, with patches of white on top. The serrated tail flukes, like the belly, are also white on the undersides and frequently lifted clear of the water prior to diving. The broad back is usually a slate grey colour. A close view will enable one to observe the characteristic fleshy knobs on the head, called "tuberosities". There are similar bumps on the flippers and a series of small knobs behind the dorsal fin. Feeds on small fish in Arabian waters, entering very shallow coastal waters to do so. However, they also occur well offshore. There are no confirmed records of this species in the Arabian Gulf and only two recent records on the UAE east coast. Development and the use of fishing nets has probably caused an irreversible decline in the population and its former range.

TOOTHED WHALES AND DOLPHINS

Toothed whales and dolphins, the odontocetes, are smaller, on average, than the baleen whales, but far more numerous, including at least 67 species. Those found off the UAE show a remarkable diversity of size, form and behaviour, from the tiny finless porpoise, well under two metres in length, which finds retreat in coastal shallows, to the colossal, deep water sperm whale that may exceed 50 tonnes and grow to 20 metres, the largest toothed whale of the UAE and indeed the entire world.

Details of the remarkable sonar system of the odontocetes remain a mystery. No man-made sonar system even approaches its sophistication and complexity. This extraordinary sensory mechanism can allow some dolphins,

Sperm whale.

for example, to discriminate between almost identical objects, too similar to be distinguished by sight alone, and over distances at which the sense of sight would anyway be ineffectual. This they can do in a noisy environment and can whistle, communicate with other dolphins and echolocate at the same time. They can also emit exploratory beams at right angles to the main beam and can echolocate on near and distant targets simultaneously. Even more impressive is their ability to analyse the sounds, compare them for subtle differences, process and interpret them in the large portion of the brain set aside for this, and respond accordingly. As sound travels over four and a half times faster in water than in air and because the dolphins may be performing these tasks whilst in high-speed pursuit of fleeing prey, all this must be done in a matter of seconds.

203

DESCRIPTIONS OF THE TOOTHED WHALES AND DOLPHINS

Finless porpoise
(*Neophocaena phocaenoides*)
Family Phocoenidae
As its common name implies, the most obvious distinguishing feature of the finless porpoise is the lack of a dorsal fin. Otherwise, it is similar in shape to the other five species of porpoise found elsewhere in the world, with a blunt head, small flippers and notched tail flukes. Finless porpoises are small, measuring well under 2m at adulthood. They are a uniform grey colour, with a ridge along the back and many tiny bumps on the back and on the back of the head. They surface in an irregular pattern, appearing slow on the surface, but underwater they move at some speed.
Hunts in the shallow water channels that weave their way between the sandbanks and mangrove-lined islands so typical of the western UAE waters

Humpback dolphin.

of Arabian Gulf. This region provides cover for the secretive habits of the finless porpoise, whose habitat in the rest of the Arabian Gulf and elsewhere in the world has been drastically reduced. The species range is extremely limited and a single record of a dead animal found on the island of Murawah in western UAE waters is all that is known of the species in this country.

The tiny bumps, called 'tubercles', that line a ridge along the adult's back are thought to provide grip for calves, which are reputedly carried by their parents. This behaviour is unknown in any other cetacean. Local fishermen call this species 'Fa'ima' and claim that it enters water less than a metre deep to give birth, usually at night.

Indo-Pacific humpback dolphin
(*Sousa chinensis*)
Family Delphinidae
Rarely reaches over 2.5m in length. On surfacing, the long snout is pushed out of the water and the head and body roll over in a gentle arc. Indo-Pacific humpback dolphins are most readily distinguished by the raised, fleshy hump on the back, from which the backward-curving dorsal fin rises. Body colour is uniform lead-grey, although paler and darker individuals may occur. The shape of the head bears some resemblance to that of the bottlenose dolphin, although the snout is usually more elongate and the forehead, or melon, less distinct. The Indo-Pacific humpback dolphin is one of the most frequently observed species of cetacean in the UAE, commonly in groups of between 2 and 20 individuals. They tend to be fairly shy and sedate, not easily approached by boat or underwater. This species is restricted to warm, shallow waters where it feeds, primarily over sand, but also over reefs. It is found throughout UAE Arabian Gulf waters, where the depth does not exceed 30m. Schools of over 30 animals have been sighted on more than one occasion. Smaller groups are resident in the natural and man-made channels near the city of Abu Dhabi and off beaches near Dubai. Local fishermen call this dolphin 'Dukhs'. It has not so far been recorded along the UAE east coast shores, which is odd as this species is known from Musandam.

Bottlenose dolphins.

Bottlenose dolphin

(*Tursiops truncatus*)

Family Delphinidae

Largest of the dolphins. In the UAE, some have been measured to be a little under 3m in length. Even from a fair distance, one may notice the robust head and relatively short and stubby beak, from which this dolphin gets its name. Close up, it is possible to see the clear crease that separates the beak from the bulbous forehead, or melon. Along with the Indo-Pacific humpback dolphin, the bottlenose is the only other dolphin likely to be seen regularly from land. It is bulkier and usually a darker colour than the Indo-Pacific humpback dolphin.

Larger adults often bear white or pinkish scars from aggressive behaviour. Typically in groups of about 5-35 individuals, bottlenose dolphins are fast, powerful swimmers often riding the bow wave of boats, and as their reputation in aquaria attests, they are inquisitive and playful and are capable of some spectacular aerial acrobatics. Feeds over deep water, and over sand, seagrass and reefs in shallow water. One of the commonest cetaceans in the UAE and the species most likely to be seen close to cities such as Abu Dhabi, Dubai, Sharjah and Fujairah. Those that live close inshore are relatively placid, not displaying the acrobatic energy of their slightly larger counterparts further out to sea.

The bottlenose dolphin is considered to be one of the most intelligent of cetaceans. In the UAE this is a species that will often find you, before you find it. As well as seeking human company, bottlenose dolphins also frequently swim with other species, ranging from Indo-Pacific humpback dolphins in the Arabian Gulf to sperm whales in the Gulf of Oman.

Spinner dolphin.

Spinner dolphin
(*Stenella longirostris*)
Family Delphinidae
The spinner dolphin is usually less than 2m in length, with a long, slender beak. The dark black back and top of the head are separated from the distinct white belly by a broad grey flank band. A dark stripe, runs from the flipper to the eye (the stripe runs from the flipper to the beak in the common dolphin), adding contrast to the stark white throat. The dorsal fin is relatively small and

tends to have a darker trailing edge. Look out too, for the black-tipped beak, which is a diagnostic feature. Spinner dolphins can offer hours of fun. They will frequently bowride, mounting spectacular displays of leaping, spinning and somersaulting. Their habit of leaping up to three metres in the air and spinning like a barrel, before slapping back down into the water, sets them apart from all other species and gives this dolphin its common name. Spinners often school in large numbers, groups of over 300 having been seen in UAE waters.

Spinner dolphins live well offshore in deep water, where they feed on small fishes, relying on speed, agility and social cooperation to hunt. Its presence in the Arabian Gulf was first evidenced by skulls found on UAE offshore islands in 1995. Sightings have since been made 20 kms off the city of Dubai, but its range here continues to at least 100 kms west of Abu Dhabi and stretches eastwards around the Musandam peninsula into the Indian Ocean. Fishermen of Fujairah claim to encounter it and its close relatives, the spotted dolphin (*S. attenuata*) and striped dolphin (*S. coeruleoalba*), well offshore.

Common dolphin
(*Delphinus delphis*)
Family Delphinidae
Like the spinners, common dolphins are slender and streamlined. They are slightly larger than spinners growing up to 2.5m in length. The common dolphin can be recognised by its conspicuous hourglass coloration pattern. The dark grey colour of the back extends down to the flanks as a V-shaped saddle. A distinct yellow patch in front of the saddle and grey patch behind create the hourglass effect. No other dolphin in the UAE has this colour pattern. A closer view will show a narrow dark stripe running from the flipper to the beak. Although common dolphins may bowride and leap out of the water, they do not spin. Schools of up to 100 common dolphins may be seen. The species generally inhabits deep water offshore, but may come into shallower water to the west of Abu Dhabi. Its presence in UAE waters is known only from skeletal remains discovered in western Abu Dhabi, but it is likely to be more common

off the UAE east coast. Sometimes called 'Abu Salaama' by local fishermen, a name that translates as 'Father of Peace'.

False killer whale

(*Pseudorca crassidens*)

Family Delphinidae

False killer whales have been estimated to reach a length of 6 m in the UAE, females being slightly smaller. Its name comes from the large, conical teeth which resemble quite closely those of the killer whale. Beyond this, however there is little obvious similarity. Although slightly paler underneath, the false killer whale's long, slender body is basically all black. The head is blunt and slightly bulbous and a close inspection may reveal lighter coloured patches around the eye and mouth. The dorsal fin is small for the size of the body, rounded, and curves gently backwards. Small odd-looking flippers, which are sharply curved, as if jointed by an elbow. The false killer whale is very playful, gregarious and inquisitive. The sight of a full grown whale leaping clear of the water, or riding wake and bow waves, matching even fairly powerful boats for speed and acceleration, is quite breathtaking. Snorkelling with these fantastic creatures, that may occur in pods of ten to a hundred or more in the UAE, is also thrilling. Their natural curiosity causes them to approach within touching distance, and their fixed broad smile remains imprinted in one's memory. Listen too, for their high-pitched calls.

Generally live in deep water, but will enter shallow waters at times. It takes all the ingenuity of highly organised packs of whales to locate and catch their prey of large fish, such as tuna, one of the ocean's fastest fishes. Sometimes it is easier to follow boats and take the bait off their lines - behaviour which has earned the false killer whale has a poor reputation among fishermen. It is relatively common off the UAE east coast in deep water. They also live in the Arabian Gulf waters of the UAE. False killer whales may be mistaken for the short-finned pilot whale (*Globicephala macrorhynchus*), which occurs widely in tropical latitudes and, although it has not been recorded, possibly occurs in deeper water off the UAE

Killer whale

(*Orcinus orca*)

Family Delphinidae

Biggest and most powerful of all the dolphins, it is difficult to mistake an adult killer whale for any other species. In some parts of the world they may reach 10m in length, and weigh up to eight tonnes. The black and white coloration is striking and diagnostic. The throat, chest and belly are white with patches extending onto the flanks at the rear. There is also a distinctive white, oval patch just above the eyes on the large tapered head. A creamy-grey saddle behind the dorsal fin varies in shape and size, conspicuous in some, less so in others. An adult male is unmistakable for its huge, triangular dorsal fin, sometimes 1.5m or more high. The flippers of both male and female are large and paddle-shaped. They tend to travel in close-knit family pods, that may number as many as 30.

Killer whales live in the open ocean, but will occasionally enter shallower water. Their prey in the UAE probably includes other cetaceans as well as turtles, seabirds and cold-blooded species such as fish and squid. Regular reports, mostly by pilots, of their presence in the Arabian Gulf have yet to be confirmed. However, they are found off the east coast, well out to sea.

Risso's dolphin

(*Grampus griseus*)

Family Delphinidae

A large dolphin, measuring up to 4m in length, as the Risso's dolphin dives, you may also notice the deeply incised, serrated tail flukes. The throat is very pale and there is a clear anchor-shaped, white pattern on the belly. When it surfaces close to you, the deep furrow from blowhole to snout along the forehead should be clearly noticeable. Generally a fast moving species that may come up close for a quick look at a boat, snorkeller or diver, before racing away. Although not acrobatic, this dolphin will breach and slam down in the water and often "spyhop", raising its head up to look around and view nearby boats. They also have a habit of rolling over on the surface revealing good

Sperm whale. views of the diagnostic colour patterns and markings. The scars on the body are mostly teeth marks, a result of some vigorous social interactions within the group. This is a deep water species, diving for squid and fish over underwater canyons and at the edge of the continental shelf.

Sperm whale
(*Physeter macrocephalus*)
Family Physeteridae

By far the largest of the toothed cetaceans, comparable in size to some of the UAE's baleen whales, growing to 20m in length. Sperm whales are dark grey-brown in colour, often paler around the belly, throat and mouth. The distinctively shaped head can be a third of the entire body length with a single blowhole at the very front of the blunt snout. Look out for the diagnostic blow, which shoots forward. Following a deep dive, the explosive blow of a sperm whale can be heard from quite a distance. If you are able to get close, you may notice the smooth skin of the head and the wrinkly, corrugated appearance of the rest of the body.

The dorsal fin is more of a hump than a fin, and is set well back on the body. Behind it, smaller knuckle-like lumps reach back to the tail flukes. Unlike the humpback whale, with which it may be confused from a distance, the sperm whale has broad tail flukes, with a straight edge, that are uniform in colour. Sperm whales also lack the long, white flippers and white tail markings of the humpback whale.

Individuals observed thirty nautical miles due east of Fujairah were positioned directly above the edge of the continental shelf, where the water depth suddenly changes from less than 600m to well over 1,000m. This is ideal habitat for feeding sperm whales, which may remain submerged for over an hour, hunting giant squid and other prey by use of their sonar.

Risso's dolphin. Relatively common in the deep water off the coasts of Fujairah and Sharjah, where they may appear in groups of over 30 or they may be in single pairs. They have often been seen with other species, such as sperm whales, false killer whales and bottlenose dolphins. From a distance, may be confused with female or young killer whales, which could account for some of the supposed sightings of this species in the UAE. However, the killer whale differs in that it does not have the heavily scarred appearance of the Risso's, and shows very striking black and white markings, not to mention its much larger size.

CARING FOR WHALES AND DOLPHINS

The waters of the UAE are part of the Indian Ocean Whale Sanctuary, designed to offer protection to whales and dolphins, and are of extreme importance to this group of marine mammals. Relatively little is known about whales and dolphins in the UAE and yet they have featured in the lives of local fishermen for centuries. Fishermen's stories about baleen whales not only indicate a respect for these giant sea-mammals but also include an element of fear and mystery. The jaw bones of beached whales are collected and kept as a symbol of good fortune and prosperity. On some offshore islands whale bones are erected to form the arches of doorways or are hoisted into the air and secured to a wooden framework where they are clearly visible from both land and sea. Whales and dolphins offer numerous potential economic values, including the possibility of using them as early warning signals of pollution damage and their role in the ecotourism industry. However, as elsewhere in the world, the cetaceans of the UAE are under threat.

The fishing industry, and particularly the use of nets, kills a significant number of whales and dolphins in UAE waters each year. Most at risk are species like the bottlenose dolphin, the Indo-Pacific humpback dolphin and the finless porpoise, due to their preference for shallow, coastal water where the majority of fishing takes place. Other threats include pollution from substances like oil, heavy metals, polychlorinated biphenyls (PCBs) and general litter, noise pollution from shipping traffic and other offshore industrial sounds, and coastal and offshore development, which may include land reclamation, dredging, construction of marinas, harbours, ports and other facilities. These kinds of development alter the habitat of cetaceans and may often cause their prey species to vanish from the area. In many cases the cetaceans simply move away, but this is not always possible. Alternative habitats nearby may also have been changed by new patterns of erosion and siltation created by development or may already be used for other purposes such as human recreation. The behaviour of coastal cetaceans, many of which have specific 'home ranges' may further restrict where they can go.

In the UAE the desire to conserve cetaceans and their environment has led to proposals to ensure that development and conservation go hand-in-hand. There are few other countries that have the potential to guide and command conservation measures so readily. Detailed scientific study, initiation of comprehensive management procedures, especially including the use of protected areas and regulation of fisheries activities, and co-operation with international conservation organisations will help to ensure the continued survival of the UAE's cetaceans for the benefit of both present and future generations.

Sperm whale.

209

DUGONGS

Besides whales and dolphins, the only other marine mammal that lives in the waters of the UAE is the dugong (*Dugong dugon*). The Arabian Gulf hosts the world's second largest population of dugongs, thought to number at least 5,000. Fishermen still talk of them as bearing some resemblance to human beings, particularly women. Similar beliefs can be found in many parts of the world and it is believed that it was dugongs that gave rise to the legend of the mermaid, whose plaintiff calls once lured sailors on passing ships to their deaths.

Dugong's are placed in a distinct order, the Sirenia, which they share with the Manatees, or sea cows, of the Americas. Their closest land relative, based on similarities of bone structure, is the elephant. Their ancestry is not well known, but they are generally thought of as relatively primitive mammals. In the UAE, archaeological finds including the bones of dugongs suggest that they have lived in the area for many thousands of years. Today they are still quite numerous and the Arabian Gulf hosts the world's second largest population, thought to number at least five thousand. The rich and extensive seagrass beds in the waters of the United Arab Emirates form habitat that has been identified as the most important for dugongs in the Arabian Gulf and probably includes the majority of this population. Worldwide dugongs were once far more common than they are today. Australian waters host by far the largest remaining populations, the Red Sea has a population about halve the size of that in the Arabian Gulf and the rest of the world's countries combined support even fewer than this. Having been largely ignored by scientists and conservationists, it has become clear in recent years that the dugong is now in danger of extinction. The species is tied to the waters of a relatively few countries, such as the UAE, which are vital to its continued survival.

They are relatively frequently seen in Arabian Gulf waters of the UAE (for information on their range see the descriptive notes below). Coastal development, former hunting pressure and accidental entanglement in fishing nets have probably been the root cause of population decline in the last 30 years, forcing dugongs away from areas where they were once abundant, such as the coastal waters of cities like Dubai. However, even today, it is possible to see small herds of dugongs just a few kms from Abu Dhabi, against the sky-rise backdrop of this modern, bustling capital.

Surveys have revealed that the waters of western Abu Dhabi are where most of the UAE's dugongs are found. This area is rich in marine life and is characterised by low-lying islands surrounded by shallow water with scattered coral communities and reefs, sand banks and bars that appear and disappear with the tide, together with extensive seagrass beds.

The best time to find dugongs is between April and August when the sea is still and calm. It can take a great deal of time and patience to locate dugongs, but there are certain tips that may make the task easier. They seem to travel between seagrass beds on the changing tide, using natural channels between sandy shallows. This is the time when they are most likely to be seen as they remain at the surface for longer periods of time. They are less likely to be disturbed by a slow moving boat that is travelling at a constant speed in one direction. Scan the horizon for any signs of a wet, glistening back arching to dive or the 'blow' of an exhaling dugong. Dugongs in the UAE characteristically surface two to three times at roughly 30 second intervals, before raising the tail flukes and diving for several minutes. Large individuals sometimes 'tailslap', raising the tail flukes and slapping the water with force, and 'spyhop', lifting the head and torso above the water, as if to view the surface surroundings. Binoculars are an obvious advantage for locating dugongs and polarising sunglasses help to pick out the ochre or tan coloured shape of a dugong against a blue sea. If you are travelling over seagrass beds look out for narrow tell-tale trails of bare sand about six inches wide that indicate where a dugong has been feeding. On really calm days it is sometimes possible to see a swirling disturbance at the water's surface where a dugong is about to surface, or has just dived.

Once you have located an animal or a herd, try and assess in which direction they are travelling and position yourself several hundred metres in front of them. Undisturbed, dugongs move quite slowly, travelling at less than 2km/h. However, they can swim at some speed and sensing danger, rapidly change direction underwater before surfacing at an unexpectedly great distance from where they were last seen. It is probably best to turn off the engines and keep quite still as dugongs often vanish at the first sign of potential danger. Local fishermen claim that they can hear even a rope dropping in the hull of a boat. Certainly the best sightings of dugongs have been from stationary boats that have gone undetected and the animals have come to within a few yards of thrilled enthusiasts. It is still possible to find herds of dugongs numbering over one hundred individuals in the UAE. Look out too for calves which will swim close to their mothers. A single calf, that measures about one metre at birth, is most common, but the mother-calf bond is strong and the calf may suckle for 18 months.

Dugong.

All evidence clearly points to the fact that the dugong is a species requiring special management if it is to survive. Threats to dugongs in the UAE are much the same as elsewhere in the world, including the effects of development. The greatest threat to dugongs, however, both here and worldwide, is the fishing net. Some studies have been conducted in western Abu Dhabi in an attempt to estimate the impact of fisheries on dugongs. Formerly, dugongs of the Arabian Gulf were hunted for their meat, which is considered a delicacy in many parts of the region, but this practice has been outlawed in the UAE and no evidence

Dugong.

of the continuing practice was found. However, it is unlikely that any dugongs found live in nets are released and dugong meat is still prized and eaten or sold. The number of animals caught by direct hunting methods has never been documented, but it is likely that incidental net captures equal or exceed this number. Increasing gill net fisheries, fuelled by a strong market for shark fins, may be a major cause of dugong mortality.

DESCRIPTION OF THE DUGONG

Dugong

(*Dugong dugon*)

Order Sirenia

May reach 3m in length and weigh almost 500 kgs. They have a thick layer of fat giving them a distinctly rotund posture, small paddle-like flippers positioned far forward on the body and a broad, flattened, powerful tail that resembles the tail of whale.

The ochre brown skin appears smooth, but a really close view reveals a rough surface covered in pits from which grow short, thick hairs. At the front end of the large head are two nostrils born on a muscular fleshy lip that, when tensed curls upwards to aid breathing at the surface. The mouth is surrounded by fleshy lobes and thick, bristly hairs, presumably sensory. Males, which are considerably larger than females, have ivory tusks believed to be used in fighting during male-male rivalry and for uprooting seagrasses. The eyes are positioned on either side of the head and are small and often go unnoticed. Locally, dugongs are known as "Aroos al-Bahr" which means "Bride of the Sea", or "Baghr al-Bahr, the "sea-cow". Feeding grounds are in shallow water over seagrass beds.

Dugongs in the UAE mostly inhabit the shallow waters around the islands of Murawah and Bu Tina to the west of Abu Dhabi, but their range extends further west to the border of Qatar and beyond and there is still the occasional sighting to the east around Jebel Ali, Umm-Al-Quwain and Ras al-Khaimah. There are no confirmed records of dugongs in the Gulf of Oman.

The rich and extensive seagrass beds in the waters of the United Arab Emirates form habitat that has been identified as the most important for dugongs in the Arabian Gulf and probably includes the majority of this population.

This species, which is thought to have given rise to the myth of the mermaid, is now threatened with extinction.

TERRESTRIAL MAMMALS

Christian Gross

Opposite page:
*Large herd of
sand gazelles on
Sir Bani Yas.*

WEDGED BETWEEN EURASIA AND AFRICA at a time when neither the Red Sea nor the Arabian Gulf existed, the land now forming the Arabian Peninsula was the natural meeting place for animals from all of these land masses. During this period, Arabia enjoyed what was probably one of the most agreeable climates in the world, with regular rainfall, dense forests and lush grasslands. Whilst an equable climate prevailed here, large parts of Europe and Asia were covered with ice during successive ice ages, forcing certain mammals southwards, in search of better living conditions. With the subsequent shifts of climate and the separation of the continents, some of these animals were unable to adapt to the changes taking place in their surroundings. The Arabian landscape was becoming increasingly arid and many species died out. A few however, like the wolf, red fox and wildcat, managed to survive by adapting to this changing world.

*A herd of Arabian
oryx with a
young calf at Sir
Bani Yas.*

The most characteristically Asian species among the UAE's mammals is the Arabian tahr, while the Arabian oryx is a species unique to Arabia, which has clear roots in Africa. There are some animals that are endemic to Arabia, of which the origin could be either in Africa or in Asia, since relatives occur in both places. The most prominent amongst this group is certainly the Arabian leopard since the leopard is the most widespread of all of the world's large cats. It is distributed widely in Asia, extending to eastern Europe in the west, and it inhabits all of Africa except the Sahara desert. Unable to cross the open deserts, the Arabian leopard has lived in isolation for thousands of years in the mountains along the Red Sea and the eastern coast of the Arabian Peninsula, and it has adapted superbly to the hot climate and the harsh terrain. Prolonged genetic isolation from other members of its species has led to small differences developing between the Arabian leopard and its cousins, sufficient for scientists to describe it as a sub-species, unique to Arabia. The cheetah, also with both African and Asian relatives, was widespread in Arabia until some 30 years ago, when it seems likely that the last animals were killed.

Most Arabian mammals have suffered dramatic declines, both in numbers and range, over the last half century. Man, with his firearms and vehicles, destroyed in the blink of an eye the adaptations evolved over millions of years. The process of extinctions from the wild continues even today, especially with respect to the larger species of Arabia's wildlife. The Arabian ostrich and the Arabian cheetah, both relatively recent inhabitants of the Emirates, are both gone forever whilst the Arabian oryx and the Arabian dorcas gazelle, no longer found in the wild, have been the focus of captive breeding programmes.

Hunting is now banned in most parts of the Arabian Peninsula, and certainly in the United Arab Emirates. Despite this, recovery of many species has continued to be hampered by Man's activities which have damaged natural habitats. Such impacts range from the inevitable effects of large scale infrastructural developments to utilisation of the desert as a playground for four-wheel drive vehicles. Pumping of ground-water for agriculture has had its own impact on the water-table and natural flora, taking its toll on mammalian habitats. Vegetation is frequently destroyed by feral goats and donkeys, both of which are hardy animals that can survive under harsh circumstances. Since they will consume just about anything that is remotely edible, they leave a trail of devastation wherever they occur, denying indigenous species such as gazelles and tahr a chance for their populations to recover from the sharp drops they suffered in the days of uncontrolled mechanised hunting.

ARABIAN ORYX

The Arabian oryx (*Oryx leucoryx*) once roamed the entire Arabian Peninsula and as mentioned earlier, it became extinct as a wild species in the early 1960's. However, H.H. Sheikh Zayed bin Sultan al Nahyan had a few captive animals that bred well, and today there are several herds at various locations in the emirate of Abu Dhabi. Hopefully, once the time is right, it may be possible to reintroduce this beautiful animal into the wild. Its precise natural range within the United Arab Emirates is not clear but they were probably found in and around the Liwa, as well as on the plains adjacent to the mountains that stretch to the northern Emirates. They are the largest of the Arabian antelopes and are creatures of the open desert being able to live in areas without trees or standing water. Instead they rely on the moisture obtained from their food and can conserve water by a special adaptation of their kidneys. Their bodies are distinctly white, whilst their legs are clearly marked dark brown as far as the last joint above their hoofs, with the last part to the hoofs being white. The tail is black-tipped and they have distinct dark facial markings that extend down to the lower part of the neck. The white body colour helps to deflect the sunlight. The skin below the hair however is dark and acts as a barrier against ultra-violet rays. Both male and female carry a pair of symmetrical horns, very slightly curved to the back. As the horns of a healthy animal are so symmetrical that they appear as one if seen in profile, it is assumed that the oryx was the origin of the legendary unicorn. The horns can grow to a length of 90 cms, and their sharp points are deadly weapons amongst bulls that are fighting for superiority in a herd. They can have calves all year round, with peaks in spring and autumn. The cow has only one young at a time. When born, it is sandy-brown in colour which blends in superbly with its natural habitat. During the first days of its life, the oryx calf lies in a shallow scrape for most of the day, relying on its camouflage to avoid predators, and only when it is able to keep up with the herd will it follow the mother throughout the day.

SAND GAZELLE

The sand gazelle *(Gazella subgutturosa marica)* is the second largest of the antelopes that occur in the UAE and weighs up to 22 kgs. Virtually extinct in the wild, there are occasional reports from the Liwa of small groups of these beautiful creatures. The elegantly curved horns of both males and females are considerably longer than those of other gazelles occurring in the area. The animals are very light in colour, the head completely white in older animals, with back and flanks being light beige. The belly is white and there is no darker stripe between the white underside and the beige flanks and back of the gazelle. Contrasting with the overall pale body, are the black eyes, nostril and mouth. Their colouring is obviously an adaptation to the habitat they favour, which is the open sands. They are absent from the mountains. The sand gazelle is the only antelope in this area that regularly gives birth to twins, and this usually in spring and autumn. The young spend their first days in shallow scrapes, or under a small bush, until they are strong enough to move with the adults.

ARABIAN MOUNTAIN GAZELLE

Found on the gravel plains, the sand deserts and the mountains is the Arabian mountain gazelle *(Gazella gazella cora)*. Its natural range extended right across the northern Emirates, only avoiding the very soft sandy areas of the Liwa into which only the sand gazelle would venture. It has a delicate body, weighing only 10 to 14 kgs and can reach speeds of 65 kms per hour if it needs to escape danger. The mountain gazelle has a pure white belly with a dark to black stripe on its flanks that changes to dark beige or brown on the back, the neck and the head. The facial markings consist of various shades of brown with two white stripes extending from the eyes towards the nostrils. Females give birth to their single fawn during any month, but with natural peaks in spring and autumn. Most grazing activity takes place at dawn and dusk. They rest during the hottest hours of the day under any shelter available, which may be a cave for those that inhabit the mountains.

Usually moving in small groups of four to six animals, they are highly territorial, with the dominant male continuously marking its territory with a wax-like substance which it produces in glands below the eyes. The substance is deposited by rubbing its head against a bush, a branch or a stone. The group also maintains several places within its territory which they establish as "toilets". The animals usually only defecate and urinate at these sites. As with oryx and sand gazelle they do not need to drink water, but will readily do so if water is available.

The sand gazelle (above left) is larger and paler in colour than the Arabian gazelle seen here.

Arabian tahr (female and young), photographed in the wild during a wildlife survey in the Shimailiyyah mountains of the UAE. This was important confirmation that tahr still exist in the Emirates, albeit in isolated pockets.

ARABIAN TAHR

In contrast to the mountain gazelle the Arabian tahr *(Hemitragus jayakari)* needs to drink water every day. An agile climber, this animal is found only in the mountains, where it dwells on steep cliffs, feeding on the sparse grass and shrubs growing amongst the rocks. They descend regularly into the wadis to find a pool from which to drink. The tahr's existence on top of Jebel Hafit near Al Ain had been mentioned by Wilfred Thesiger some 45 years ago. After a last carcass of a tahr was found near a water pool on this mountain in 1982 and no further evidence of this secretive animal came to light from either Jebel Hafit or any of the other mountains, it was generally thought that the tahr was extinct outside the Sultanate of Oman. However, reports received from local people living in the mountains indicated that an animal different from a gazelle was being seen from time to time in various areas in the northern Emirates. Then, in 1995, during a survey conducted by T. and C. Stuart on behalf of the Arabian Leopard Trust a female tahr, together with her kid, was photographed when both animals descended to drink at one of the water pools!

Tahr have long reddish-brown hair, with a dark stripe down their back and short, goat-like, stubby horns. Older males sport a beard, which is absent in the younger animals. The calves are grey in colour at birth, changing to greyish-brown around the same time when the horns start to grow. No doubt the Arabian leopard was the tahr's natural enemy, but today it is the destruction of their natural habitat by feral goats, as well as poaching, that keep their numbers dangerously low.

HARE

Absent from the mountains but otherwise widespread in the United Arab Emirates is the hare *(Lepus capensis)*. Adapted to the harsh environment, the local hare is much smaller than its European counterpart and is therefore often mistaken for a rabbit, which does not occur in Arabia. Unlike the rabbit, the hare does not live in burrows, but spends the day motionless, with its ears folded back, relying totally on its camouflage, remaining in shallow scrapes under a bush or even in the open. The young hares, or leverets, are born fully furred with their eyes open and are able to survive without their mother from the seventh to the tenth day of their lives. The baby hares are left by the mother in separate locations, where she visits them a couple of times a night to let them suckle. The advantage of this system is, that if one young is found by a fox or another predator, only that individual will be killed and not the whole

218

litter. Should the mother vanish, then the babies, as mentioned earlier, are able to fend for themselves from a very early age. As with the other mammals that have adapted to the desert life, the hare does not need to drink water, obtaining enough moisture from the grasses and shrubs it eats.

territorial. Young wolves are blind at birth and are weaned at the age of about eight weeks, at which time the adults start regurgitating food for the pups. When hunting, the Arabian wolf will attack animals up to the size of a goat. It will also readily eat any carrion that is encountered.

Far left:
The Arabian wolf, though extinct in the UAE, is still present in southern Oman, Yemen and Saudi Arabia.

Left: *Striped Hyaena.*

ARABIAN WOLF

The Arabian wolf (*Canis lupus arabs*), is probably not present in the UAE at the time of writing. However, they are able to travel up to 60 kms in a night and may therefore appear suddenly in an area where they have not been seen for a long time. In Oman the wolf population has increased significantly since hunting was banned, and there is a strong possibility that they will reappear in the United Arab Emirates in the relatively near future. Smaller than the European or American wolves, the local animals have shorter hair and are greyish-beige in colour. The pure Arabian wolf's eyes are yellow with black pupils. Today many are found with brown eyes, a certain sign that they are not of pure blood anymore and that their ancestors have interbred with feral dogs. This poses a very serious threat to the survival of this species. They do not live in large packs but hunt in pairs or groups of three to four animals. Their cubs are born in a den and it is probably only during this time that the wolves are

STRIPED HYAENA

Another predator, occurring in Arabia, that has a liking for carrion is the striped hyaena (*Hyaena hyaena*). As with the wolf, there have been no confirmed sightings of this carnivore in the Emirates for a number of years. It too can travel vast distances in a short period of time and might appear in an area suddenly. Furthermore, the hyaena is very secretive, solitary and totally nocturnal, so that an animal feeding quietly on a rubbish dump might be overlooked for months. However, since the animal appears to be absent from northern Oman at the present time, the chances of the hyena reoccurring in the United Arab Emirates seem to be slim.

Arabian Red Fox.

Rueppell's sandfox cub basking in the early morning sun at the entrance of its den in the Liwa sand dunes.

ARABIAN RED FOX

Widespread, and certainly not endangered in the region is the Arabian red fox (*Vulpes vulpes arabica*). Highly adaptable, it inhabits virtually every environment and lives in the cities along the coast, the desert and the mountains. However, it does not seem to penetrate areas such as the Liwa with soft sand and high dunes. An omnivorous animal it will eat almost anything, from dead fish on the beach, to dates, carrion and of course small mammals and birds, which it actively hunts during the night. The cubs, numbering up to six per litter, are raised in a burrow that the vixen excavates herself and often uses year after year. They are born in early spring, fully furred but blind and their eyes open after about 10 days. At the age of four weeks they start taking solid food and this is also the time when they begin exploring the surroundings of their burrow. Soon after this they follow the vixen on short hunting trips. As they lack the long dense fur of the European fox they appear to have thin bodies and long legs, but proportionally they are the same, with the exception of their ears. These are larger and have thousands of tiny blood vessels that help the fox to maintain its body temperature. Reddish to sandy-brown, their colour has adapted to the environment in which they are living.

BLANDFORD'S FOX

Blanford's fox (*Vulpes cana*) was confirmed in the area only in 1995 during the survey mentioned above that led to rediscovery of the Arabian tahr in the UAE. It is smaller than the Arabian fox, with a large bushy tail, very big ears and black facial markings. Its overall greyish colour blends in superbly with its natural habitat. This fox is only found in the mountains and is absent from the open desert, thus avoiding competition with the red fox. It feeds on small mammals, birds, insects and during the season also thrives on fruits such as dates and zidr apples.

SAND FOX

The counterpart to Blanford's fox in the sands is the even smaller Rueppell's or sand fox (*Vulpes rüpellii sabaea*). Although rarely seen, it appears to be widespread in the Liwa and in the soft sand dunes south of Al Ain. Some old records also mention it from Jebel Ali near Dubai, but this has not been reconfirmedduring recent years. Similar in build to Blanford's fox it is a little smaller, with a bushy tail, large ears and reddish-brown facial markings. The animal is very light in colour, which helps it deflect the sunlight and serves as camouflage in the dunes. Active at night, when it hunts rodents, birds and insects, it spends the day in any place that provides shelter from the scorching sun.

ARABIAN LEOPARD

Undoubtedly the most famous mammal of today is the Arabian leopard (*Panthera pardus nimr*). The reason for its present fame is sadly, that it is on the brink of extinction. A spate of killings by hunters in the early 1990s triggered a conservation effort, spearheaded by the Arabian Leopard Trust, which aims at preserving the mountain habitat with all its wildlife. At about 30 kgs for the male and around 20 kgs for the female, the Arabian leopard is much smaller than most of the African and Asian races. Very light in colour, the deep golden yellow between the black rosettes is only present on the animal's back, whilst the rest of the body is beige to greyish-white. Leopards are not animals of the open desert and only occur in the mountains, where permanent water sources exist. In this arid terrain they require large territories in order to find enough food, which means that even at the best of times there have never been many leopards in this area. As they are solitary animals, the territory is fiercely defended against intruders. Whilst the area of a male might overlap with the territories of several females, no other animal of the same sex is allowed near what the leopard considers to be the core of its range.

A female in heat attracts a male over quite some distance and mating, which is very vocal, takes place over a period of about five days. During this period they may mate several hundred times. The gestation period extends approximately 100 days, after which time she gives birth to between one and four cubs. They are born in a sheltered area, such as a small cave or under a rock overhang. During the first few weeks of life the female frequently moves her cubs to different hiding places. The blind young open their eyes after about 10 days and are weaned at the age of three month, but stay with their mother until the age of about 16 months. Although leopards do occasionally bring food to their young, they usually prefer to take the young to the kill. As the natural prey species such as the tahr and the mountain gazelle are virtually extinct, leopards often have to turn to domestic stock, mainly goats, for food. They also prey on foxes, or any other small mammal or bird and will also readily eat carrion. These secretive animals hunt mainly around dawn and dusk but stay active throughout the night, while spending the hot hours of the day in a shady place that has an unobstructed view.

CARACAL

Much smaller than the leopard is the handsome caracal (*Caracal caracal schmitzi*). Standing some 40 cms at the shoulders, it is the second largest of the wild cats that occur in the United Arab Emirates. Once widespread in the open desert as well as the hills it is now confined to the mountains where it cannot be hunted so easily by man. Light brown to sandy in colour it has strong black facial markings, with the back of the ears and the long tufts also being black. It has the typical square lynx appearance, with long legs and a relatively short, slender but strong body and a short blunt tail. A very agile hunter, it preys mainly on birds and small mammals and reptiles but has little difficulty in killing tahr, gazelles or goats. Breeding probably takes place all

The Arabian leopard is on the brink of extinction both in the UAE and the rest of Arabia, but efforts are being made on national and international levels to save the species.

Young female caracal from the Ras al-Khaimah mountains.

The Gordon's wildcat likes to spend the daytime in a tree. In 1986 a captive breeding program was started in Dubai to save this subspecies from extinction.

year round but with seasonal peaks, and after a gestation period of about 75 days, the female gives birth to litters of two to three cubs. The young caracals are born blind in a burrow excavated by another animal, or in any other sheltered place that is suitable. Since they seem to be active also during daylight hours, they are more easily observed by hikers and hunters than the other Arabian carnivores. Most of the time, however, they hunt at night and spend the day resting, giving preference to a shady place with a good field of vision. The ALT survey in 1995 indicated that caracal numbers are still relatively high, but this will only remain so if killing of the animals by hunters is kept to a minimum.

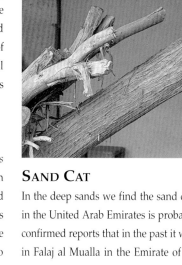

ARABIAN WILDCAT

The Arabian wildcat (*Felis silvestris gordoni*) is found in the mountains, on the gravel plains, as well as in the sand deserts of the northern Emirates but it is probably absent from the sands of the Liwa. Although they do not require to drink water, they need a regular supply of prey species such as gerbils, jirds and jerboas through which they obtain the

Baby wildcats.

The sandcat has a very placid nature contrary to the Gordon's wildcat, which is infamous among the bedu for its fierceness.

required moisture. They also hunt birds and will occasionally eat large insects. Wildcats are ash-grey to buff in colour with fine darker grey speckling on back and flanks and a whitish underside. The back of their ears is orange and the slightly bushy tail has three black rings ending in a black tip, while the underside of all four feet is also black. It is a shy animal that hunts at night and spends the day in hiding. Adapted to life in the wild, the wildcat is very strong and agile and can defend itself fiercely if it is cornered. They breed all year around, the female giving birth to a litter of two to three kittens in a rock crevice, hollow tree or an empty fox burrow. Similar in size to the domestic cat, it unfortunately interbreeds readily with the latter, which will probably result in the species becoming extinct.

SAND CAT

In the deep sands we find the sand cat (*Felis margarita*). Its present distribution in the United Arab Emirates is probably limited to the Liwa, although there are confirmed reports that in the past it was also found at Jebel Ali, near Dubai, and in Falaj al Mualla in the Emirate of Umm al Quwain. Orange-grey to buff in

colour, with a white belly, it is the smallest of the Arabian wild cats. A large sand cat barely reaches half the size of an average domestic cat. The tip of the back of its ears is black, it has black stripes on its elbows and dark rings at the end of its tail which ends with a black tip. The sand cat has long tufts of hair growing between its toes that help it to cross soft sand and also protect the naked foot pads from the hot desert surface in summer. Living in areas where there is no natural shelter available, the sand cat is the only cat in Arabia that digs its own burrow, in which its lives all year around. Active at night, the sand cat emerges from its burrow to hunt at dusk. Insects and reptiles form a large part of its diet, but it will overpower mammals up to the size of a young hare.

HEDGEHOGS

Hedgehogs are represented by three species in the UAE, the largest and most common being Brandt's hedgehog (*Paraechinus hypomelas*). It has an overall dark to black appearance with only the tip of its muzzle and the inside of its ears being grey. The top of its body is evenly covered with spines, whilst it has a bold patch on the top of the head between its ears. Slightly smaller than the Brandt's hedgehog is the Ethiopian hedgehog (*Paraechinus aethiopicus*). This animal is much lighter in colour, the bases and the tips of the spines are white and as is its hairy underside. The ears are slightly rounded at the tip, it has a bald patch without spines on the top of its head and a dark grey to black facial mask, surrounded by a lighter coloured band. Very similar but again smaller in size is the long-eared hedgehog (*Hemiechinus auritus*). Its spines are also white at the base and the tip, and its underside is white, but its ears are longer and more pointed. It lacks the bald patch at the top of the head and has a grey muzzle but no facial mask. Hedgehogs are solitary nocturnal animals, spending the day in a sheltered location, emerging at dusk when they start to hunt for insects and reptiles. As their spines offer poor protection against the cold they hibernate during the cool season, even in Arabia! In the Emirates they are found in the mountains, as well as in the desert and the coastal plains. Only the little long-eared hedgehog seems to favour the proximity of cultivations.

Ethiopian hedgehog.

Brandt's hedgehog.

Sheath-tailed bat.

Mouse-tailed bats in a cave in UAE.

BATS

Several insectivorous species of bats, as well as one fruit-eating bat, occur in the UAE. The most common insect-eating bats are the mouse-tailed bat (*Rhinopoma muscatellum*) and the sheath-tailed bat (*Taphozous nudiventris*) followed probably by the leaf-nosed bat (*Asellia tridens*). These are small bats with bodies only a few cms in length and a wingspan of 20 to 25 cms. All three are active at night, spending their days suspended from the ceiling of a cave, in rock crevices, hollow trees or under the roofs of old buildings. They are gregarious animals that may gather in quite large numbers. Pregnant females separate themselves from the main group towards the end of the gestation period, and in an undisturbed corner they give birth to their young while hanging upside down. The young bats are born blind, without fur and immediately cling to the mother. After a few days their eyes open and soon thereafter they leave the mother's body to hang by themselves, but they are still dependant on the mother's milk. As several females often use the same quiet corner of a colony's cave to give birth, the nurseries can contain considerable numbers of young bats.

The Egyptian fruit bat (*Rousettus aegyptiacus*) also lives in colonies, but might not be present in the UAE throughout the year, since the animals tend to migrate, depending on the availability of ripe fruit. With a body length of approximately 15 cms and a wingspan of around 60 cms it can be distinguished from other bats that occur in the region by its size. The fruit-eating bat is also only night active, sleeping in caves or old buildings during the day. It used to be present in considerable numbers at certain times of the year, but excessive use of pesticides seems to have taken a heavy toll amongst this species and today it is only rarely seen.

JERBOAS

Rodents are the largest group of mammals in the United Arab Emirates. The most unusual in shape is certainly the lesser jerboa *(Jaculus jaculus)*. It has greatly enlarged hind legs with large hair tufts on its back feet, which enable it to move in leaps in a similar gait to the kangaroo. The long tail is tipped with an extended, flat, rudder-like tuft that helps the jerboa keep its balance when taking leaps that can cover more than one metre. The jerboa often sits on its back legs using the tail as a third leg, like a tripod. It is sandy-beige in colour with a white belly, rather large, rounded ears and conspicuous big black eyes.

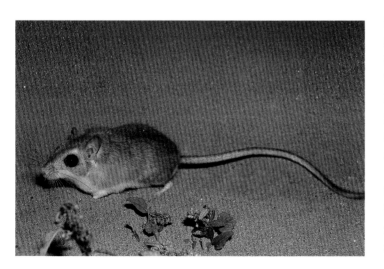

GERBILS

Cheesman's gerbil *(Gerbillus cheesmani)* is also widespread in the Emirates and has many similarities with the lesser jerboa. Although it is smaller than the latter and its hind legs are not as elongated, it can still take considerable leaps. In the Emirates the jerboa seems to favour the deserts towards the gravel plains, whereas Cheesman's gerbil is found all over the country. It is also sandy-beige in colour, with large black eyes, a white belly and a tail that seems more in proportion, in comparison with its body, than that of the jerboa.

Another gerbil that is widespread in the area, and occupies similar habitats, is the Baluchistan gerbil *(Gerbillus nanus)*. It is much darker in colour, greyish-brown with small white spots behind the ears. The tuft at the tip of the tail is not very well developed and consists of dark hair. It too has the typical large, round, black eyes of the nocturnal desert mice.

Top left: *The lesser jerboa lives in the sandy desert and is entirely nocturnal.*

Above: *Cheesman's gerbil.*

Left: *A Baluchistan gerbil - common and widespread.*

225

Sundevall's jird, hiding in a bush.

The Egyptian spiny mouse was not photographed alive in the UAE until a wildlife survey in the spring of 1995.

JIRDS

The largest rodents in the UAE are the jirds. They are represented by two species that are very difficult to separate from each other, the Libyan jird (*Meriones libycus*) and Sundevall's jird (*Meriones crassus*). They are both heavily built, greyish-brown in colour with a black tuft at the tip of the tail. The head is quite broad and has features similar to those of a hamster. The only visible difference between the two animals are the claws. The Libyan jird's claws are dark to black, whilst the Sundevall's jird's claws are of ivory colour. This of course can only be detected if the animals are handled. They favour the same habitat, desert with shrubs and small bushes, and appear to be absent from the mountains.

EGYPTIAN SPINY MOUSE

A typical mountain dweller in the UAE is the Egyptian spiny mouse (*Acomys cahirinus*). It was first recorded here in 1995, during the same survey that confirmed the presence of the tahr and Blanford's fox. Dark to reddish-brown in colour with a pale underside, it has a white patch under each eye and behind the relatively large ears. The hair on its back is replaced by relatively strong spines but it is unclear to what extent they help to protect the animal. It is said that domestic cats do not like to eat spiny mice, since they find them difficult to swallow. Absent from the open desert, they feed on seeds, vegetable matter and insects.

TRADITIONS AND WILDLIFE

Christian Gross & Marijcke Jongbloed

The barbary falcon, indigenous to Arabia, was one of the first falcons to be used in falconry. Migratory falcons such as the peregrine and sakers falcons are now preferred as hunting birds .

ALTHOUGH PETROGLYPHS IN REMOTE WADIS indicate that hunting occurred in ancient times, in recent history it has not played a major role in the United Arab Emirates. Animals large enough to provide meat for a family were hard to come by in the harsh environment of the desert and few people relied on hunting alone for their livelihood. However, all tribal people would, if the opportunity arose, catch any animal to supplement their diet.

Trap construction required materials that were not generally available in the desert. The extensive desert 'kites' used to kill gazelle in parts of central and northern Arabia do not appear to have been much used in the Emirates. Obtaining the materials for making bow and arrows was also a problem, as was approaching the prey, across open landscape, to within bow and arrow range of 30 metres or less. In more recent years firearms were brought into the desert, but these were almost exclusively used in tribal wars or for self-defence against camel raiders and bandits.

Until very recently a father, upon his death, would have left his treasured, antiquated and richly decorated rifle, together with whatever ammunition he had, to his eldest son. Since ammunition was both difficult and expensive to obtain, he would only use it to defend his family when attacked or maybe fire it once during a family wedding. In this way, he might have expended only three or four bullets during his entire lifetime, before the weapon was again passed on to his heir, together with the remaining ammunition.

Since all the materials required to manufacture a bullet had to be imported from far-away countries, it is obvious that the price for one shot was probably many times the meat value of a little desert gazelle of barely 10 kgs . One must also take into account that these shy animals could be easily missed and a precious bullet would have ended up in a sand dune. Thus, hunting wild game on a big scale in southern Arabia was not a practical proposition until perhaps 40 or 50 years ago. The first animals to be seriously hunted were the large species, such as oryx and ostrich, where value of the meat exceeded the cost of ammunition. The ostrich was hunted not only for its meat but also to supply the world demand for the much sought-after plumes - Arabian ostrich feathers were said to be superior to those of its African counterpart. The ostrich became extinct in Arabia by late 1940. The oryx survived in the wild until early 1960, while the Arabian cheetah, persecuted as vermin, probably vanished around the same time. These extinctions are more a consequence of modern civilisation than of the traditions of gathering food.

One of the most fascinating interactions between nature and man is that which takes place between the bird and its handler in Arabian falconry. During autumn the houbara (Macqueen's) bustard flies from the northern hemisphere to Arabia and Africa to over-winter. The houbara, with a weight of two to three kilograms, is large enough to provide food for several people, but was nevertheless too small to be shot with a precious bullet. The bedouin needed an alternative method to capture this nutritious and tasty bird.

The houbara's migration is preceded by that of the birds of prey, and the people of the desert captured the peregrine and saker falcons on their passage to Africa. There were numerous ways to trap the falcons, depending on the availability of materials, the most ingenious system was certainly also the simplest one. If a bedouin located a falcon sitting on a dune in the first light of dawn, he would return to the same location on the following morning, riding together with a friend on a single camel. As soon as they found the bird again, they positioned themselves upwind from the falcon and dismounted, keeping the camel between themselves and the bird of prey. Hidden behind the camel one bedouin buried the other one in the sand leaving only the head and one arm exposed, following which the falconer was further concealed by branches of a bush. The other bedouin then remounted and rode briskly away, whilst at the same time the man left behind in the sand let fly a pigeon, that was tethered by the legs with a string.

Apparently the falcon did not realise that only one man was riding away with the camel, whereas there were two riders when it arrived. It also looked as if the helplessly fluttering pigeon had been disturbed by the passing camel. Since falcons recognize pigeons as suitable prey, and with their sharp eyes would have been able to detect the fact that the bird was handicapped, and a potentially easy catch, they were encouraged to attack the bird as soon as the

camel and rider were some distance away. With the bedouin positioned upwind from the falcon, and the pigeon flying against the wind, the falcon also dived on and killed the pigeon upwind from the buried hunter. The pigeon prey was of course tied to a string so the falcon could not carry it away and it would eventually settle down to start eating the dead bird. Falcons do not like the wind ruffling their feathers from behind so whilst eating, the enticed bird always faced into the wind, turning its back to the buried bedouin who was down-wind from the falcon and the dead pigeon. Pulling the string slowly towards him, the hunter thus brought the dead pigeon, with the falcon sitting on top, closer to his outstreched arm which was also hidden under the sand. The falcon, tricked into thinking that the pigeon was still alive kept attacking it fiercely whilst the hunter pulled it ever closer until the moment when he could grab its legs and throw a cloth over his quarry.

The bedouin had considerable powers of observation and a deep insight into the environment in which they were living, and thus managed to trap animals with the simplest of methods. Another way they used to trap falcons was again very simple and based purely on the fact that the hunter understood the behaviour of his quarry. Knowing that falcons are very opportunistic feeders

Falconry is still carried out in the traditional manner in the United Arab Emirates.

The houbara bustard is the tradional quarry of falconers in the UAE, although other prey is also hunted.

and are strongly attracted to vulnerable prey, the falconer kept, or caught in late summer, a kestrel. Kestrels are resident breeders in the UAE and at the same time the smallest and most defenceless falcons in the area. Once the large peregrines and sakers started to arrive in autumn, the hunter waited in a hide with his kestrel outside, tied to a block. Attached to the kestrels legs was a bundle of feathers that was laced with very fine snares. With its eyesight that is many times better than that of man, the kestrel would observe a large approaching falcon long before the falconer could see it. As soon as the

falconer noticed that his kestrel started to become agitated, he would release it and the kestrel, irritated by the bundle of feathers tied to its legs, would immediately start flying.

The large falcon would see the kestrel and mistake the bundle of feathers for freshly killed prey and immediately try to rob the kestrel. Stooping at the kestrel, it would pass underneath the latter and turning on its back in mid-air would try to sink its talons into the feather bundle under the fleeing bird, thus becoming entangled in the snares. Now attached to each other, both falcon and kestrel would be unable to fly and would finally come down to the ground in a fluttering tangle of feathers. The waiting bedouin would throw a cloth over the struggling pair.

These were probably the two main traditional methods of trapping falcons in the Emirates. Later, in more prosperous times, when pigeons became more affordable, a third capture technique was adopted, using a pigeon that wore a harness on its back to which snares were attached. Handicapped by the harness, the pigeon did not have its natural fast and straight flight. The falcon, tempted by the handicapped pigeon, would stoop and become entangled in the snares. Along the UAE coastline, and on its islands, falconers also installed more complicated traps, using nets that were flicked over the falcon by a man sitting in a hide, waiting motionless and patiently often for days on end.

Once the falconers managed to trap one of the highly prized birds, they had only two to three weeks to train it before the migrating houbaras started to arrive. The freshly captured falcon's eyes were covered by threading a hair from a horse tail through the lower eyelids, bringing it together and tying in a knot on top of the head. The falcon's eyes were permanently shut and stayed like this for several days during which time the falconer kept his bird with him for 24 hours of the day. He carried the bird with him wherever he went, stroked it, talked to it and kept calling it the name he had chosen. This was to calm the wild bird, to make it used to sitting on the falconer's gauntlet, called *mangalah*, and to get it to know the voice of the falconer. When the hair thread was removed after about three days, the first thing the falcon would see was the man whose voice he had heard and started to trust during his days of temporary blindness. The falconer then also offered his bird some food from

The monitor lizard was one of the great delicacies of the bedouin. It was hunted by a variety of methods.

231

The dhub lizard remains one the great delicacies of the traditional desert dwellers. Over-hunting has resulted in protective measures being taken to save the lizard in the UAE.

his hand and in this way the bond of trust between a wild captured bird and a falconer was established over a relatively short period of time.

Shortly thereafter, the bird would be "cast off" the mangalah to fly a few metres to some food that was offered to him, whilst still being attached to the falconer's glove with a long string. The flight distance was constantly increased and eventually the bird was left to fly free. The bird was also introduced to the lure which was made from a pair of houbara wings, which the falconer had retained from the previous year. In this way the falcon, which would not necessarily kill bustards in the wild, or which might have come from a region where there were no houbaras, became familiar with the quarry that the bedouin wished it to hunt.

Ideally, the training of the falcon was completed by the day when the first houbaras arrived and the bedouin would hunt the bustards with his falcon throughout the winter months. In the early morning hours they searched for houbara tracks in the sand, which they then followed, knowing that this night-active bird spent the day resting under a bush. Once a houbara was found and "brought up", the falcon was released, to hopefully capture and kill it. After a successful hunt, the falconer would feed his bird with the head and the neck of the bustard and keep the rest for himself and his family. The traditional way of cooking a houbara was to bury the bird as it was, with feathers and offal in the glowing fire where it was left to cook through. When the bird was considered to be done, it was taken out of the fire, the charred feathers and skin were removed, revealing the delicious white flesh that had cooked in its own juice.

On days when they did not manage to capture any prey with the falcon, the falconer's children were sent out at night to catch a jird, gerbil or jerboa to feed the falcon and on occasion the falconer and his bird stayed hungry and had to try twice as hard the following day. In spring, when the houbaras returned to their breeding grounds in the north, there was no prey small enough for the

falcon to kill, and at the same time large enough to feed the falconer and his bird. That was the time when the bedouin took his hunting companion and set him free again, hoping that the coming autumn would give him a new bird with which to train and hunt.

In some areas falcons were also used to hunt gazelles, together with saluki dogs. The falcon attacked the fleeing gazelle's head and irritated the animal in such a way that the salukis had a chance to catch up with it and to bring the gazelle down, so that the bedouin could move in and kill it. It appears that the falcons used for this were trained with tame gazelles, that had pigeon meat attached to their horns. This was certainly not a very common way of hunting and was probably more of a sport for people who could afford it rather than a way of supplementing a very basic diet.

Once the bedouin had released his falcon he started hunting for hare in the desert with his dogs. The hare could also be hunted with the falcons, but the chances of a falcon breaking its feathers in a fight on the ground with a struggling hare were so great, that the bedouin did not take this risk. The salukis ran wild around the camps throughout the year. They lived off scraps and caught the various desert mice and rats as well as reptiles and generally looked after themselves, coming back to the camp only for water.

In winter, when the temperature was cool and the food plentiful, the hares were fit and "jumpy". At the slightest disturbance they bolted from their hiding place under a bush and made for safety, thus becoming very difficult for the saluki to catch. In summer this was quite different. Little food is available and running during the heat of the day uses a lot of energy and water. Therefore the hare would try to rely on its camouflage until the very last minute and only run when the saluki was almost upon him. This was the time of the year when the partnership of bedouin and saluki could successfully hunt hare . As with the houbara, the hare was large enough to provide food for the saluki as well as for the hunter. The bedouin would never take the prey away from his hunting assistant without sharing it with either dog or falcon.

In order to catch hare, the hunter, on his camel, followed fresh tracks until he located his prey, generally crouching under a bush. Taking his saluki into his arms, he rode his camel as closely to the hare as possible, never riding straight at the prey, but making several passes, each one being a little closer. In this way he managed to come to within a distance of ten metres or less, by which time he would then throw his saluki towards the hiding hare, prompting the latter to bolt. If the dog was unable to catch the animal within a chase of 50 m or less he would abandon the chase and the bedouin would have to find a new hare.

Good salukis were on occasion able to catch gazelles, but usually only young and inexperienced animals, or the old and weak. This depended so much on luck, that the bedouin never relied on it, but when the opportunity arose, he most certainly took it. If the bedouin was on his own and a gazelle was caught, he deboned, washed, salted and then dried the meat on clean sand. The procedure of washing, salting and drying was repeated several times until the meat was completely dry and as light as potato chips. Then it could be transported very easily and stored for several weeks. In this form it could be eaten as it was, or boiled with rice in a byriani.

Dhabs or spiny-tailed lizards were also eaten, in some areas as a delicacy, in others only when there was no other food available. These vegetarian reptiles grow to about 60 cms in length, live in deep burrows in the open desert, and were usually caught in snares set by children. Once an inhabited dhab hole was found, the snares were set outside the burrow in the evening, and the lizard was then caught the next morning when it tried to leave the hole to find a place in the sun to warm up. A major advantage of catching dhabs was that they could be attached with a collar to a small post and kept alive for several days without requiring food or water. Carried in a hessian bag that allowed a reasonable airflow, they could also be easily transported on a camel saddle and served as fresh meat in remote areas. Not only the tasty meat was eaten, but also the tough leather was used to make strings, small bags and purses.

Where bushes and trees grew, any of the small birds, resident or migratory were snared, or caught with small traps, by children and brought home to enhance the staple diet. Along the coast where the francolin was found, and in the mountains, the habitat of the partridges, traps were made with little baskets and a set of sticks, ingenuously put together. Once the bird tripped one of the sticks, the basket toppled over and the bird was caught.

Along the beaches gulls were caught with small fishing hooks that were hidden in sardine and attached to strings weighted down by rocks, covered with sand. It was a cruel method of catching food, but since they were caught to be eaten, and considering the harshness of the surroundings where people were often on the brink of starvation, anything that would provide food was acceptable.

Other delicacies the beaches provided were eggs from turtles, as well as from the seabirds, mainly the Socotra cormorants. During the laying season the

The trap shown here ensnares the dhub lizard as it emerges from its burrow.

233

people would go to the islands where the huge cormorant colonies were located and collect the eggs by the bucketful. The impact on the cormorant populations was virtually nil, since the local people wanted fresh and not partly incubated eggs and therefore they only raided the nests at the very beginning of the breeding season, after which they left the colonies alone. A female cormorant who lost her egg soon after laying, would produce a new one after a few days.

Turtles' nests were found early in the morning by following the tracks a female had left during the night when she came onto the beach for egg laying. The eggs provided protein rich food and could be kept in a shady place for several weeks before going bad. Turtle meat was also eaten, the flesh having a texture between veal and chicken with a rather neutral but slightly fishy taste. The impact on the turtle population was negligible since live animals were caught only rarely.

Fishing was mainly carried out with fish traps. The wire traps that are widely seen today are a rather recent developement, as are fishing hooks attached to nylon line. Before metal and nylon were available, the domed 'garghour' traps were made of ribs of the leaves of date palms. These were then weighed down with rocks to keep them from floating. Other traps, the 'hadra', were a complicated "V"-shaped system of wooden sticks that were deeply embedded in the sand. With the incoming tide, the fish that swam with it towards the shore would follow the rows of sticks, that were set closer and closer to each other the nearer they were to the beach, leading to the final trapping chamber. The last compartment was funnel-shaped and once the fish were inside, they were unable to find their way out. At low tide the family who owned a trap would then go and collect the fish, which very often needed to be speared, since the trapping chamber at low tide still had a depth of about 60 cms of water. A properly built fish trap was a significant asset and was maintained by a family throughout their lives and passed on from one generation to the next.

At an early stage, nets were used to fish the numerous creeks along the shores of the Emirates. These were made of natural fibre and were up to a hundred metres in length. In the centre the net was funnel-shaped and ended in a large bag. At high tide, when the maximum number of fish was inshore, such a net was placed across the mouth of a creek, sealing it effectively for all of the fish that wanted to return to deeper water before low tide. When the water level was at its lowest, rows of men on either side of the creek, started to slowly pull the net in and gradually drag it up the creek until they reached its top end where the two parties met and in this way closed the net. It was then pulled onto the beach, with the bag in the centre leaving the water last. One haul with a large dragnet was a day's work for maybe 20 men but could yield several hundred kilograms of fish. In times of plenty, the surplus fish were dried on a clean stretch of beach, or salted and stored in wooden barrels if available, or just kept covered under a pile of salt. Salt was found in abundance on the flats along the coast, where the water evaporated naturally, leaving the salt crystals behind. These were then harvested during the later months of summer. Salt was also exported, as were cuttlefish "bones", that were used to manufacture scouring powder.

Shellfish also contributed to the people's diet and were collected by the women and children along the beaches and in the mangroves. A major natural resource exploited in the old days was created by the pearl oyster. Large oyster-banks occured off the coast and oysters there frequently attach themselves to sponges or soft corals. During strong storms wave turbulence dislodged many of these from their attachments, causing them to float to the surface, carrying oysters with them. Washed onto the beaches, they were then collected and eaten. No doubt this was the way in which the first pearl was discovered, thousands of years ago.

Soon the demand for pearls was greater than the natural harvest along the beaches could provide and the people started using boats and divers to find more of these precious gems. The pearling dhows stayed out for weeks at a time, with very little drinking water available, and divers living on a diet of dates and fish. This was a hard existence and many pearlers died in pursuit of the oyster's bounty. Until the arrival of cultured pearls, the pearling cities along the Arabian Gulf shores enjoyed relative wealth and prosperity.

the desert; the palm tree did almost the same for the bedu of the plantations in the oases and along the coast. Palm tree trunks supported the roofs of the lovely mudbrick castles and towers. The ribs of the palm leaves were used to weave the walls of the huts or to provide the floating bulk of the interesting small fishing boats, called *shasha*. The *garghour* or domed fishing traps were also made from these palm leaf ribs before the advent of nylon and plastic. Dried palm leaves were tied together to make barusti, which was (and is) used for a multitude of purposes: shades, roofs, separating walls, and making enclosures. The fibre on the tree trunk was collected and used to make rope or to weave baskets, mats and the typical pyramid-shaped covers that protect food from flies.

All over the Arab world, different types of dates are produced. These different varieties must have developed, because plantations were far removed from one another and the palms grew on soils of widely varied chemical and mineral content. Most dates are eaten raw, but some types are boiled before being used. Pliny's *Natural History*, an interesting if often inaccurate account of flora and fauna some 2000 years ago, already lists 49 varieties of dates. In Arabic, there are said to be 500 different names for the date, which must be an indication about its importance to the life of a desert Arab.

Wendell Phllips, in his book *Unknown Oman*, mentions that a knowledgeable bedu housewife would be able to give her husband a different date dish on each day of the month. He also recounts the story of a man who received a letter one evening, but had no light by which to read it. His resourceful wife kneaded a small cup from some dates, poured into it a little melted fat and made a wick from a few threads, taken from a piece of cloth. The man read the letter by the light of the lamp, and when he was finished he threw out the wick, drank the fat and ate the cup, so consuming his lamp!

In a land where little or nothing could be bought even if one had money, living off the land has always been of paramount importance. Even now, when everyone shops in the supermarket, old customs persist. An early rain has the people out in droves looking for the coveted *faqah*, (*Trefezia sp*) a subterranean mushroom that lives in symbiosis with a small perennial plant called

Research carried out at Al Ain University is investigating the medicinal properties of traditional herbal plants.

TRADITIONAL USES OF PLANTS AND TREES

The relationship of the bedu and their palm trees is as important as that between man and his camel. Even though both date palm and dromedary cannot be considered to be truly wild now, it was the bedu that tamed both and put them to good use for his daily life. Whereas the camel provided housing, clothing and useful objects (besides meat and milk) to the bedu of

235

Roots of the red-thumb plant, Cynomorium coccineum, *formed part of the traditional diet.*

Helianthemum lippii. It is often called a truffle, but it is more likely to be a bovid. It is quite a palatable fungus, but cannot be compared with the European true truffle in taste or appearance.

The roots of the parasitic plant *Cynomorium coccineum* are eaten in the same way as asparagus is served: boiled in slightly salted water. But one has to be very hungry indeed to enjoy this particular vegetable- a bitter fibre, that sets the teeth on edge!

Spring rains provide other delicacies for the bedu : the tangy vitamin-C rich mountain sorrel *Rumex vesicarius*, and the juicy *Caralluma*, a cactus-like member of the Euphorbia family. Also the new shoots on *arta, Calligonum comosum*, are gathered as a vegetable in the spring. Among the *Calligonum* plant's multiple uses is that of sand stabilization; it being used to protect fields against blowing sands. Large bushes provide the firewoodwhich is needed to keep the tribesmen warm during the cold winter nights. In some books there is also mention of the use of the lampion-like seeds as a spice for rice dishes, but I have not been able to find anyone that would verify this use in the UAE. The flowerbuds of the caper plant *Capparis spinosa*, are also edible. Pickled, they are used as a condiment even in Europe. Another edible flowerbud popular with the bedu is the bud of the large bush *Leptadenia pyrotechnica*. It is a plant of the sandy desert, bordering on the sabkhas, which in turn are the habitat for the strange fern *Ophioglossum polyphyllum*. In spite of the species name, suggesting many leaves, this plant only has two to three leaves, at the base of the stalk that carries the sporophore. These leaves are collected as a salad green by the bedu.

Much sought after are the small sour apples of the *sidr, Zizyphus spina-christie*. Both the wild and the cultivated kinds are appreciated. In addition to the fruits providing food for man and beast, the blossoms of the *sidr*, that drop to the ground after flowering, seem to be a favourite fodder for the ubiquitous goats in mountain villages, as well as for the wild mountain gazelles.

Wild herbs played a major role in folklore medicine. Nowadays the local Arabs still make good use of medicinal herbs but these are often brought in from India and are sold in the suqs in packages that do not reveal what they are. Still, some local plants are used even today to combat certain ailments. Perhaps the best known is the seed of *Cassia italica*, the senna plant. Used all over the world as a laxative, the bedu claim it will heal any kind of stomach pain. It is often mixed with rosewater to combat that most common of local complaints: gases!

The seeds of the desert squash, *Citrullus colocynthis*, are also highly acclaimed as a cure for diabetes. Ingestion of four seeds a day is said to be sufficient to control diabetes of the elderly. Many of the perennial plants have medicinal actions ascribed to them; in fact a comprehensive list of medicinal uses of local plants could fill a book by itself. Almost every part of a plant could be used: as poultices, brews, or mixed with fat as ointments. The bitter sap of the milkweed *Calotropis procera* was even dried and used to fill aching hollow teeth, while the woody parts of this plant were burned to make charcoal, which was an ingredient for gunpowder in the old days. Poultices made of the leaves were applied to joints to heal rheumatism. The leaves also

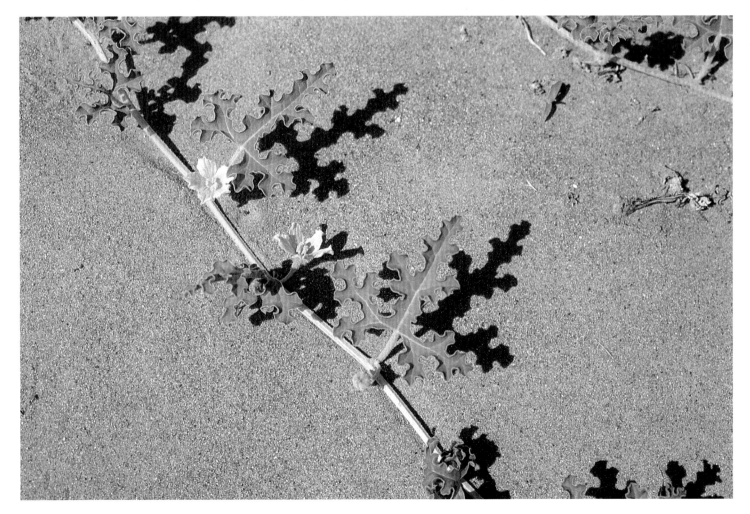

Citrullus colocynthis was an acclaimed cure for diabetes.

237

Pergularia tomentosa was used in the tanning process as an aid to removing hairs from hides.

served as fertiliser - dug into the ground around the roots of an ailing palm tree, they help to make the tree more vigorous.

Another plant, that has toxic latex, was used to remove hair from the hides of goats and gazelles before tanning. *Pergularia tomentosa* shoots were crushed to a paste and then spread over the hairy side of a hide, rolled up and left buried for some days. Later, the hair could just be brushed off, providing not too much of the plant had been used, in which case the hide could have been

damaged by burns. Local people claim that bunches of twigs of *Taverniera glabra*, a shrubby perennial of the mountains, were used to beat the water of a wadi pool in order to stun fish, which could then easily be caught by hand.

Some plants, like *Salsola imbricata* and several *Suaeda* species, were dried and powdered to be used as snuff to clear the sinuses and provide a mild high. Others were used by women as dyes for clothing or as cosmetics: the roots and twigs of *Arnebia hispidissima* provided rouge for lips and cheeks while blue colours were extracted from the *Indigofera* plants. The best known cosmetic use of a plant is that of henna to dye hair and to beautify hands and feet on special days like weddings and Eid celebrations. To make the henna paste, crushed dried berries and leaves are mixed with medicinal herbs, including one containing a blue dye, and applied to the skin in intricate designs. Poultices of the henna plant leaves are also used to calm down headaches.

The poisonous plant *Rhazya stricta* is used in small quantities to settle gastric upsets in people, while *Zygophyllum qatarense* is eaten by camels for the same purpose. It is assumed that the diarrhoea which follows ingestion of these plants, clears the system of toxins or irritants. An important plant for combating fevers is *Teucrium stocksianum,* a most fragrant herb, similar to a sage. The seeds of *garat* (*Acacia nilotica*) are ground to a powder to dry out second degree burns. According to one source, the skin underneath the powder application grows in like a baby's skin, without scarring. Plants that are still used regularly these days are *Salvadore persica*, of which twigs are chewed to clean teeth, and *Aerva javanica*, that produces woolly seeds, used for stuffing pillows and camel saddles.

CHECKLIST OF THE COMMON BIRDS OF THE UNITED ARAB EMIRATES

(in taxonomic order after Voous)

COMMON NAME	SCIENTIFIC NAME	SPECIES NOTES FOR THE UAE
Little grebe	*Tachybaptus ruficollis*	Resident, breeds all months. Also migrant September to March.
Black-necked grebe	*Podiceps nigricollis*	Localised winter visitor September to early April.
Great cormorant	*Phalacrocorax carbo*	Common winter visitor November to March, occ. to May.
Socotra cormorant	*Phalacrocorax nigrogularis*	Resident, with huge flock movements noted off some coasts.
Night heron	*Nycticorax nycticorax*	Common passage migrant and winter visitor from September to April, with few locally oversummering.
Little green heron*	*Butorides striatus.*	Breeding resident along all coasts, with some local movements to nearby freshwater wetlands particularly in autumn.
Indian pond heron*	*Ardeola grayii*	Regular winter visitor to Khor Kalba October to mid April.
Cattle egret	*Bubulcus ibis*	Increasingly common passage migrant and winter visitor mid October to April, occasionally other months.
Western reef heron*	*Egretta gularis*	Common breeding resident, few on passage, dispersive in winter.
Little egret	*Egretta garzetta*	Common passage migrant and winter visitor September to March, occasionally in summer.
Great white egret*	*Egretta alba*	Fairly common winter visitor September to April, few in summer.
Grey heron*	*Ardea cinerea*	Very common passage migrant and winter visitor, many oversummering.
Purple heron	*Ardea purpurea*	Passage migrant in small numbers, most common late August to October.
White stork	*Ciconia ciconia*	Irregular autumn migrant, some remaining in winter. Rare from March to early May, occasionally June.
Glossy ibis	*Plegadis falcinellus*	Regular passage migrant and winter visitor September to April, occasionally in summer.
Spoonbill	*Platalea leucorodia*	Regular passage migrant and winter visitor, usually in groups and occasionally in summer.
Greater flamingo	*Phoenicopterus ruber*	Common migrant and winter visitor, flocks of 200+ regular. Has attempted to nest.
Wigeon	*Anas penelope*	Localised winter visitor October to March, rarely to April.
Teal	*Anas crecca*	Common and widespread passage migrant and winter visitor September to March, occasionally August and April, rarely in May.
Mallard	*Anas platyrhynchos*	Very common winter visitor mid October to April.
Pintail*	*Anas acuta*	Fairly common winter visitor October to March, occasionally September to April.
Garganey	*Anas querquedula*	Fairly common passage migrant February to April and late August to October.
Shoveler	*Anas clypeata*	Common migrant and winter visitor mid-September to March, occasionally to April.
Egyptian vulture*	*Neophron percnopterus*	Local breeding resident.
Lappet-faced vulture	*Torgus tracheliotus*	Resident, assumed breeding in UAE territory or very close to border in Omani enclaves of Mahdah and Buraimi.
Short-toed eagle	*Circaetus gallicus*	Uncommon migrant mainly September to April, but recorded in all months.
Marsh harrier	*Circus aeruginosus*	Common migrant and winter visitor September to early April, occasionally May.
Pallid harrier	*Circus macrourus*	Common passage migrant and winter visitor September to March, few remaining to early May.
Montagu's harrier	*Circus pygargus*	Common migrant, few in winter, with peak passage August to October and March to early April.
Sparrowhawk	*Accipiter nisus*	Regular passage migrant and winter visitor in small numbers September to April, occasionally in May.
Long-legged buzzard*	*Buteo rufinus*	Passage migrant and winter visitor September to April. Breeds in remote desert areas in winter months, and appears to be dispersive (or migratory) at other times.
Spotted eagle	*Aquila clanga*	Regular passage migrant and winter visitor late October to March, occasionally in summer.
Imperial eagle	*Aquila heliaca*	Scarce and irregular passage migrant and occasional winter visitor September to March.
Booted eagle	*Hieraaetus pennatus*	Scarce passage migrant and winter visitor September to April, rarely late August and early May.

Bonelli's eagle	*Hieraaetus fasciatus*	Uncommon breeding resident in mountain areas, with post-breeding dispersal from September to March. Migrants may also occur.
Osprey	*Pandion haliaetus*	Common breeding resident on isolated coasts and islands, nesting November to March. Migrant and winter visitor September to April.
Lesser kestrel	*Falco naumanni*	Localised spring migrant mid March to mid April. Less common during autumn passage mid-September to November.
Kestrel	*Falco tinnunculus*	Common migrant and winter visitor peaking September to April. Also breeding resident, nesting in mountain areas, rocky outcrops and more recently noted amongst high-rise buildings.
Sooty falcon	*Falco concolor*	Breeding visitor to rocky islands, April to October, with nesting commencing in June.
Saker falcon*	*Falco cherrug*	Scarce winter visitor September to April. Favoured species of Middle East falconers and many are trapped during peak passage October to November. Escaped birds are regularly reported.
Peregrine falcon	*Falco peregrinus*	Uncommon winter visitor September to April, occasionally later. Many migrants are trapped and there are regular reports of escaped birds still wearing leg jesses.
Barbary falcon	*Falco pelegrinoides*	Uncommon breeding resident in high remote mountain areas.
Sand partridge	*Ammoperdix heyi*	Common and widespread mountain resident.
Grey francolin	*Francolinus pondicerianus*	Very common resident in northern Emirates, rarely far from water. Fewer in south and west.
Quail	*Coturnix coturnix*	Common passage migrant March to April and August to early November, occasionally other months. Heard calling January-July and may be a regular breeding visitor.
Moorhen	*Gallinula chloropus*	Common passage migrant peaking March and late August to December, scarce winter visitor and local breeding resident in reedbeds, young in June.
Coot	*Fulica atra*	Common winter visitor October to March, occasionally April and September.
Houbara bustard	*Chlamydotis undulata*	Scarce winter visitor October (rarely from September) to March. Reported as a former breeder. Traditional prey of falconers, and many tracked and hunted.
Oystercatcher	*Haematopus ostralegus*	Locally common migrant and winter visitor, few in summer.
Black-winged stilt	*Himantopus himantopus*	Common opportunist breeder, migrant and winter visitor.
Crab plover	*Dromas ardeola*	Localised passage migrant and winter visitor. Nests May to August.
Cream-coloured courser*	*Cursorius cursor*	Resident and dispersive. Also occurs on migration.
Collared pratincole	*Glareola pratincola*	Rather uncommon passage migrant mid April to May, occasionally June, more common July to October.
Little ringed plover*	*Charadrius dubius*	Breeding visitor and passage migrant late February to early September, rare October to January.
Ringed plover	*Charadrius hiaticula*	Common passage migrant and winter visitor, peak passage mid August to October, small numbers recorded May to mid July.
Kentish plover*	*Charadrius alexandrinus*	Very common and widespread breeding resident, and common winter visitor. Nests from late March, peak hatching period from late May to June.
Lesser sand plover	*Charadrius mongolus*	Very common passage migrant and winter visitor, few oversummering.
Greater sand plover	*Charadrius leschenaultii*	Locally common passage migrant and winter visitor, some in summer.
Pacific golden plover*	*Pluvialis fulva*	Regular migrant and winter visitor late August to early May, sometimes in large groups.
Grey plover	*Pluvialis squatarola*	Common passage migrant and winter visitor, few oversummering.
Red-wattled lapwing	*Hoplopterus indicus*	Opportunist breeding species, confined mainly to Northern Emirates, resident in agricultural and other suitable areas.
Sanderling	*Calidris alba*	Regular passage migrant and winter visitor, mostly on exposed sandy beaches and never very common.
Little stint	*Calidris minuta*	Common passage migrant and winter visitor, widespread at pools and mudflats mid August to May, few in summer months.

Temminck's stint	*Calidris temminckii*	Common passage migrant and winter visitor mid August to early May, though never numerous.
Curlew sandpiper*	*Calidris ferruginea*	Abundant autumn migrant, less common in winter.
Dunlin	*Calidris alpina*	Very common passage migrant and winter visitor.
Broad-billed sandpiper	*Limicola falcinellus*	Locally common passage migrant and winter visitor, mostly at Khor Dubai. Few over-summer.
Ruff	*Philomachus pugnax*	Common passage migrant and winter visitor August to April, occasionally to mid May.
Common snipe	*Gallinago gallinago*	Common and widespread passage migrant and winter visitor, late August to April.
Black-tailed godwit*	*Limosa limosa*	Regular passage migrant and winter visitor, though never common.
Bar-tailed Godwit*	*Limosa lapponica*	Very common passage migrant and winter visitor to all tidal mudflats.
Whimbrel	*Numenius phaeopus*	Common passage migrant, localised in winter.
Curlew	*Numenius arquata*	Common passage migrant and winter visitor.
Redshank	*Tringa totanus*	Very common and widespread passage migrant and winter visitor.
Greenshank	*Tringa nebularia*	Regular passage migrant and winter visitor August to April.
Green sandpiper	*Tringa ochropus*	Fairly common passage migrant and winter visitor July to April.
Wood sandpiper	*Tringa glareola*	Common passage migrant and rather scarce winter visitor August to mid May.
Terek sandpiper	*Xenus cinereus*	Common passage migrant and winter visitor late July to mid May, though rather localised.
Common sandpiper	*Actitis hypoleucos*	Common winter visitor and passage migrant July to mid May.
Turnstone	*Arenaria interpres*	Common passage migrant, less common in winter and few in summer.
Red-necked Phalarope*	*Phalaropus lobatus*	Common passage migrant mid March to April and late July to early November. Large numbers winter offshore in Gulf of Oman.
Pomarine skua*	*Stercorarius pomarinus*	Common passage migrant and winter visitor.
Arctic skua	*Stercorarius parasiticus*	Common passage migrant, with peak passage mid March to mid April and mid August to September.

Sooty gull	*Larus hemprichii*	Breeding visitor to few remaining undisturbed Gulf islands, eggs May to June.
Great black-headed gull*	*Larus ichthyaetus*	Common late winter visitor most occurring mid December to March.
Black-headed gull	*Larus ridibundus*	Very common and widespread winter visitor mid November to mid April.
Slender-billed gull*	*Larus geneii*	Common non-breeding visitor, present throughout the year on mainland coasts and lagoons.
Lesser black-backed gull	*Larus fuscus.*	Passage migrant and winter visitor late August to April.
Yellow-legged gull	*Larus cachinnans*	Sometimes considered a form of Herring Gull *L.argentatus*, the nominate form of which is still unconfirmed in the UAE. However this species may in fact be more closely related to Lesser Black-backed Gull. Very common winter visitor September to April.
Gull-billed tern	*Gelochelidon nilotica*	Common passage migrant and winter visitor late July to March.
Swift tern	*Sterna bergii*	Breeding summer visitor, some resident and dispersive.
Lesser crested tern	*Sterna bengalensis*	Common summer breeding visitor, small numbers present all year.
Sandwich tern	*Sterna sandvicensis*	Very common winter visitor and passage migrant.
White-cheeked tern*	*Sterna repressa*	Very common breeding summer visitor from April to November, occasionally in other months.
Bridled tern	*Sterna anaethetus*	Very common pelagic breeding summer visitor late March to October.
Saunders' little tern*	*Sterna saundersi*	Common breeding visitor.
Lichtenstein's sandgrouse	*Pterocles lichtensteinii*	Scarce and elusive breeding resident of mountains and gravel plains.
Chestnut-bellied sandgrouse*	*Pterocles exustus*	Common resident, sandy and gravel areas including coastal scrub.
Collared dove	*Streptopelia decaocto*	Abundant resident, dispersive and partly migratory.
Turtle dove	*Streptopelia turtur*	Common passage migrant and breeding visitor April to September.
Palm dove*	*Streptopelia senegalensis*	Very common and widespread resident.
Rose-ringed parakeet	*Psittacula krameri*	Introduced, common breeding resident, dispersive and spreading.
Striated (Bruce's) scops owl*	*Otus brucei*	Uncommon breeding resident, with some local movement or migration recorded. Nests from April and young noted June to August.

Eagle owl	*Bubo bubo*	Widespread breeding resident of rocky outcrops and larger trees even in sand desert areas. The (sub)species which occurs, *B.(bubo) ascalaphus* may be a distinct species, Desert Eagle Owl.
Little owl	*Athene noctua*	Common, apparently sedentary breeding resident.
Common swift*	*Apus apus*	Common passage migrant, mostly late February to early May.
Pallid swift	*Apus pallidus*	Very common passage migrant and breeding visitor.
White-collared kingfisher*	*Halcyon chloris*	Very localised sedentary resident on East Coast. Present only at Khor Kalba where less than 50 pairs remain.
Kingfisher	*Alcedo atthis*	Common passage migrant and winter visitor mid August to April.
Little green bee-eater*	*Merops orientalis*	Common breeding resident in north and east.
Blue-cheeked bee-eater	*Merops superciliosus*	Common passage migrant, mid February to mid May and August to October, and local breeding summer visitor.
European bee-eater*	*Merops apiaster*	Common passage migrant late March to April and mid August to mid October. Breeds locally.
European roller	*Coracias garrulus*	Common passage migrant, April to early May and mid August to October. Breeds locally.
Indian roller*	*Coracias benghalensis*	Common breeding resident in north and east.
Hoopoe	*Upupa epops*	Very common passage migrant, localised winter visitor and thinly distributed breeding resident.
Black-crowned finch lark*	*Eremopterix nigriceps*	Common breeding resident, subject to nomadic or seasonal movements outside the breeding season.
Desert lark	*Ammomanes deserti*	Common, app. sedentary breeding resident.
Hoopoe lark*	*Alaemon alaudipes*	Fairly common breeding resident.
Crested lark	*Galerida cristata*	Very common and widespread breeding resident.
Skylark	*Alauda arvensis*	Common winter visitor November to early March.
Sand martin	*Riparia riparia*	Common passage migrant late March to early May and late August to mid-October.
Pale crag martin	*Hirundo obsoleta*	Common breeding resident of mountains, foothills and high-rise buildings near Gulf coast.
Swallow	*Hirundo rustica*	Very common passage migrant, occasionally all months.
Tawny pipit	*Anthus campestris*	Common passage migrant and winter visitor mid September to mid April.
Tree pipit	*Anthus trivialis*	Common passage migrant March to mid-April and September to October.
Red-throated pipit*	*Anthus cervinus*	Common passage migrant and localised winter visitor mid September to mid May.
Water pipit	*Anthus spinoletta*	Common winter visitor mid October to March.
Yellow wagtail	*Motacilla flava*	Common passage migrant, though in irregular numbers annually, peaking late February to mid May and late August to October.
Grey wagtail	*Motacilla cinerea*	Widespread passage migrant mid February to mid April and late August to October.
White wagtail	*Motacilla alba*	Very common winter visitor October to early April.
White-cheeked bulbul	*Pycnonotus leucogenys*	Locally common breeding resident, particularly in Dubai and Abu Dhabi.
Yellow-vented bulbul	*Pycnonotus xanthopygos*	Common breeding resident of mountains, wadis and nearby cultivations.
Red-vented bulbul	*Pycnonotus cafer*	Very common and localised introduced breeding resident.
Nightingale	*Luscinia megarhynchos*	Fairly common passage migrant late March to mid May and late August to mid October.
Bluethroat	*Luscinia svecica*	Common and widespread winter visitor and passage migrant. Widespread mid Oct-March.
Black redstart	*Phoenicurus ochruros*	Fairly common winter visitor late October to early March.
Redstart	*Phoenicurus phoenicurus*	Very common spring passage migrant, scarce in autumn, rare in winter.
Stonechat	*Saxicola torquata*	Common passage migrant and winter visitor September to March.
Isabelline wheatear	*Oenanthe isabellina*	The commonest migrant and wintering wheatear, present mid August to April.
Pied wheatear	*Oenanthe pleschanka*	Very common passage migrant mid February to mid April. Much less common late August to mid November.
Desert wheatear	*Oenanthe deserti*	Common passage migrant and winter visitor September to April.
Red-tailed wheatear	*Oenanthe xanthoprymna*	Common winter visitor, regular on passage.
Eastern pied wheatear*	*Oenanthe picata*	Localised but regular winter visitor to stony plains adjacent to foothills, occasionally marginal land, September to early March, passage birds to late March.

Hooded wheatear	*Oenanthe monacha*	Local resident and rare migrant in south and west only.
Hume's wheatear	*Oenanthe alboniger*	Sedentary breeding resident of mountains.
Rock thrush	*Monticola saxatillis*	Common passage migrant, mostly mid February to April, stragglers to mid May.
Song thrush	*Turdus philomelos*	Common winter visitor November to March.
Graceful warbler	*Prinia gracilis*	Common breeding resident, spreading in proportion to increase in irrigated gardens and agriculture.
Scrub warbler	*Scotocerca inquieta*	Uncommon sedentary breeding resident of mountain areas only.
Marsh warbler*	*Acrocephalus palustris*	Common passage migrant April to early June.
Reed warbler	*Acrocephalus scirpaceus*	Fairly common passage migrant from late February to May and late July to early November. Casual breeding summer visitor to suitable (man-made) reed habitat.
Clamorous reed warbler	*Acrocephalus stentoreus*	Locally common breeding resident, regular passage migrant/winter visitor Aug-May.
Olivaceous warbler	*Hippolais pallida*	Common passage migrant and localised breeding visitor.
Booted warbler	*Hippolais caligata*	Very scarce passage migrant late March to May and mid August to November.
Upcher's warbler	*Hippolais languida*	Regular passage migrant mid March to mid May and mid July to early October.
Ménétries' warbler*	*Sylvia mystacea*	Regular passage migrant late September to April, localised in winter.
Desert warbler*	*Sylvia nana*	Common winter visitor, locally on passage, mid September to mid April.
Orphean warbler	*Sylvia hortensis*	Uncommon passage migrant, localised and irregular in winter.
Lesser whitethroat*	*Sylvia curruca*	Common passage migrant September to November and mid February to mid May.
Desert lesser whitethroat*	*Sylvia minula*	Common winter visitor, fewer on passage.
Hume's lesser whitethroat*	Sylvia althaea	Uncommon passage migrant mid January-early April and October-early December.
Common whitethroat*	*Sylvia communis*	Common passage migrant February to May and mid August to October.
Plain leaf warbler	*Phylloscopus neglectus*	Regular winter visitor October to March, exceptionally to early April, to dry mountain wadis and adjacent savannah plains.
Chiffchaff*	*Phylloscopus collybita*	Very common passage migrant and winter visitor October to April.
Willow warbler	*Phylloscopus trochilus*	Common passage migrant late March to May. Fewer in autumn, mid August to October.
Spotted flycatcher	*Muscicapa striata*	Common passage migrant late March to June and late August to October
Arabian babbler	*Turdoides squamiceps*	Common breeding resident, mostly on plains in north and east and in wadis with denser vegetation and usually in small groups.
Purple sunbird	*Nectarinia asiatica*	Very common breeding resident, dispersive, wandering in response to food availability.
Golden oriole	*Oriolus oriolus*	Common passage migrant late April to May and mid August to mid October.
Isabelline shrike	*Lanius isabellinus*	Common passage migrant and winter visitor September to mid May.
Red-backed shrike	*Lanius collurio*	Common passage migrant, in variable numbers annually. Most common April to May, with fewer September to mid November.
Great grey shrike	*Lanius excubitor*	Common and widespread breeding resident, passage migrant and winter visitor.
Woodchat shrike	*Lanius senator*	Common passage migrant mid February to April. Scarce and irregular mid August to October.
House crow	*Corvus splendens*	Common, locally abundant breeding resident.
Brown-necked raven	*Corvus ruficollis*	Thinly distributed desert breeding resident.
Common mynah	*Acridotheres tristis*	Common, locally abundant breeding resident. Rapidly expanding range throughout whole region.
House sparrow	*Passer domesticus*	Ubiquitous breeding resident, numbers increasing and colonising even outer islands.
Spanish sparrow	*Passer hispaniolensis*	Rare winter visitor late November to early March and localised resident.
Pale rock sparrow	*Petronia brachydactyla*	Common spring passage migrant late February to early April, often in flocks of several hundred. Very localised summer breeding visitor.
Yellow-throated sparrow	*Petronia xanthocollis*	Widespread breeding summer visitor and uncommon passage migrant late March to mid September.
Indian silverbill	*Euodice malabarica*	Very common and widespread breeding resident and common escape from bird markets (sometimes with colour-dyed plumage).
House bunting	*Emberiza striolata*	Common breeding resident of mountains, dispersing to lower levels in winter.

INDEX

GENERAL INDEX

Abu al Abyadh, 67-68, 150, 153
Abu Dhabi, 12, 14-20, 24-25, 28-30, 42-45, 47, 52-55, 58-60, 65-69, 84, 93, 112, 136, 139, 144-145, 157, 163, 165, 196, 204-206, 210, 212, 216, 239-240
Abu Dhabi Environmental Group, 20
Abu Musa, 43
ADCO, 12, 16, 19, 42, 46, 48, 50
Aden, 43, 115, 179, 189
ADMA-OPCO, 16
Afro-Arabian continent, 22-23, 34
Afro-Arabian plate, 22, 34-35, 37
Afrotropical, 101
Al Ain, 12, 16-18, 20, 43, 48, 52, 54, 73, 92-93, 106, 114, 157-158, 163, 165, 218, 220, 235, 239
Al Ain Zoo, 18
Al Aqqa, 67
Al Faqit, 67
Al-Wigan, 93
amateur naturalists, 18, 20
Arabian falconry, 229
Arabian Gulf, 12, 22, 24-26, 29, 37, 42-44, 47, 50, 66, 68-69, 136, 144-148, 150, 161, 168, 170, 173, 176-178, 180-181, 189, 192, 196-197, 200, 202-204, 206-207, 210, 212, 214, 234, 240
Arabian Leopard Trust, 18, 20, 72, 218, 221, 240
Arabian Platform, 22, 24-26, 33-36, 39
archaeology, 14-15, 17, 19
arthritis, 81
Barchan dunes, 26
barchans, 27, 29
Baynunah, 29, 44-47
Baynunah Formation -, 29, 45, 47
Baynunah formation -, 29, 45, 47
Bazam Al Gharbi, 67-68
beach, 43, 48, 76, 78, 82, 139-144, 146, 148, 190, 196, 220, 234
Beach-combing, 76
bedouin, 16, 60, 129, 229, 231-233
biodiversity, 20, 55, 72, 74, 104, 109
biodiversity, 20, 55, 72, 74, 104, 109
Biodiversity Conservation Committee, 20, 74
Bird List, 14-15, 17, 19
birds, 12, 14-17, 19-20, 47, 52-55, 60, 62-69, 71, 73, 76, 84, 101-102, 113, 116, 118, 124, 126-129, 150-

151, 153, 155, 158-159, 161, 163, 165-166, 220-222, 228-229, 231, 233, 240
birdwatchers, 19
breeding colonies, 69
Buraimi, 92
Butinah, 67-68
Captain Atkins Hamerton, 12
children, 73, 106, 112, 232-234, 239
Christian Gross, 18, 122, 214, 228, 240
climate, 26, 37, 65, 72, 74, 87, 108, 118, 214
clothes moths, 98
coast, 12, 20, 23, 26, 29, 33-34, 38, 44, 62, 65-69, 76, 79, 82, 84, 86, 89, 93, 125-126, 139, 145, 150, 161, 168-170, 173-176, 179-183, 186, 192, 195-196, 200, 202-204, 207, 214, 220, 233-235, 240
coastal zone., 82
coastline, 19, 22, 30, 45, 48, 64, 66, 71, 86, 161, 231
coastlines, 50, 66, 192, 195
communication, 54
conservation, 16, 20, 52, 55, 63, 68, 72, 74, 81, 102, 104-106, 138, 142, 166, 209, 221, 239-240
Conservation, 16, 20, 52, 55, 63, 68, 72, 74, 81, 102, 104-106, 138, 142, 166, 209, 221, 239-240
conservationists, 16, 79, 81, 138, 210
continental shelf, 23, 200, 208
cookie-cutter sharks, 202
Cretaceous-, 24-26, 34-39, 42-43, 48-50, 239
cultivation, 53
D.F. Vesey-Fitzgerald, 12, 14
Dalma, 43
Dam Formation, 44
Dama dama, 62
Das, 15, 25, 43
dead dolphins, 79, 82
Desert and Marine Environment Centre, 19
desert, 12, 14, 16-17, 19-20, 26-30, 32, 37, 52-56, 65, 74, 77, 86-87, 89, 92-94, 96, 104-106, 108-111, 113, 118, 122, 125-129, 131, 133, 154, 157-158, 161, 163, 165, 214, 216, 219-221, 223, 225-226, 228-229, 232-233, 235-237, 240
Desert Protected Areas, 54-55
desert squash, 93, 237
Dhadnah, 67

Dibba, 35, 39, 73, 87, 158, 195-196
Dibba Zone, 35
diversity, 49, 77, 84, 108, 117, 150, 161, 203
diving, 186, 202-203, 208, 210
dolomite, 30-31
dolphin watching, 200
Donald Hawley, 14
Dr. Sheikh Sultan bin Mohammed Al Qassimi, 20
drought, 29, 93-94
Dubai, 12, 14, 17-18, 20, 43, 48, 52, 54, 66-67, 86, 92, 116, 145, 153, 157, 161, 163, 165-166, 204-206, 210, 220, 222, 239-240
Dubai Natural History Group, 17, 239-240
Dubai Zoo, 18
dune, 26-29, 32, 82, 93, 228-229
dune patterns, 26-27
dune ridges, 27-29, 32
Ecotourism, 73, 209
eggs, 17, 54, 78, 113-114, 139-142, 177, 189, 195-196, 233-234
Emirates Bird Records Committee, 19, 65, 166, 240
Emirates Environmental Group, 20
Emirates Natural History Group, 15, 19-20, 54, 93, 239
Empty Quarter., 24, 26-27, 31, 93, 157
endemic, 74, 129, 153, 179, 214
ENHG, 15-17, 239
Environment Friends Society, 20
Environmental-, 42, 48
Eocene, 42, 48
evolution, 93, 96, 119
exoskeleton, 108
extinction., 16, 61-62, 72, 81, 86, 136, 141, 210, 212, 221-222
F.E. Warr, 19
falconer, 229-232
falconry, 16, 20, 53-55, 228-229, 240
farmers -, 72-73, 94
FEA, 20, 74
Federal Environ. Agency, 20, 74
fish traps, 170, 234
fishermen, 15, 59, 69, 78, 145-146, 168, 172-173, 175, 186, 204, 206-207, 209-211
fishes, 15, 76, 84, 142, 168-173, 175-176, 182, 184, 186, 188-189, 196-197, 200, 206-207, 240
fishing, 17, 60, 67, 81-82, 142, 144, 146, 161, 203, 209-210, 212, 233-235, 240

fishing industry, 209
flora, 14-15, 18, 20, 26, 50, 84, 86-87, 94, 97, 106, 108, 214, 235
flotsam, 69, 76
flounders, 171, 190
fodder, 53, 68, 93-94, 157, 236
folklore, 86, 236
footprints, 72
fossil horses, 45
fossils, 19, 25, 37-39, 42-50, 239
freshwater, 29, 43-44, 66-67, 74, 182, 184
Fujairah, 12, 20, 43, 48, 50, 67, 89, 102, 139, 161, 173, 205-206, 208
Gary Feulner, 22, 239
geologists, 14, 23-26, 30, 33, 38-39, 42, 45-46, 59
glaciation, 26, 29, 31, 37
grazing, 26, 53-55, 73, 86, 168, 217
Gulf of Oman, 66, 144-145, 147-148, 161, 179, 186, 202-203, 206, 212
gun, 16
gypsum, 25, 30, 43
habitats, 43, 52, 55, 57, 59, 61, 63, 65, 67-68, 74, 82, 84, 89, 96, 99, 104, 109, 113-115, 122, 126, 128, 138, 142, 150, 163, 209, 214, 225
Hafeet, 12, 92
Hajar Mountains, 22, 24-26, 32-33, 35-38, 42-43, 48-49, 94, 111, 153
Hajjar, 89
Hatta, 35, 39, 89, 92, 157
heat, 52, 93, 122, 129, 141, 221, 233
heavy metals, 209
hima, 52
Hulaylah, 67
hunting, 16-17, 19, 54-55, 97, 115, 134, 141, 146, 208, 210, 212, 214, 219-220, 228, 232-233
Indian Ocean, 42, 48, 50, 67, 71, 136, 150, 161, 195, 206, 209
Indian Ocean Whale Sanctuary, 209
insect life, 96
Iraq, 12, 45, 48, 106
islands, 12, 15, 19, 25, 43, 48, 59, 66-69, 74, 139, 143-145, 153, 168, 173, 196, 204, 206, 209-210, 212, 231, 234, 239
J.G. Lorimer, 12
Jacobson's organ, 124
Jebel Ali, 25, 174, 190, 202, 212, 220, 222
Jebel Buhays, 43, 48
Jebel Dhana, 25
Jebel Fayah, 37-38

Jebel Hafit, 12, 14, 37-38, 42, 48, 73, 92, 158, 218
Jebel Huwayyah, 43, 48
Jebel Rawdah, 43, 48-49
Jebel Rowdhah, 37-39
jetsam, 69, 76
Jirnain, 43
Jordan, 45, 48
Khor Kalba, 67, 71, 89, 153, 161
Khorfakkan, 73, 179-180, 195-196
land reclamation, 209
law, 16-17, 20, 150
Liwa, 27-29, 32, 44, 48, 52, 93, 216-217, 220, 222
Liwa oasis, 27, 29, 32, 93
malaria, 98
Manadir, 27, 29, 32
Marijcke Jongbloed, 18, 84, 228, 240
marine pollution, 74
Marine Reserve, 67-68
marshes, 89
medicine, 99, 106, 236, 239-240
Merawah, 67-68
Merewah, 68
Mesozoic seas, 23
Mesozoic sequence, 24
Michael Gallagher, 15
migrant birds, 17, 163
migration, 24, 63, 150, 166, 172, 179, 229
Ministry for Higher Education and Scientific Research, 42, 50
Miocene, 19, 25, 29, 38, 42-47
mountain farmers, 72-73
mountain gazelle, 52, 59-60, 72, 217-218, 221
mountain guides, 73
mountains, 12, 14, 22, 24-26, 32-33, 35-39, 42-43, 48-49, 58, 66-67, 71-74, 86-87, 89-90, 92, 94, 96, 100-101, 106, 111, 114, 125-127, 131, 134, 153, 157-158, 214, 216-218, 220-223, 226, 233, 238
Musandam, 25, 33, 37, 42, 50, 86, 195, 204, 206
Musandam peninsula, 25, 33, 37, 206
Muscat, 12
nappes, 25, 34, 36
NARC, 19, 63
National Avian Research Center, 55
Natural History Museum -, 12, 14-15, 17-19, 42, 45-46, 49-50, 239-240
oceanic crust, 25, 33-35, 38, 43, 48

oil industry, 14, 48, 68
oil reserves, 24
Oligocene, 25-26, 37, 42, 48
Oman, 12, 18, 20, 22, 25, 27, 39, 66, 68-69, 73-74, 104, 108, 113, 119, 131, 136, 144-145, 147-148, 161, 166, 179, 186, 200, 202-203, 206, 212, 218-219, 235, 239
ophiolites, 33, 35-36, 38, 48
Palaearctic, 108, 150, 161
palaeontologists, 17, 19, 42, 45-46, 49-50
pestiferous insects, 98
petroglyphs, 228
plankton, 183
plant collector, 84
plant communities, 92
plants, 14, 16-17, 26, 47, 49, 52, 55, 65, 74, 76, 84, 86-87, 89-90, 92-94, 97-98, 102, 104, 116, 158, 163, 235-238
poisonous, 52, 92, 98-99, 110, 117, 124, 126, 193, 197, 238
polychlorinated biphenyls, 209
Professor A.A. Ghonaimy, 18
Public Hunting Triangle, 54
Qarnein, 15, 69
quartz, 26
rainfall, 29, 90, 94, 104, 214
Rams, 67
rangers, 54-55, 73
Ras al-Khaimah, 12, 15, 37, 50, 67, 86, 139, 157, 163, 212, 221
research, 17-20, 42, 50, 55, 63, 79, 82, 92, 106, 118, 136, 138, 142, 235, 239-240
reserves, 20, 24, 55, 67-68
River Tigris, 45
Rob Western, 18
Ronald Codrai, 12, 20
Royal Botanic Gardens, 15, 18
Ru'us Al-Jibal, 22, 24, 33-35, 37, 39, 73
Rub al-Khali, 44
rushes, 67
Sabkha Matti, 30-31, 47
sabkhas, 14, 30, 32, 84, 94, 131, 236
sabkhas, 14, 30, 32, 84, 94, 131, 236
salt flats, 14, 27, 157
salt, 14, 25, 27, 30-31, 43, 66, 76, 84, 93, 118, 157, 234
sand desert, 26, 30, 125, 157
sand roses, 32
sea level, 25-26, 29, 31, 37, 46
sand roses, 32
seagrasses, 76, 78, 82, 138, 141, 212

seagrasses, 76, 78, 82, 138, 141, 212
Sharjah Nat. Hist. Museum, 18, 240
Sharjah, 12, 14, 18, 20, 67, 86, 110, 117, 205, 208, 240
shasha, 235
Sheikh Hamad bin Mohammed Al Sharqi, 20
Sheikh Zayed, 16-19, 53, 58-60, 62, 65, 216
shell collecting, 67
shells, 12, 16, 20, 29, 43, 49-50, 76-77, 144, 192-193
shooting., 16, 55
Shuwaihat Formation, 46-47
silk, 99, 113
Simsima Formation, 48-50
Sinaiya, 69
Sir Abu Nu'ai, 43
Sir Abu Nu'air, 25
Sir Arnold Wilson, 12
Sir Bani Yas, 18, 25, 58-65, 68, 78, 214
Sirri, 43
skulls, 12, 76, 79, 145, 206
sonar system, 203
Southern Ocean, 202
stomach contents, 82
sulphur, 43
Sweihan, 54, 63, 117
Syria, 45, 48
tectonic movements, 22
Tertiary, 25, 37
Tethys Ocean, 22-23, 34, 39
Tethys, 22-23, 34, 39, 42-43, 48
transverse dunes, 27, 29
tree-planting, 53
Umm Al Quwain, 69, 157, 161, 222
University, 12, 16-20, 46, 106, 119, 235, 239-240
venomous lizards, 124
Wadi Bih, 87
Wadi Haqil, 37
Wadi Shawkah, 15
wadis, 25, 37, 72-74, 89, 102, 106, 114, 117, 131, 134, 158, 218, 228
watching whales and dolphins, 200
wildlife park, 18
Wilfred Thesiger, 12, 30, 218
wind directions, 26
wind, 26-27, 29, 45, 90, 229
Yale University, 17, 19, 46, 239
Yemen, 43, 72, 115, 219
Zagros Mountains, 22, 26, 42, 48
Zirku, 15, 25
zoos, 18

COMMON NAMES INDEX

addax, 62
African crowned crane, 63
African Emigrant, 96
African pompano, 172
almond, 87
ammonites, 49
amphisbaenid, 128-129
Angelfishes, 188
annulated sea snake, 146-147
antlions, 96, 99
ants, 44, 97-100, 105
Aphids, 97, 99
Arabian Babbler, 154, 157-158
Arabian Cicada, 96
Arabian gazelle, 18, 217
Arabian Gulf sea snake, 145-147
Arabian leopard, 18, 20, 72, 214, 218, 221, 240
Arabian Oryx, 12, 16, 18, 59, 61-62, 214, 216
Arabian oryx, 12, 16, 18, 59, 61-62, 214, 216
Arabian tahr, 12, 72-73, 214, 218, 220
Arabian Threadfin Bream, 186
Arabian wolf, 72, 219
arachnids, 110-111, 114, 119
Arctic Skua, 161
Areolate grouper, 195
arta, 86, 236
arthropods, 108-114, 117-120
Arzana, 43
Asiatic mouflon, 62
axis deer, 62
baleen whales, 201-203, 208-209
Barbary Falcon, 228
barbary sheep, 62
bark spiders, 115
barn swallows, 12
Barracudas, 196
bean weevils, 98
bees, 16-17, 97-100
beetles -, 96-100, 104-106, 112
beisa oryx -, 62
Bigeye scad, 173
Bigeye snapper, 182
Bimaculated Lark, 163
Biting lice, 99, 101
black francolin, 63
Black widows, 115
Black-crowned Finch Lark, 150, 157
black-crowned finch-lark, 52
Black-striped goatfish, 184
Black-tipped shark, 174
Blackfin barracuda, 196

Blackspot snapper, 182
Blackspotted grunt, 179
blacktip houndshark, 173
Blacktip reef shark, 173
blacktip reef shark, 173
blacktip shark, 173-174
blister beetles, 96, 98
Blue whale, 201-202
blue whale, 201-202
Blue-spot mullet, 184
blue-spotted emperor, 181
Bluestripe snapper, 182
Blyth's Pipit, 165
Bonefish, 168-169
Bonito, 192
Bonouk, 169
book-lice, 112
Booted Eagle, 163
booted warbler, 67, 153
Booted Warbler, 67, 153
bottlenose dolphin, 77, 79, 204-206, 208-209
bream, 186, 196
Bridled Tern, 153, 161
brine shrimps, 109
Bristletails, 99-100
Broad-billed Sandpiper, 153, 161
Broomtail wrasse, 180
brown-necked raven, 52
Brown-necked Raven, 52
Brownspotted grouper, 195
Bryde's whale, 201-202
bugs, 97-100
Butterflyfish, 174-175
caddisflies, 99, 102
camel, 30, 53, 98, 108-109, 113-114, 118, 163, 165, 228-229, 233, 235, 238
camel spiders, 108-109, 113-114, 118
camel-racing, 53
camels, 52-55, 84, 89, 92, 98, 154, 157, 238
cape hare, 12, 52
caracal, 14, 18, 72-73, 221-222
carpet beetles, 98-99
carpet viper, 125
Caspian Plover, 165
cat snake, 127-128
catfishes -, 169, 187
Catfishes -, 169, 187
cats, 18, 69, 141, 214, 221, 223, 226
Caucasian Bluethroat, 163
centipedes, 109, 117, 119
cetaceans, 19, 68, 81, 200, 205-209
Chestnut-bellied Sandgrouse, 150, 154, 165

chukar partridge, 63
Cicadas, 96, 99
Clark's clownfish, 189
Cobia, 190
Cockroaches, 98-100
Coffee, 12
comb-footed spiders, 115
common dolphin, 206
cone shells, 76
coral, 14, 20, 26, 34, 39, 48-49, 67-68, 74, 76-78, 136, 142, 144-146, 168, 170, 173-175, 179-182, 184-189, 191-193, 197, 210
Coral grouper, 195
coral reefs, 20, 26, 67-68, 74, 136, 142, 144-145, 168, 170, 173, 175, 179-182, 184-185, 187-189, 191-193, 195-197
coralfish, 174
corals, 39, 43, 48-50, 77-78, 136, 144, 168, 188-189, 234
cormorants, 17, 69, 150, 161, 233
Crab Plover, 150, 153, 161
crab plovers, 68
crab spiders -, 115, 119
crabs, 69, 71, 108, 141, 145-146, 169-170, 196
Cream-coloured Courser, 52
cream-coloured courser, 52
Crickets, 96, 98-100
crocodiles, 29, 43-45
crude oil., 24
Crustacea, 76, 108-109, 119-120
crustaceans, 109, 169, 171-174, 176-177, 179-182, 185-186, 188, 190-191, 193, 195-198
damselflies, 99
Dark butterflyfish, 174
Dark pomfret, 178
dates, 12, 220, 234-235
defassa waterbuck, 62
Delgoa Threadfin Bream, 186
desert eagle owl, 52, 165
Desert Eagle Owl, 52, 165
desert flora, 86, 94
Desert Lark, 157-158
Desert Lesser Whitethroat, 154, 157-158
Desert Warbler, 157
Desert Wheatear, 157
dhabs, 52, 54, 122, 233
dhub, 17, 232-233
Diadem, 96, 106, 128
diadem snake, 128
dolphinfish, 176
dolphins, 12, 16-18, 52, 54-55, 59-60, 68, 72-73, 93-94, 214, 217-218, 221, 228, 232-233, 236, 238
Dolphinfishes, 176

dolphins, 15, 19, 76-77, 79, 81-82, 161, 174, 200-201, 203-210, 239
Domino, 189
Dorab wolf herring, 176
dorado, 176
dorcas gazelle, 60, 214
Dory snapper, 182
dragonflies, 96, 99
Driftfishes, 169
ducks, 64, 68
dugong, 59, 68, 210-212
Eagle ray, 186
Eagle Rays, 183, 186
earthworm, 128
Eastern Black Redstart, 163
Eastern Little Tuna, 192
Eastern Pied Wheatear, 153-154, 157
echinoids, 37-38, 43, 50, 239
Eel catfishes, 187
Egyptian goose, 63
elephants, 29, 44, 202
Emperor Angelfish, 188
emu, 59, 62-63, 68
Earwigs, 99, 101
faqah, 86, 235
faqah, 86, 235
falcon, 14, 153, 228-233
fallow deer, 62
false cobra, 126
false horned viper, 125-126
False killer whale, 207
faqah, 86, 235
figs, 12, 34
Filefishes, 170, 183
Fin whale, 202
Finless porpoise, 200, 203-204, 209
Firebrat, 100
fish, 12, 15, 17, 19, 43, 47, 65, 67-69, 74, 76-79, 122, 124, 128, 131, 134, 136, 141, 145-146, 150, 168-193, 195-198, 203, 207-208, 220, 234, 238, 240
Flathead mullet, 184
Fleas, 78, 99, 102
flies, 96-100, 112, 229, 235
Flutemouth, 177
Flutemouths, 177
Flying fish, 177
Forest Wagtail, 165
francolin, 63, 233
Frigate mackerel, 192
fringe-toed sand lizard, 131
fungi, 86, 118
garfish, 170
gazelle, 12, 16-18, 52, 54-55, 59-60, 68, 72-73, 93-94, 214, 217-218, 221, 228, 232-233, 236, 238

geckos, 52, 125, 129, 131-132
geese, 68
gerbil, 44-45, 225, 232
giant crab spiders, 115
giant velvet mite, 117
giraffe, 59, 68
Goatfishes, 184
goats, 52-55, 72-73, 87, 116, 154, 157, 214, 218, 221, 236, 238
Golden-striped goatfish, 184
Gordon's wildcat, 18, 222
grain beetles, 98
Granulated guitarfish, 191
grapes, 12
grasshoppers, 96-97, 99-100, 117
Great barracuda, 196
Great Hammerhead, 196
Great Knot, 153, 161
greater flamingo, 64-65, 160
Greater Flamingo, 64-65, 160
Greater Sand Plover, 153, 161
Greater Tunb, 12
green turtle, 136, 138-139, 142-144
Grey Plover, 153
Grey reef shark, 172, 174
Groupers, 193, 195
Grunts, 179
guitarfish, 190-191
Halfbeaks, 179
Halfspotted grouper, 195
hammer oysters, 77
hamour, 195
hare, 12, 52, 218-219, 223, 232-233
hares, 17, 55, 116, 218, 233
harvestmen, 109, 114
hawksbill turtle, 136, 138-139, 144
hedgehog, 52, 223
helmeted guineafowl, 63
herbs, 87, 236, 238
hermit crab, 77
Herrings, 176
hippos, 44-45
hog deer, 62
honey badger, 52
Honeybees, 98
Hooded Wheatear, 157-158
Hoopoe Lark, 52, 157
hoopoe lark, 52, 157
horned viper, 52, 124-126
hornet -, 98
houbara -, 19, 52, 54-55, 62-63, 150, 229-230, 232-233, 240
houbara bustard, 19, 52, 54-55, 150, 230, 240
houbara hunting, 55

House Bunting, 158
House Cricket, 96
house sparrow, 14
Hume's Lesser Whitethroat, 154
Hume's Wheatear, 150, 153, 158
humpback whale, 203, 208
hyaenas, 12, 44
hyrax, 72
ibex, 72-73
Imperial Eagle, 163
Indian lionfish, 192
Indian Pond Heron, 153
Indian Roller, 158-159
Indian threadfinned trevally, 172
Indo-Pacific humpback dolphin, 200, 204-205, 209
Indo-Pacific Sailfish, 179
insects, 16-17, 53, 55, 65, 96-106, 108-109, 111-113, 117, 119, 124, 128-129, 131-132, 134, 220, 222-223, 226
isopods, 109-110, 119
jack-pomfret, 178
jackal, 52
Japanese Threadfin Bream, 186
Java cownose ray, 186
Javan Rabbitfish, 195
Jayakar, 12
jumping spiders, 115
karowan, 54
kawkawa, 192
Kentish Plover, 150, 153
kestrel, 163, 165, 230-231
killer whales, 207-208
Killifish, 176
kingfish, 173, 192
krill, 202
lacewings, 96, 99
Lappet-faced Vulture, 73, 154, 158
Largescale mullet, 184
leatherback turtle, 136, 145
Leatherjackets, 170, 183
lemon fish, 190
lemons, 12
leopard, 12, 18-20, 44, 72-73, 105, 171, 214, 218, 221, 240
leopard sole, 171
Leopard sole, 171
leopards, 72, 221
Lesser Crested Tern, 161
lesser jerboa, 52, 225
Lesser Kestrel, 163, 165
Lesser Noddy, 165
Lesser Sand Plover, 150, 153, 161
Lesser Whitethroat, 154, 157-158, 161

Lichtenstein's Sandgrouse, 158
Lieutenant Colonel S.B. Miles, 12
Lime Butterfly, 96
lined butterflyfish, 174
lionfish, 192
Little Green Bee-eater, 150, 158
little owl, 52
Lizardfishes, 197
lizards, 12, 52, 54, 113, 116, 122, 124-127, 129, 131, 233
Locust, 12, 96
loggerhead turtle, 136, 145
Long-finned Batfish, 187
Long-legged Buzzard, 52
long-legged buzzard, 52
Long-tailed stingray, 177
Long-toed Stint, 165
Longfaced emperor, 181
mackerel, 172, 191-192
Malabar red snapper, 181
mammals, 15, 17, 43-44, 47, 52, 54-55, 59, 73, 78, 101-102, 118, 124, 126, 128, 176, 200-201, 203, 207, 209-211, 214-215, 217, 219-221, 223, 225, 240
mangoes, 12
mangrove, 17, 58, 63, 65, 67, 71, 78, 84, 89, 161, 182
mangroves, 17, 19, 64, 66-68, 77, 84, 86, 234
manta rays, 183
marine mammal, 68, 186, 210
marine mammals, 17, 78, 176, 200-201, 203, 207, 209, 211
mayflies, 99, 101
millipedes, 117
minke whale, 201
mites, 109, 112, 116-117, 119
molluscs, 43-44, 77, 145, 169-170, 177, 181, 186, 191, 195-197
monitor lizard, 129, 231
monitor, 20, 52, 129, 231
Mono, 184
Monos, 184
Montagu's Harrier, 163
moon snail, 78
Moray eel, 185
Moses sole, 171
moths, 86, 96-100
Mottled electric ray, 198
Mullets, 184
Narrow-barred Spanish mackerel, 192
Nautilus, 12, 20
Needlefish, 170
odontocetes, 203

oil beetles, 98-99
Oleander Hawkmoth, 100
olive ridley turtle, 136
olives, 12
Opliones, 110
Orange butterflyfish, 174-175
oranges, 12, 65
orb-weavers, 115
Oriental halibut, 190
Oriental Hornet, 98
Oriental Pratincole, 165
Oriental Skylark, 165
oryx, 12, 16, 18, 20, 52, 59-62, 68, 93, 214, 216-217, 228-229
Osprey, 68, 153
ostrich feathers, 228
ostrich, 14, 29, 63, 68, 214, 228-229
Pacific Golden Plover, 161
Pale Crag Martin, 158
palm trees, 74, 235
Parrotfish, 191
pearl oyster., 234
pearl oysters, 77
pearls, 234
pennant coral fish, 174-175
peregrine, 19, 228-229
pheasant, 63, 77
Pinjalo snapper, 182
pink flamingo, 65
Pintail Snipe, 165
pipefish, 197
Pipefishes, 196
Plain Leaf Warbler, 150, 153-154, 158
Plain Tiger, 96, 98
Pomarine Skua, 161
pomegranates, 12
Pomfret, 178
Preying mantises, 97, 99-100
pseudoscorpions, 109, 112-113, 119
pygmy blue whale, 202
queenfish, 171, 173
Rabbitfish, 193, 195
racing camels, 53, 92
Radde's Warbler, 165
Rainbow Runner, 172
ratel, 52
raven, 14, 52
rays, 142, 161, 170, 172, 176-177, 179, 181-183, 186, 189-190, 195-196, 198, 216
red fox, 54, 214, 220
Red-billed Tropicbird, 69, 153
red-billed tropicbird, 69, 153
Red-tailed Wheatear, 153-154, 157-158

Redspot Emperor, 181
Remora, 177, 183, 190
Remoras, 177
reptiles, 15, 17, 20, 47, 52, 54, 118, 122-125, 128-129, 131, 136-137, 139, 141-142, 145, 221, 223, 232-233
requiem sharks, 173
rhea, 63
rheem, 52, 59-60
Risso's dolphin, 200, 207-208
river snapper, 182
Round Batfish, 187
Rueppell's fox, 52
Russel's snapper, 182
Russell's lionfish, 192
saddle oysters, 77
saguro, 168
saluki, 232-233
samsum Ant, 98
sand boa, 52, 128, 131
sand cat, 52, 222-223
sand dollar, 78
sand fish, 131
sand gazelle, 18, 52, 60, 217
Sand Partridge, 158
sand snake, 126-128
Sandbar shark, 173
sardines, 172, 176
Saunders' Little Tern, 161
saw-scaled viper, 122, 125
scad, 171, 173
Scarab beetles, 97
scimitar-horned oryx, 62
Scissortail sergeant, 189
Scorpio, 111
scorpions, 108-114, 118-119, 129
Scrub Warbler, 158
sea bass, 193
sea cow, 68
Seabreams, 195
seahorses, 196
see se, 63
sei whale, 201-202
senna, 236
Sergeant major, 189
Shaw's sea snake, 146, 148
sheet-web spiders, 115
short-finned pilot whale, 207
Short-toed Eagle, 158
shovelnose ray, 190
shrimps, 49, 109, 169
Siberian Stonechat, 163
sicklefin lemon shark, 173
Silver pomfret, 178
Silverfish, 99, 112
silverfish, 99, 112

Silversides, 169
Sirenia, 210, 212
skink, 52, 130-131
Slender-billed Gull, 161
Slipmouths, 180
Snakes, 122, 124-129, 136, 145-148
snakes, 122, 124-129, 136, 145-148
Snappers, 179, 181
Snowflake moray, 185
Socotra Cormorant, 69, 150, 153, 161
Socotra cormorant, 69, 150, 153, 161
sohal, 168
Soles, 171
solifugid, 113-114
solifugids, 109, 113-114
Sooty Falcon, 153
Sooty Gull, 69, 150, 153-154, 161
sorrel, 236
sperm whale, 200, 203, 208-209
spiders, 108-109, 113-115, 118-119
spinecheeks, 186
spinner dolphin, 206
spinner shark, 173
spiny-tailed agamids, 17
spiny-tailed lizard, 122, 124, 129
spiny-tailed lizards, 52, 54, 122, 127, 233
spottail shark, 173
spotted dolphin, 206
Spotted Eagle ray, 186
Spotted Eagle, 161, 186
Spotted grunt, 179
Spotted halfbeak, 179
Spotted puffer, 197
Spotted stingray, 177
spring-tails, 112
Springtails, 99-100
squash, 93, 237
steppe eagle, 14
Steppe Great Grey Shrike, 163
Stick insects, 99, 101
Stingray, 177
stone curlew, 54
Stonefish, 192-193
striped dolphin, 206
Striped eel catfish, 188
striped hyaena, 52, 72, 219
sucker fish, 177
Sucking lice, 99-100
Sunfish, 183
surgeon fishes, 168
Sweetlips, 179
swift, 68-69, 161
Swift Tern, 161

tadpoles, 134
Talang Queenfish, 173
tawny eagles, 14
Terek Sandpiper, 161
termites, 98-100, 117, 128
Termites, 98-100, 117, 128
terrapin, 134
thread snake, 128
Threadfin bream, 186
threadfin breams, 186, 195
threadfinned trevally, 172
Thrips, 99-100
ticks, 109, 116, 119
tiger beetles, 106
tiger shark, 173-174
Tiger sharks, 173
toad-head agama, 129, 131
Toothed flounders, 190
toothed cetaceans, 208
Toothed flounders, 190
trevally, 171-172
triggerfish, 170
Triggerfishes, 170, 183
True bugs, 99
turtle nesting, 68
turtles, 15, 17, 29, 43, 68, 76, 81-82, 136, 138-145, 161, 174, 207, 233-234
tusk shells, 77
Two-bar bream, 196
Upcher's Warbler, 154, 157
Violet damselfish, 189
vipers, 122, 124-126
vultures, 14
wadi racer, 128
warbler, 52, 67, 150, 153-154, 157-158, 161, 165
wasps, 17, 96-100
Web-spinners, 99
whaler shark, 173
whales, 19, 76, 79, 81, 200-204, 206-210, 239
whales, 19, 76, 79, 81, 200-204, 206-210, 239
Wheat, 12
wheatear, 52, 150, 153-154, 157-158
whip scorpions, 109, 114
whip scorpions, 109, 114
white stork, 12
White-capped Bunting, 165
White-cheeked Tern, 150, 161
White-collared Kingfisher, 67, 71, 153, 161, 163
white-collared kingfisher, 67, 71, 153, 161, 163
White-spotted shovelnose ray, 190

White-throated Bee-eater, 165
Whitecheek shark, 173
Whitefin wolf herring, 176
wild goat, 72-73
wild sheep, 62
Wilson's Storm-petrel, 161
wolf spiders, 115
wolf, 52, 72-73, 115, 176, 214, 219
wolves, 12, 219
Yellow sea snake, 146-148
yellow-bellied sea snake, 146, 148
Yellow-throated Sparrow, 150, 154, 157
Yellow-vented Bulbul, 153, 158
Yellowbar Angelfish, 188
Yellowfin jack, 172
Yellowfin tuna, 192
Yellowtail barracuda, 196
Yellowtail surgeonfish, 168
zebra, 68

Scientific Names Index

A. crassicauda, 111-112
A. thazard, 192
Abalistes stellaris, 170
Abudefduf saxatilis, 189
Abudefduf sexfasciatus, 189
Abudhabia baynunensis, 45
Abutilon pannosum, 89
Acacia, 87, 89, 96, 154, 157-158, 238
Acacia nilotica, 238
Acacia tortilis, 87, 157
Acanthastrea, 78
Acanthodactylus gongorhyncatus, 15
Acanthodactylus schmidti, 131
ACANTHURIDAE, 168
Acanthurus sohal, 168
Acari, 109-110, 112, 116, 119
Acherontia styx, 104
Acheta domestica, 96
Acropora, 78
Addax nasomaculatus, 62
Adiantum capillus-veneris, 89
Aerva javanica, 86, 238
Aetobatus narinari, 186
Aetomyleus nichofii, 186
Agelenidae, 115, 120
Albula vulpes, 169
ALBULIDAE, 168
Alectis ciliaris, 172
Alectis indicus, 172
Alectoris chukar., 63
Alepes mate, 172
Aloe vera, 86
Alopochen aegyptius, 63

Amblyomma, 116
Amblypygi, 109, 114, 120
Ammoperdix griseogularis, 63
Amnotragus lervia, 62
Amphiprion clarkii, 189
Amygdalus arabicus, 87
Anacanthotermes ochraceous, 100
Anagallis arvensis, 86
Anax parthenope, 100
Androctonus, 111-112, 120
Androctonus australis, 112
Androctonus crassicauda, 111, 120
Anopleura, 99
Anoplocnemis curvipes, 101
Anthemis odontostephana, 87
Antilope cervicapra, 62
Anvillea garcinii, 92-93
Apistobuthus, 111
Apithobuthus pterygocercus, 111, 120
Aponomma, 116
Apterygota, 99-100
Aquila nipalensis, 14
Araneae, 109, 119
Argas, 116
Argiopidae, 115, 120
Argyrolobium roseum, 89
ARIIDAE, 169, 187
ARIOMMIDAE, 169
Arius thalassinus, 169
Arnebia hispidissima, 238
Arothron stellatus, 197
Asteriscus pygmaeus, 90
Astigmata, 116, 120
Astragalus species, 86
Astragalus spinosus, 87
ATHERINIDAE, 169
Atriplex leucoclada, 84
Avicennia marina, 65, 84, 161
Axis axis, 62
B. pantherinus, 171
Bacopa monnieri, 89
Balaenoptera acutorostrata, 201
Balaenoptera borealis -, 201
Balaenoptera edeni, 201-202
Balaenoptera musculus, 201-202
Balaenoptera physalus, 202
Balaenopteridae, 201-203
Balearica regulorum, 63
BALISTIDAE, 170, 183
BELONIDAE, 170
Bleparis ciliaris, 94
Blepharis ciliaris, 90
Boerhaavia elegans, 89
Boidae, 128
Boophilus annulatus, 116, 120

Boophilus, 116, 120
BOTHIDAE, 171
Bothus pantherinus, 171
Bufo arabica, 134
Bufo dhofarensis, 134
Bufo dhufarensis, 12
Buthacus yotvatensis nigroac-uleatus, 110-111, 120
Buthus, 111
C. nudus, 176
Buthus, 111
Calligonum comosum, 86, 89, 236
Calotropis procera, 86, 237
Capparis cartilaginea, 93
Capparis spinosa, 89, 236
Capus lepensis, 12
Caracal caracal, 14, 18, 221
Caracal caracal schmitzi, 18, 221
caracal lynx, 18, 72
Caralluma, 90, 93, 236
Caralluma flava, 90
CARANGIDAE, 171-172
Carangoides bajad, 171-172
Carangoides chrysophrys, 172
Carangoides malabaricus, 172
Carangoides sexfasciatus, 172
Caranx ignobilis, 172
Caranx sem, 172
CARCHARHINIDAE, 173
Carcharhinus brevipinna, 173
Carcharhinus dussumieri, 173
Carcharhinus limbatus, 173-174
Carcharhinus melanopterus, 173
Carcharhinus plumbeus, 173
Carcharhinus sealei, 174
Carcharhinus sorrah, 173
Caretta caretta, 136, 145
Cassia italica, 236
Catopsilla florella, 96
Cenchrus pennisetiformis, 94
Centaurium pulchella, 89
Cephalopholis hemistiktos, 195
Cephalopholis miniata, 195
Cerastes cerastes gasperetii, 126
Cerithidea., 77
Cervus porcinus, 62
Chaetodon lineolatus, 174
Chaetodon melapterus, 174-175
Chaetodon obscurus, 174
Chalcides ocellatus, 131
Cheilinus lunulatus, 180
Chelicerata, 108-110, 112-116, 120
Cheliceridae, 113
Chelonia mydas, 136, 143
Cheumatopsyche capitella, 102
Chirocentrus dorab, 176
Chirocentrus nudus, 176

Chlamydotis undulata, 19, 62, 150
Chlamydotis undulata macqueenii, 19
Ciconia ciconia, 12
Circopeltis, 50
Citrullus colocynthis, 93, 237
Cleome pruinosa, 94
Cleome rupicola, 89
CLUPEIDAE, 176
Codiopsis lehmannae, 50
Coelachyrum piercei, 94
Collembola, 99, 112
Coluber rhodorachis, 128
Compsobuthis arabicus, 111, 120
Compsobuthus, 111
Convolvulus arvensis, 86
Convolvulus deserti, 92
Cornulaca monacantha, 86
Coryphaena hippurus, 176
CORYPHAENIDAE, 176
Crotalaria persica, 86
Cryptostigmata, 116, 120
Ctenolepisma ciliata, 100
Cynomorium coccineum, 86, 236
Cyperus arenarius, 84
CYPRINODONTIDAE, 176
Cypselurus oligolepis, 177
Danaeus chrysippus, 96
Daphnis nerii, 100
Dascyllus trimaculatus, 189
DASYATIDAE, 177
Dasyatis kuhlii, 177
Delphinidae, 204-207
Delphinus delphis, 206
Dermaptera, 99, 101
Dermestes frischii, 99
Dermochelys coriacea, 136, 145
Dianthus cyri, 89
Dictyoptera, 99
Dinonthrombium sp, 117
Diplectium, 49
Diplometopon zarudni, 128
Diplotaxis harra, 90
Dromaius naavaehollandiae, 63
Dugong dugon, 210, 212
E. chlorostigma, 195
ECHENEIDAE, 177
Echeneis naucrates, 177
Echidna nebulosa, 185
Echiochilon thesigeri, 93
Echis carinatus, 125
Echis coloratus, 125
Elagatis bipinnulatus, 172
Embioptera, 99, 101
Endopterygota, 99, 102
Ephemeroptera, 99, 101

Epinephelus areolatus, 195
Epinephelus chlorostigma, 195
Epinephelus tauvina, 195
Epipactis veratrifolia, 89
Eremobium aegyptiacum, 86
Eretmochelys imbricata, 136, 144
Erodium laciniatum, 89
Erucaria hispanica, 90
Eryx jayakari, 128
Euphorbia larica, 90
Euphorbia prostrata, 89
Euthynnus affinis, 192
EXOCOETIDAE, 177
Exopterygota, 99-100
Fagonia indica, 92
Falco cherrug, 19
Falco peregrinus, 19
Farsetia aegyptiaca, 93
Felis sylvestris gordoni, 18
Fistularia petimba, 197
FISTULARIDAE, 177
Formio niger, 178
FORMIONIDAE, 178
Francolinus francolinus, 63
Francolinus pondicerianus, 63
Galaxea, 78
Galeocerdo cuvieri, 174
Galeodes arabs, 114, 120
Galeodidae, 114, 120
Galeoides decadactylus, 173
Galium setaceum, 87
Gastrocotyle hispida, 89
Gazella dorcas, 60
Gazella gazella., 18, 59-60, 217
Gazella gazella cora, 60, 217
Gazella, 12, 18, 59-60, 62, 217
Gazella granti, 60
Gazella subgutterosa, 18, 60
Gazella subgutterosa marica, 60
Geophilomorpha, 117
Glabrobournonia arabica, 49
Gladiolus italicus, 87, 89
Globicephala macrorhynchus, 207
Gnathanodon speciosus, 172
Gnathosidae, 115
Goniopygus arabicus, 50
Grampus griseus, 200, 207
Gymnarrhena micranthus, 93
Gymnothorax favagineus, 185
H cyanocynctus, 146-147
H spiralis, 146
H stipulacea, 138
Haemaphysalis, 116
Halcnemum strobilaceum, 84
Halodule uninervis, 138

Halopeplis perfoliata, 84
Halophila ovalis, 138
Haloxylon salicornicum, 84
Haplophyllum tuberculatum, 89
Helianthemum lippii, 86, 236
Helichrysum somalense, 93
Heliotropium kotschyi, 84
Hemidactylus flaviviridus, 132
Hemiptera, 99
Hemipteronotus hypospilus, 180
HEMIRAMPHIDAE, 179
Hemiramphus far, 179
Hemiscorpius, 111
Heniochus acuminatus, 174-175
Heterodiadema buhaysensis, 50
Hexaplex kuesterianus, 77
Hibiscus micranthus, 90
Himantura gerrardi, 177
Himantura uarnak, 177
Hippocampus histrix, 197
Hippocampus kuda, 197
Hyalomma hyalomma anatolicum, 116, 120
Hyalomma, 116, 120
Hydrophiidae, 145, 147-148
Hydrophis lapemoides, 145, 147
Hyoscyamus muticus, 89
Hyplimnas misippus, 96
Hypocolius, 165
Hypogaleus hyugaensis, 173
Hypogalius balfouri, 174
Hyporhamphus sp, 179
Indigofera intricata, 94
Indopacetus pacificus, 79
Iphiona aucheri, 92
Isoptera, 99-100
ISTIOPHORIDAE, 179
Istiophorus platypterus, 179
Isurus oxyrinchus, 173
Ixiolirion tataricum, 87, 89
Ixodidae, 116, 119-120
Jaubertia aucheri, 92
Kickxia hastata, 89
Kobus ellipsiprymnus defassa, 62
Koweitoniscus tamei, 110, 120
Labidura riparia, 101
Labroides dimidiatus, 180
Lacerta cyanura, 15, 132
Lacerta jayakari, 131
Lactrodectus hysterix, 115
Lactrodectus pallidus, 115
Lactrodectus spp, 115
Lagocephalus lunaris, 197
Lapemis curtus, 146, 148
Launaea, 86, 89, 93
Launaea massauensis, 89

Launaea spinosa, 93
LEIOGNATHIDAE, 180
Leirus, 111
Lepidochelys olivacea, 136
Lepisma saccharina, 100
Leptadenia pyrotechnica, 94, 236
Leptotyphlos macrorhynchus, 128
LETHRINIDAE, 181
Lethrinus lentjan, 181
Lethrinus miniatus, 181
Lethrinus nebulosus, 181
Leucas inflata, 89
Limonium axillare, 84
Linum corymbulosum, 89
Linyphiidae, 115, 119
Lippia nodiflora, 89
Littrorophiloscia stronhali, 110, 120
Liza macrolepis, 184
Lotus halophilus, 86
LUTJANIDAE, 181
Lutjanus argentimaculatus, 182
Lutjanus ehrenbergi, 182
Lutjanus fulviflamma, 182
Lutjanus johni, 182
Lutjanus kasmira, 182
Lutjanus lineolatus, 182
Lutjanus malabaricus, 181
Lutjanus russelli, 182
Lycium shawii, 87
Lycosidae, 115, 120
Makaira indica, 179
Makaira mazara, 179
Mallophaga, 99, 101
Malpolon moilensis, 126
Malva parviflora, 86
Matricaria aurea, 87
Mauremys caspica, 134
Megalaspis cordyla, 172
Megaptera novaeangliae, 203
Mesalina brevirostris, 12
Mesostigmata, 116, 120
Metastigmata, 116, 120
Milliolite, 43
Misopates orontium, 89
MOBULIDAE, 183
Mola mola, 183
Mola ramsayi, 183
MOLIDAE, 183
Moltkiopsis ciliata, 84
Monacanthidae, 170, 183
MONODACTYLIDAE, 184
Monodactylus argenteus, 184
Monsonia nivea, 86
Montipora, 78

Moringa peregrina, 87
Mugil cephalus, 184
MUGILIDAE, 184
MULLIDAE, 184
Mulloides flavolineatus, 184
Mulloidichtys auriflamma, 184
MURAENIDAE, 185
Muscaris longipes, 87, 89
MYLIOBATIDAE, 186
Mylo bifasciatus, 196
mysticetes, 201
Negaprion acutidens, 173
NEMIPTERIDAE, 186
Nemipterus delagoae, 186
Nemipterus japonicus, 186
Nemipterus tolu, 186
Neophocaena phocaenoides, 200, 204
Neophron percnopterus, 14
Nerium mascatense, 89
Neuroptera, 96, 99
Notostigmata, 116, 120
Numidia meleagris, 63
Nummulites, 37-38, 48
Odonata, 99
Olipiidae, 113, 120
Ophioglossum polyphyllum., 94, 236
Orcinus orca, 207
Ornithodorus, 116
Orobanche cernua, 94
Orthochirus, 111-112, 120
Orthoptera, 99
Oryx dammah, 62
Oryx gazella beisa, 62
Oryx leucoryx, 12, 18, 62, 216
Ovis ammon, 62
P. anguilaris, 188
P. arab, 188
Pachycondyla sennaarensis, 98
Paederus fuscipes, 99
Pampus argenteus, 178
Panicum turgidum, 84, 94
Panthera pardus nimr, 18, 221
Papaver dubium, 89
Papilio demoleus, 96
Parabuthus liosoma, 111, 120
Parabuthus, 111, 120
Paracaryum intermedium, 89
Paramonacanthus choirocephalus, 183
Paramonacanthus oblongus, 183
Parembia persica, 101
Parupeneus cyclostomus, 184

Parupeneus macronema, 184
Passer domesticus, 14
Pauropoda, 117-118, 120
Pavona, 78
Pelamis platurus, 146, 148
Pennisetum divisum, 84, 94
Pergularia tomentosa, 89, 238
Periploca aphylla, 87
Petalabrissus rawdahensis, 50
Phasianus colchicus, 63
Phasmida, 99, 101
Phoenocopterus ruber, 65
Phragmites australis, 89
Phrenocephalus arabicus, 131
Physeter macrocephalus, 200, 208
Physorrhynchus chaemarapistrum, 89
Pinjalo pinjalo, 182
PLATACIDAE, 187
Platax orbicularis, 187
Platax teira, 187
Platygyra, 77
Platypleura arabica, 96
Plectorhynchus fangi, 179
Plectorhynchus gaterinus, 179
Pleistocene, 26, 29, 37, 43
Pleuronectiformes, 190
PLOTOSIDAE, 187
Plotosidae, 187
Plotosus lineatus, 188
Pocillopora, 78
POMACANTHIDAE, 188
Pomacanthus imperator, 188
Pomacanthus maculosis, 188
POMACENTRIDAE, 188
Pomacentrus sindensis, 189
Porcellio assimilis, 110, 120
Porcellionides pruninosus, 110, 120
Prionocidaris emiratus, 50
Pristotis jerdoni, 189
Pristurus rupestris, 132
Prosopis cinerea, 86, 157
Prosopis juliflora, 87
Prostigmata, 116, 120
Protracheneonisus inexpectatus, 110, 120
Psammophis schokari, 126
Psettodes erumei, 190
PSETTODIDAE, 190
Pseudocerastes persicus, 125
Pseudogaillonia hymenostephana, 90
Pseudorca crassidens, 207
Pseudorhombus arsius, 171

Pseudoscorpiones, 109, 112, 119-120
Pseudotrapelus sinaitus, 131
Pseudotriacanthus strigilifer, 183
Psocidae, 112
Pterois miles, 192
Pterois russelli, 192
Pterygota, 99
Ptyodactylus hasselquisti, 132
Pulicaria arabica, 89
Pulicaria glutinosa, 92
RACHYCENTRIDAE, 190
Rachycentron canadus, 190
Radianthus, 189
Reseda aucheri, 89
Rhagodidae, 114, 120
Rhazya stricta, 92, 238
Rhea americana, 63
Rhinecanthus assasi, 170
RHINOBATIDAE, 190
Rhinobatis annulatus -, 190
Rhinobatus granulatus, 190
Rhinoptera javanica, 186
Rhynchobatus djiddensis, 190
Rhynchosia minima, 94
Rumex vesicarius, 236
S. doriae, 131
S. mirabilis, 117
S leptocosymbotis, 131
Salsola imbricata, 84, 238
Salticidae, 115, 119-120
Salvadore persica, 238
Salvia aegyptiaca, 87
Salvia spinosa, 89
Saurida tumbil, 197
Saurida undosquamis, 197
SCARIDAE, 191
Scarus scaber, 191
Schizopeltida, 109, 114, 120
Schweinfurthia papillonacea, 92
Scincus mitranus, 131
Scolopendrida mirabilis, 117, 120
Scolopendrida, 109, 117, 120
Scolopendromorpha, 117, 120
Scolopsis ghanam, 186
Scolopsis ruppelli, 186
Scomberoides commersonianus, 172-173
Scomberoides lysan, 173
Scomberomorus commerson, 192
Scomberomorus lysan, 172
SCOMBRIDAE, 191
SCORPAENIDAE, 192
Scorpiones, 109-110, 120

Scrophulariacea, 94
Scutigeromorpha, 117
Seriola dumerili, 172
Seriolina nigrofasciata, 172
SERRANIDAE, 193
Setaria verticillata, 94
Setodes sugdeni, 102
Sida urens, 89
SIGANIDAE, 195
Siganus , 195
Silene villosa, 56, 86
Siluriformes, 187
Siphonaptera, 99, 102
Solifugidae, 109
Solpugidae, 114
Somalodillo paeninsulae, 110, 120
Sousa chinensis, 200, 204
Spalerosophis diadema, 128
Sparassidae, 115, 120
SPARIDAE, 195
Sphyraena flavicauda, 196
Sphyraena qenie, 196
SPHYRAENIDAE, 196
Sphyrna mokarran, 196
SPHYRNIDAE, 196
Sporobolus arabicus, 84
Stendactylus leptosymbotes, 15
Stenella longirostris, 206
Stenodactylus arabicus, 131
Stephanolepis diaspros, 183
Stethojulis interrupta, 180
Stipagrostis plumosa, 94
Stoichactis, 189
Struthio camelus syriacus, 14, 63
Stylophora, 78
Suaeda, 238
Sufflamen albicaudatus, 170
Sufflamen capsitratus, 170
Sufflamen chrysopterus, 170
Sygnathus analaricens, 197
Symphyla, 117-118, 120
Symphyllia, 78
Synanceia verrucosa, 192-193
SYNGNATHIDAE, 196
SYNODONTIDAE, 197
Syringodium isoetifolium, 138
Taeniura melanospila, 177
Tamarix, 84
Tardigrada, 118, 120
Taurotragus oryx, 62
Taverniera glabra, 94, 238
Taverniera spartea, 86
Telescopus dhara, 127
Tephrosia apollinea, 89, 92

Teratoscincus scincus, 131
Terebralia palustris, 77
Tetragnathidae, 115, 120
TETRAODONTIDAE, 197
Tetrapturus audax, 179
Tetrastigmata, 116, 120
Teucrium stocksianum, 90, 238
Thalassoma lunare, 180
Thelyphonida, 109, 114, 120
Therapon puta, 197
Therapon theraps, 197
THERAPONIDAE, 197
Theridiidae, 115
Thermobia domestica, 100
Thomisidae, 115, 119-120
Thomisus citrinellus, 115, 120
Thunnus albacares, 192
Thysanoptera, 99-100
Thysanura, 99-100
Thysanurana, 112
TORPEDINIDAE, 198
Torpedo panthera, 198
Trachinotus blochi, 172
Trachycormocephalus, 118
Trefezia sp, 235
Triacanthus biaculeatus, 183
Tribulus, 15, 19-20, 93, 239
Trichoptera, 99, 102
Turbinaria, 78
Tursiops truncatus, 205
Typha domingensis, 89
Ulua mentalis, 172
Umbonium vestiarium, 77
Upeneus asymetricus, 184
Upeneus sulphureus, 184
Upeneus tragula, 184
Uromastix microlepis, 129
Vachoniolus globimanus, 111, 120
Vachoniolus minipectibinus, 111, 120
Vachoniolus, 111-112, 120
Valamugil seheli, 184
Varanus griseus, 129
Vernonia arabica, 89
Vespa orientalis, 98
Vicia sativa, 87
Vicoa pentanema, 87
Viola cinerea, 89
Zebrasoma xanthurum, 168
Zebrasoma xanthurus, 168
Zizyphus spina-christie., 236
Zygophyllum, 77, 84, 93, 238
Zygophyllum mandavillei, 84
Zygophyllum qatarense, 238